ECONOMIC LIBERALISATION AND PUBLIC ENTERPRISES

About the Authors

Professor R. K. Mishra is currently Professor and Dean, Institute of Public Enterprise, Hyderabad. He is a Graduate of International Management Programme, SDA Bocconi, Milan, Italy. He has had research stints at London Business School and Maison Des Sciences De L'Hommes, Paris. He has been the recipient of British Council, Commonwealth, IIAS, IASIA, ICSSR, UGC and UN Fellowships. He has taught at the University of Bradford, United Kingdom and was a visiting Professor at Maison Des Sciences De L'Hommes, Paris. He was on action research at North-West Province of South Africa at the invitation of DFID, UK. He has undertaken many institutional researches and consultancy projects on various aspects of public enterprises, public systems and finance. He has also been a researcher for Planning Commission, Finance Commission, Prime Minister's Economic Advisory Council, Indian Council of Social Science Research, Commonwealth Secretariat, International Civil Service Consortium, State Bureaus of Public Enterprises, Financial Institutions and Banks. He is Vice-President (Asia), International Association of Schools and Institutes in Administration, Brussels.

Ms. Ch. Lakshmi Kumari is currently Research Associate at the Institute of Public Enterprise, Hyderabad. She is a resource faculty to various MBA programmes. She has been associated with various Training Programmes organised for national and international agencies.

B. Navin is currently Knowledge Manager at the Centre for Good Governance, Hyderabad. He has worked for his Doctoral thesis on Asset Pricing Behaviour in Indian Stock Market. He has been associated with the Asian Development Bank Project and at the Institute of Public Enterprise, Hyderabad. He is also involved in teaching Managerial Economics and Financial Services at the Post-Graduate Level.

P. Geeta is currently Knowledge Manager at the Centre for Good Governance, Hyderabad. She has completed her Doctoral study on Memorandum of Understanding in Public Sector Enterprises in India. She has also worked in the area of Social Safety Net for the State Level Public Enterprises in Andhra Pradesh.

ECONOMIC LIBERALISATION
AND
PUBLIC ENTERPRISES

R.K. MISHRA
CH. LAKSHMI KUMARI
B. NAVIN
P. GEETA

CONCEPT PUBLISHING COMPANY, NEW DELHI-110059

Cataloging in Publication Data—DK
Courtesy: D.K. Agencies (P) Ltd. <docinfo@dkagencies.com>

Psychological perspective of HIV & AIDS / edited by M. Rajamanickam.
p. cm.
Contributed articles.
Includes bibliographical references (p.)
Includes index.
ISBN 8180692280

1. AIDS (Disease). 2. AIDS (Disease)—India. 3. HIV Infections. 4. HIV Infections—India. 5. AIDS (Disease)—Patients—India—Psychology. I. Rajamanickam, M. (Muniappa), 1925-

DDC 616.979 200 954 21

ISBN 81-8069-257-4

First Published 2006

Published and Printed by
Ashok Kumar Mittal
Concept Publishing Company
A-15/16, Commercial Block, Mohan Garden,
New Delhi-110 059 (India)

Phones : 25351460, 25351794
Fax : 091-11-25357103
Email : publishing@conceptpub.com

PREFACE

Public Enterprises (PEs) occupy the central stage in terms of the ongoing debate about their place in the Indian Economy. Their future role in terms of contribution to Gross Domestic Product (GDP), employment creation, vehicle of social transformation and an instrument of mobilization of savings is being debated in different national and international fora. The present volume addresses to vital issues of the place of PEs in the future of the Indian Economy and the organizational mix that these enterprises would have to adopt in the years to come. The scope of the volume has been extended to cover even the State Level Public Enterprises. The relevance of some strategic innovations in PE management such as MoU, Navaratna and Miniratna and Corporate Restructuring has been examined at great length. The status of PEs in terms of new policy measures such as liberalization, privatisation and globalization has been critically examined to arrive at a balanced view.

The present volume is the result of policy research taken up by the authors for a host of national and global agencies including the Planning Commission, Finance Commission, PM's Economics Advisory Council, Department of Public Enterprises (GoI), Inter-State Council (GoI), Common Wealth Secretariat, International Association of Institutes in Administration, Indian Council of Social Science Research, and Ministry of Disinvestment (GoI).

We hope that the Volume would be found useful by policy makers, researchers, Public Enterprise executives, industry associations, management community and the post-graduate students.

Hyderabad

R.K. Mishra
Ch. Lakshmi Kumari
B. Navin
P. Geeta

CONTENTS

1

PUBLIC ENTERPRISES IN THE ERA OF ECONOMIC LIBERALISATION

Public Enterprises Policy

Public Enterprises (PEs) have acted as an instrument for self-reliant economic growth of India in order to develop agriculture and industry, diversify public economy and overcome economic backwardness. The predominant considerations for continued large investments in PEs were to accelerate the growth of core sectors of economy; to serve the equipment needs of strategically important sectors such as railways, telecommunications, nuclear power, defence etc., enable the government to exert a countervailing power on the operation of private monopolies and multinationals in selected areas; and, provide strength for the economy to achieve a significant degree of self-sufficiency in the critical sectors.

The Industrial Policy Resolution of 1956 gave the public sector a strategic role in the economy. Massive investments have been made over the past five decades to set up a number of PEs. Many of these enterprises successfully expanded production, opened up new areas of technology and built up a reserve of sectoral competence. Nevertheless, after the initial concentration of public sector investment in key infrastructure areas, public enterprises began to spread into all areas of the economy including non-infrastructure and non-core areas.

In order to improve the performance of PEs in a liberalised economy, the Government of India announced on 24th July, 1991 as a part of the 'Statement on Industrial Policy', a statement on Public Sector also. The following major decisions were taken in respect of the public sector:[1]

"(i) Portfolio of public sector investments will be reviewed with a view to focus the public sector on strategic, high-tech and essential infrastructure. Whereas some reservation for the public sector is being retained, there would be no bar for area of exclusivity to be opened up to the private sector selectively. Similarly, the public sector will also be allowed entry in areas not reserved for it.

(ii) Public enterprises which are chronically sick and unlikely to be turned around will, for the formulation of revival/ rehabilitation schemes, be referred to the Board for Industrial and Financial Reconstruction (BIFR), or other similar high-level institutions created for the purpose. A social security mechanism will be created to protect the interests of workers likely to be affected by such rehabilitation packages.

(iii) In order to raise resources and encourage wider public participation, a part of the Government's shareholding in the public sector would be offered to mutual funds, financial institutions, general public and workers.

(iv) Boards of public sector companies would be made more professional and given greater powers.

(v) There will be a greater thrust on performance improvement through the Memoranda of Understanding (MoU) system through which managements would be granted greater autonomy and will be held accountable. Technical expertise on the part of the Government would be upgraded to make the MoU negotiations and implementation more effective.

(vi) To facilitate a fuller discussion on performance, the MoU signed between Government and the public enterprises would be placed in Parliament. While focusing on major management issues, this would also help place matters on day-to-day operations of public enterprises in their correct perspective".

The main elements of the present Government policy towards PEs as stated in the Economic Survey presented to the Parliament in February 2003 are:[2]

- Bring down Government equity in all non-strategic PEs to 26 per cent or lower, if necessary;
- Restructure and review potentially viable PEs;

- Close down PEs which cannot be revived; and
- Fully protect the interest of workers.

Performance of Public Enterprises

According to a study of the comparative performance of public and private sector conducted by the Centre for Industrial and Economic Research[3] on behalf of the Standing Conference of Public Enterprises (SCOPE), the growth in operating profit between 1991-92 and 1992-98 of the CPEs was 29 per cent against 14.7 per cent registered by the private sector during the same period. According to the Confederation of Indian Industry (CII), the public sector giants are in the limelight as they have emerged as top players in earning profits as compared to the private enterprises. In this context, it is relevant to discuss the robust performance of the Oil and Natural Gas Corporation (ONGC) in terms of profit earning[4]. During 2002-03, ONGC earned a profit of over Rs. 10,000 crore and its capital expenditure is proposed around Rs. 16,000 crore for the year 2003-04. As soon as a public sector chief is about to retire, he is lapped by giving double the salary. A large number of PEs follow latest management techniques such as business re-engineering, total quality management, resources planning, online performance appraisal, etc. Quite a few of them are recognised as ISO 9000 and ISO 14000 companies. The National Thermal Power Corporation (NTPC) was the first to achieve the ISO 9002 certification amongst super thermal power stations of India. The Indian Oil Corporation's Mathura Refinery is the first in Asia and third in the world to have won the ISO 14000 environment management system award. The Bharat Heavy Electricals Ltd. (BHEL) has developed social objectives as extension of its business practices. PEs continue to give top priority to the welfare of the weaker sections of the society. The scheduled castes, scheduled tribes and other backward classes constitute nearly 27 per cent of the total employment generated by PEs. In pursuing their objective of promoting balanced development of the entire country, PEs have contributed 21 per cent of their capital deployment as compared to 12.5 per cent by the private sector[5].

There are areas of great concern relating to PE performance. PEs have excessively invested in capital employed. Their marketing organisations are not strong enough to achieve a better turnover/

Table 1.1: Trends of Profitability of Public Enterprises during the last ten years (1992-93 to 2001-02)

(Rs. in crore)

S.No.	*Particulars*	*92-93*	*93-94*	*94-95*	*95-96*	*96-97*	*97-98*	*98-99*	*99-00*	*00-01*	*01-02*
1.	No of operating Enterprises	239	240	241	239	236	236	235	232	234	230
2.	Capital employed (CE)	140110	159836	162451	173948	231178	249855	265093	302367	331401	390261
3.	Profit before dep. Int. and tax (PBDIT)	25227	27707	33384	40161	44457	53062	56495	62212	69287	89619
4.	Depreciation	9270	9151	10754	12574	13542	15856	16768	19942	20520	26362
5.	Profit before int. and tax (PBIT)	15957	18556	22630	27587	30915	37206	39727	42270	48767	63257
6.	Interest	10881	11901	12862	13966	15537	17990	20025	20233	23800	24958
7.	Profit before Tax	5076	6655	9768	13621	15378	19216	19702	22037	24967	38299
8.	Tax provisions	1805	2110	2581	4047	5192	5634	6499	7706	9314	12254
9.	Net profit	3271	4545	7187	9574	10186	13582	13203	14331	15653	26045
10.	Profit of profit making PEs	7384	9768	12070	14763	16125	20279	22508	24633	28494	36432
11.	Loss of loss incurring PEs	4113	5223	4883	5188	5939	6697	9305	10302	12841	10387
12.	PEs in Profits	131	121	130	132	129	134	126	126	123	119
13.	PEs in Losses	106	116	109	102	104	100	107	105	110	109
14.	PEs in no profit/loss	2	3	2	5	3	2	2	1	1	2
15.	Dividend	792	1028	1436	2205	2836	3609	4932	5455	8260	8067
16.	Dividend tax	—	—	—	—	261	464	537	790	842	9
17.	Retained profit	2479	3517	5751	7369	7089	9509	7734	8086	6551	17969
	Financial Ratio (%)	—	—	—	—	—	—	—	—	—	—
A.	PBDIT to CE	18.0	17.3	20.6	23.1	19.2	21.2	21.3	20.5	20.9	23.0
B.	PBIT to CE	11.4	11.6	13.9	15.9	13.4	14.9	15.0	14.0	14.7	16.2
C.	Dividend payout	24.2	22.6	20.0	23.0	27.8	26.6	37.4	38.1	52.8	31.0

Source: Department of Public Enterprises (Government of India, New Delhi), Public Enterprise Survey: Vol. 1, 2001-2002, p. 25.

capital employed ratio. They neglected the issues connected to brand development, globalisation, optimal product mix, efficient cost management, and reduction in interest burden. There is no denying the fact that many of these concerns have not been resolved to the fullest extent due to the backseat driving by the political executive and civil servants.

Table 1.1 shows the performance of public enterprise during 1992-93 to 2001-02. The salient features of the table are as follows:

(i) The capital employed has increased by 350 per cent between 1992-93 to 2001-02.

(ii) PEs obtained a cash profit of 18 per cent in 1992-93 which increased to 23 per cent in 2001-02.

(iii) Profit Before Interest and Tax (PBIT) to Capital Employed ratio was 11.4 per cent in 1992-93 which increased to 16.2 per cent in 2001-02.

(iv) The Capital Employed to Turnover/Operating Income ratio was 1.05 per cent in 1992-93 which increased to 1.22 per cent in 2001-02.

(v) The Dividend Pay-out ratio increased from 24.2 per cent in 1992-93 to 31.0 per cent in 2001-02.

Disinvestment

In its PE policy, the Government did not outline the basic principles governing disinvestment. However, in a *suo moto* statement laid in both the Houses of Parliament on 9th December, 2002, the Government indicated that the disinvestment specifically aimed at the modernisation and upgradation of public enterprises, creation of new assets, generation of employment, retiring of public debt and creation of disinvestment fund. The disinvestment in PEs commenced in 1991-92. The following is the chronology of evolution of the Government thinking on disinvestment:

Table 1.2: Chronology of Evolution of Government thinking on Disinvestment

Date	*Event*
1991-92 Interim Budget	Government announced its intention to divest upto 20 per cent of government equity in selected PSUs in favour of public sector institutional investors.
Budget Speech 24th July, 1991	In the case of selected enterprises, part of government holdings in the equity share capital of the enterprises was decided to be disinvested in order to provide further market discipline to the performance of public enterprises.
Rangarajan Committee Report, April 1993	It emphasized the need for substantial disinvestment, and stated that while the percentage of equity to be divested was to be not more than 49% for industries explicitly reserved for the public sector, it could be either 74% or 100% for others.
Budget speech : 1998-99	Government decided that in the generality of cases, the Government shareholding in public sector enterprises was being brought down to 26 per cent. In cases of public sector enterprises involving strategic considerations, Government was to continue to retain majority holding. The interest of workers was to be protected in all cases.
Budget speech: 1999-2000	Government strategy towards public sector enterprises was to continue to encompass a judicious mix of strengthening strategic units, privatizing non-strategic ones through gradual disinvestment of strategic sale and devising viable rehabilitation strategies for weak units.
Cabinet decision of March 16, 1999	Public Sector Undertakings (PSUs) were classified into **strategic and non-strategic entities for** the purpose of disinvestment. Strategic PSUs belonged to the areas of: (a) *Arms and ammunitions* and the allied items of defence equipment, defence aircrafts and warships; (b) *Atomic energy* (except in the areas related to the operation of nuclear power and applications of radiation and radio-isotopes to agriculture medicine and non-strategic industries);

(contd.)

Table 1.2 (contd.)

Date	*Event*
	(c) *Railway transport* : All other PSUs were to be considered as non-strategic. For the non-strategic PSUs, it was decided that the reduction of government stake to 26% would not be automatic. Decision in regard to the percentage of disinvestment i.e., Government's stake going down to less than 51% or to 26%, were to be taken on the following considerations: (a) Whether the industrial sector requires the presence of the public sector as a countervailing force to prevent concentration of power in private hands, and (b) Whether the industrial sector requires a proper regulatory mechanism to protect the consumer interests before Public Sector Enterprise are privatised.
Budget Speech: 2000-01	In order to secure the presence of the public sector as a countervailing force, the Government took the decision of not going for disinvestment of GAIL, IOC and ONGC, and retaining them as flagship companies.
CCDs Decision dated September 7, 2002	Central Public Sector Undertakings (PSUs), Central Government owned Cooperative Societies (where Government's ownership is 51% or more) were not permitted to participate in the disinvestment of other PSUs as bidder. If in some specific cases any deviation from these restrictions is considered desirable in public interest, the Ministry/Department concerned was to bring an appropriate proposal for consideration of the Core Group of Secretaries on Disinvestment.
Suo moto statement made in both the Houses of Parliament on 9th December 2002 by Minister of Disinvestment	"The main objective of disinvestment is to put national resources and assets to optimal use and in particular to unleash the productive potential inherent in our public sector enterprises. The policy of disinvestment of Parliament specifically aims at: — Modernisation and upgradation of Public Sector Enterprises; — Creation of new assets; Generation of employment; Retiring of Public Disinvestment Debt.

(contd.)

Table 1.2 (contd.)

Date	*Event*
	Government would continue to ensure that disinvestment does not result in alienation of national assets, which, through the process of disinvestment, remain where they are. It will also ensure that disinvestment does not result in private monopolies. In order to provide complete visibility to the government's continued commitment of utilization of disinvestment proceeds for social and infrastructure sectors, the government would set up a Disinvestment Proceeds Fund. This Fund will be used for financing fresh employment opportunities and investment, and for retirement of public debt. For the disinvestment of natural asset of companies, the Ministry of Finance and the Ministry of Disinvestment will work out guidelines." — The Ministry of Finance was also to prepare for consideration of the Cabinet Committee on Disinvestment a paper on the feasibility and modalities of setting up an Asset Management Company to hold, manage and dispose the residual holding of the government in the companies in which government equity was disinvested to a strategic partner. With these objectives as the guiding principles, the government took the following specific decisions: — To disinvest through sale of shares to the public in Bharat Petroleum Corporation Ltd. (BPCL). — To disinvest in Hindustan Petroleum Corporation Ltd. (HPCL) through strategic sale. — To allot, in both cases of BPCL and HPCL, a specific percentage of shares to the employees of the two companies at a concessional price.

Source: Department of Public Enterprises (Government of India, New Delhi), Public Enterprise Survey: Vol. 1, 2001-2002, pp. 81-83

Table 1.3 shows the monies realised from disinvestment from April 1991 till October 2002 and methodologies adopted for disinvestment.

Table 1.3 : Actual Disinvestment from 1991-92 to 2002-03 and Methodologies Adopted

(Rs. in crore)

Year	*No. of Cos. in which equity sold*	*Target receipt for the year*	*Actual receipts*	*Methodology*
1991-92	47 (31 in one tranche and 16 in other)	2500	3038	Minority shares sold by auction method in bundles of "very good", "good", and "average" companies.
1992-93	35 (in 3 trenches)	2500	1913	Bundling of shares abandoned. Shares sold separately for each company by auction method.
1993-94		3500	Nil	Equity of 7 companies sold by open auction but proceeds received in 1994-95.
1994-95	13	4000	4843	Sale through auction method in which NRIs and other persons legally permitted to buy, hold or sell equity allowed to participate
1996-97	1	5000	380	GDR (VSNL) in international market
1997-98	1	4800	902	GDR (MTNL) in international market
1998-99	5	5000	5371	GDR (VSNL)/Domestic offerings with the participation of FIIs (CONCOR, GAIL) Cross purchase by 3 Oil sector companies i.e. GAIL, ONGC and Indian Oil Corporation.
1999-00	2	10000	1829	GDR—GAIL VSNL—domestic issue, BALCO restructuring MFIL's strategic sale and others
2000-01	4	10000	1869	Strategic sale of BALCO, LJMC, KRL (CRL), CPCL (MRL)
2001-02	10	12,000	5632#	Strategic sale of CMC—51%, HTL—74%, VSNL—25%, IBP—33.58%, PPL—74%, and other modes; ITDC, HCI, STC, MMTC.
2002-03	6	12,000	3336@	Strategic sale of HZL—26%, MFIL—26%, IPCL—25% and other modes: HCI, ITDC and Maruti.
Total	**48***	**71,300**	**29481 #**	

Source: Department of Public Enterprises (Government of India, New Delhi), Public Enterprise Survey, Vol. 1, 2001-2002 and Ministry of Finance, GOI, Economic Survey, 2003, p.149

* Total number of companies in which disinvestment has taken place so far.

\# Figures (inclusive of amount realized by way of control premium, dividend/ dividend tax and transfer of surplus cash reserves prior to disinvestment etc.)

@ Till 31.1.2003.

Table 1.3 shows that the actual receipts from disinvestment turned out to be 37.6 per cent of the targeted receipts. The disinvestment could never show up as a dominant source of bridging the fiscal deficits. A review of disinvestment policy raises questions relating to the method of sale, organisation for sale, identification of PEs for sale, eligibility for bidding and involvement of concerned PEs in the process. The method of sale has attracted a severe criticism.

Table 1.4 shows that during 1992-2000 strategic disinvestment ruled the roost. The government has openly preferred the strategic sale. However, the Initial Public Offer (IPO) of Maruti Udyog Ltd. hitting the Indian capital market in June 2003 brings altogether a different experience. The retail investor has gained much in terms of allotment of shares. The capital market has tremendously benefited from Maruti IPO in terms of increased capitalisation and wider distribution of its shareholdings. The market capitalisation of PEs has gone up by 25 per cent of PEs.[6] Such IPOs by PEs will not allow the formation of monopolies. This method is bound to improve the corporate governance in India as the vigilant shareholders would insist on wealth creation which would benefit all the stakeholders. The strategic sale suffers from many demerits. Besides, propping up monopolies, it gives unfettered rights to the strategic buyer to bring about far reaching changes which might go against the interests of the workers and the government.

Table 1.4 : Strategic Disinvestment since 1999-2000

S.No.	*Name*	*GoI/ Equity sold*	*Realisation (Rs. Crores)*
	1999-2000		
1.	MFIL	9.63	105.00
A	**Total for the year 2000-01**	**9.63**	**105.00**
2.	BALCO	112.52	826.50
3.	LJMC	0.77	2.53
B	**Total for the year 2001-02**	**113.29**	**829.03**
4.	CMC	7.73	152.00
5.	HTL	11.10	55.00
6.	IBP	7.44	1153.68
7.	VSNL ^	71.25	3689.00
8.	PPL	320.16	151.70
	ITDC		
9.	Agra	1.70	3.61
10.	Bodhgaya	0.44	1.81

(contd.)

Table 1.4 (contd.)

S.No.	*Name*	*GoI/ Equity sold*	*Realisation (Rs. Crores)*
11.	Hassan	0.21	2.27
12.	Mamallapuram	0.83	6.13
13	Madurai	0.71	4.97
14.	Bangalore*	0.96	39.41
15.	Qutab	0.83	34.46
16.	Lodhi	0.96	71.93
17.	LVPH, Udaipur	0.55	6.77
	HCI	—	—
18.	Juhu, Bombay	8.95	153.00
19.	Ragir	1.72	6.51
20.	STC	—	40.00
21	MMTC	—	60.00
C	**Total for the year 2002-03**	**435.54**	**5732.25**
22	Hindustan Zinc Ltd.	109.85	445.00
23.	Maruti Udyog ^^	66.00	1000.00
24.	IPCL	64.50	1490.84
25	MFIL—Phase II	3.38	44.00
	ITDC		
26.	Manali	0.63	3.65
27.	Kovalam	1.85	40.39
28.	Aurangabad	1.16	16.50
29.	Airport Kolkata	0.66	19.39
30.	Khajuraho	0.97	2.19
31.	Varanasi	1.74	8.38
32.	Kanishka	1.90	92.37
33.	Indraprastha (AYN)	0.80	43.39
34.	Chandragiri Project	7.00	17.27
35.	Airport Mumbai	4.00	83.00
	Hotel Corpn. of India		
36.	Ranjit	3.20	29.20
D.	**Total for the year**	**267.64**	**3335.57**
E	**Maruti** **^^**		**1424.00**
F	**JESSOP****		**18.18**
	Grand Total (A to F)	**826.10**	**11344.03**

Source: Department of Public Enterprises (Government of India, New Delhi), Public Enterprise Survey: Vol. 1, 2001-2002, pp.85-86

* Including NPV of future earnings on MGAP and lease rentals

** expected ^ Including dividend and dividend Tax ^^ (minimum amount to be received over trenches; could go up to Rs. 3158 cr) Sr. No. 3, 18, 19, 34, 35 and F are subsidiaries. Sales at F to be approved by Govt./BIFR.

The government has defended strategic disinvestment in terms of a superior price to earnings ratio obtained in the case of the disinvested units as compared to those obtained in the case of PEs where shareholdings were disinvested to mutual funds, financial institutions, etc. Table 1.4 shows the price to earning ratio in the case of sale of shares viz., strategic disinvestment route to privatised PEs. The government continues to fail to appreciate the superiority of the IPO to other routes of disinvestment by not distinguishing between sale of shares to the general investor and off-loading shares to mutual funds, banks and financial institutions Nonetheless, the strategic disinvestment would be appropriate for the sale of small units. The IPO method was frequently employed for disinvesting shares in PEs in the United Kingdom (UK). The demand to consider management-employee buy out as an alternative to strategic sale was conceded to after a prolonged delay in April 2003. As per the decision of the Cabinet Committee on Disinvestment (CCD) if the employees' bid is not the highest, it shall be considered only if the said bid is within 10 per cent of the highest bid.[7] Even in the employees' bid, the government is keen to promote competition as 15 per cent or 200 employees, whichever is lower, could make a bid paving the way for multiple bids from workers. Such bids will be exempted from minimum turnover criteria. The government would do well to take a leaf from the British experience of disinvestment wherein the UK Government had directed the Bank of England to finance the employee buy out through a specially designed loan scheme.

The eligibility criteria for bidding suffer from many inconsistencies. The Reliance Industries Ltd. was allowed to bid for the Indian Petrochemicals Corporation Ltd. (IPCL) contrary to the recommendation that it would create a monopoly. Since privatisation, there has been a steady rise in the prices of the products of IPCL While creating a monopoly in petrochemicals, the ONGC is not allowed to bid for HPCL, although ONGC share of refining even after acquisition of Mangalore Refineries and Petrochemicals Ltd. (MRPL), HPCL will be less than the capacity of single private sector refinery. Now, ONGC has not been allowed to bid for HPCL on the ground that the public sector company should not participate in disinvestment. The logic of this is far from clear. Indian Oil Corporation (IOC) was allowed to bid for I.B.P Co. Ltd. (IBP) and the government obtained a very high bid from IOC for IBP. Close on the heels of the decision there was a decision to allow ONGC and the Gas Authority of India Ltd.(GAIL) to bid the Engineers India Ltd (EIL) This flip-flop points to the lack of consistency in the disinvestment policy of the government. It is to be kept in mind that the government finances are different from PE finance. PEs are independent legal entities. The companies are different from shareholders. Participation of PEs will enhance the bidding levels. The government has projected disinvestment exercise as a money spinner to improve its finances. However, the study of disinvestment in the case of Jessop & Co. Ltd (Jessop) and Paradeep Phosphates points out a completely different picture. In the case of Jessop, the government committed on disinvestment to sell 72 per cent stake to Ruia Cotex for Rs. 18.18 crore. Finalising the package for forwarding to Board for Financial and Industrial Reconstruction (BIFR) for approval, CCD also decided to give a financial support of Rs. 63 crore to clear liabilities of bank and others apart from non-fund support of Rs. 140 crore by way of writing off the interest and government loans to Ruia Cotex. There was hardly any difference in the case of Paradeep Phosphate in which case the government sold its 74 per cent stake to the sole bidder Zuari-Maroc combine at Rs. 151.7 crore. The sale was much below a reserve price of Rs. 176 crore. As per the government philosophy to stop financial haemorrage in the loss making PEs, the government went for negative bidding in the case of Paradeep Phosphate. The government approved a financial restructuring package entailing over Rs. 200 crore including waiver of interest and conversion of loan into preferential capital to give a clean balance sheet to the company. The government has curbed PE initiatives for bidding by empowering the Cabinet Secretary to review the process of authorisation of bids.

The disinvestment process suffers from the executive interference caused by politicians and bureaucrats. Despite suggestions to set up an independent authority to handle disinvestment through an enactment in the Parliament and leave the entire gamut of decision making to it, the Executive perpetuates its control on disinvestment. It is because of these reasons that the sale of Hotel Corporation of India property at Airport, Mumbai, for Rs. 83 crore drew nationwide attention as it was difficult for the government to defend its decision to sell the property for Rs. 83 crore which was resold by the buyer in a very short period for Rs.120 crore making a kill of Rs. 37 crore. As part of the damage control exercise, the government later announced that properties sold through disinvestment would not be resold for a certain minimum period. It is very important to cite the case of Videsh Sanchar Nigam Ltd.(VSNL). Disinvestment wherein during the immediate post-privatisation period the board of the privatised company decided to transfer Rs.1200 crore to one of its constituent units. The nominee directors of the government were asked to explain as to why such move was not stopped as the government continue to have a sizeable shareholding in the privatised VSNL. However, the government drew a blank.

Table 1.5 : Price to Earning Ratios

S.No.	*Sale of Shares 1991-99*		*Strategic Disinvestment 1999-2000 to October 2002*	
1	IOC	4.9	BALCO	19
2.	BPCL	5.7	CMC	12
3.	HPCL	5.9	HTL	37
4.	GAIL	4.4	MFIL	Very high as earning per share was negative
5.	VSNL	6.0 (In Monopoly Days)	LJMC	-do-
6.			PPL	-do-
7.			JESSOP	-do-
8.			IBP	63
9.			VSNL	11 (inclusive of income from dividend etc. (after the end of monopoly)
10.			HZL	26
11.			MARUTI	89
12.			IPCL	58

Source: Department of Public Enterprises (Government of India, New Delhi), Public Enterprise Survey: Vol. 1, 2001-2002, p. 79

Navaratna/Miniratna PEs

The Navaratna concept which originated in the Common Minimum Programme 1996 of the United Front Government promised identification of PEs having comparative advantages to be supported in their drive to become global giants. Other profit-making PEs were to be strengthened and their management professionalised. It was however on July 4, 1997 that the government decided to confer wide powers to nine PEs as Navaratnas. Two more PEs were added to this later. The Navaratna PEs comprise:

1. Bharat Heavy Electricals Ltd. (BHEL)
2. Bharat Petroleum Corporation Ltd. (BPCL)
3. Hindustan Petroleum Corporation Ltd. (HPCL)
4. Indian Oil Corporation (IOC)
5. Indian Petrochemicals Ltd. (IPCL)
6. National Thermal Power Corporation (NTPC)
7. Oil and Natural Gas Corporation (ONGC)
8. Steel Authority of India Ltd. (SAIL)
9. Videsh Sanchar Nigam Ltd. (VSNL)
10. Gas Authority of India Ltd. (GAIL)
11. Mahanagar Telephone Nigam Ltd. (MTNL)

The first category covered enterprises: (i) making profits continuously for the last three years, with a pre-tax profit of at least Rs. 30 crore in at least one of the three years, (ii) having a positive net worth, (iii) not having defaulted on Government loans, and (iv) not receiving any budgetary support. The second category comprised PEs with pre-tax profits (no amount mentioned) during the last three years; (ii), (iii) and (iv) being the same, as for category-I. Category I PEs were empowered to: (i) incur capital expenditure upto Rs. 300 crore or equal to their net worth, whichever is lower, (ii) establish joint ventures and subsidiaries in India, and if abroad with the concurrence of the administrative ministry, with an equity limit of Rs. 100 crore or 5 per cent of the net worth in any one case, and 15 per cent of the net worth for all joint ventures and subsidiaries put together, and (iii) negotiate technology joint ventures and strategic alliances subject to Government guidelines. For category II, the figures under various heads were restricted to: (i) Rs. 150 crore or 50 per cent of the net worth, (ii) Rs. 50 crore, in any one project not exceeding 5 per cent of the net worth in any one project, or 15 per cent of the net worth of PE in all joint ventures of the subsidiaries put together.

The recognition of PEs as Navaratna /Miniratna implied the assumption that given the adequate operational and financial autonomy, PEs would weather any storm and that such empowerment would enable them to become self-sustaining entities. The author as a Member of the Working Group on Public Enterprises set up by the Ministry of Heavy Industry and Public Enterprises, Government of India, and Planning Commission, carried out a study on the functioning of the Navaratna/Miniratna PEs. This Section summarises the findings of the study in order to examine the relevance of the concept. Table 1.6 presents a picture of the operational autonomy given and availed by Navaratna and Miniratna PEs.

Financial Autonomy

Budgetary Support

Regarding budgetary support from government, a majority of the respondents stated that they are not getting any budgetary support. However, the CMD, Indian Medicines Pharmaceutical Corpn. Ltd. (IMPCL), stated that it received budgetary support from government of Rs. 51 lakh for its modernisation and expansion since its inception. The CMD, PEC Ltd., indicated that it gets government guarantee as per terms and conditions applicable to public sector enterprises.

Freedom to be given to Incur Capital Expenditure

The respondents stated that they are incurring capital expenditure in new projects, entering into new technologies, collaborations and establishing joint ventures. Powergrid Corporation and Kudremukh Iron Ore Ltd., have raised debt from domestic market.

The changing conditions call for a new approach and more freedom is required in incurring capital expenditure. Hence the respondents in general stated that more freedom is to be given by the government as there is no budgetary support from government.

The views given by some of the respondents in respect of capital expenditure are given briefly in the Table 1.7.

Table 1.6 : Operational Autonomy given and availed by PEs

Name of PE	*Operational autonomy given and availed by the PE*				
	Monitoring of Performance by the Board	*Technology and R&D*	*Product Mix*	*Fixation of Performance targets*	*Remarks*
1. HPCL	—	—	—	—	Under Navaratna package only decision-making authority accorded and no special operational autonomy given.
2. ONGC	Overall performance monitored by Board on quarterly basis.	Initiatives being taken by various R&D institutes in ONGC to acquire new technology. Except for the guidelines issued by government in January 2000 for technology joint ventures, no other change and existing tendering procedures have to be followed.	No change. Crude oil, natural gas and value-added products continue to be primary revenue earners.	Financial targets carrying 60% of weight are still as per existing directive of DPE. Physical targets and dynamic efficiency parameters modified to reflect organisation's focus on production, reserves accretion, HR, IT and R&D etc.	—
3. NTPC	Yes	Yes	Four Joint Ventures have already been formed for taking up diversification in related areas.	Yes	—

(contd.)

Table 1.6 (contd.)

Name of PE	*Operational autonomy given and availed by the PE*				
	Monitoring of Performance by the Board	*Technology and R&D*	*Product Mix*	*Fixation of Performance targets*	*Remarks*
4. SAIL	The autonomy is being availed.	Autonomy has been availed.	Yes*	Availed	It was always available after de-regulation of steel sector in 1992.
5. KIOL	Yes	Yes	Yes	Yes	Operational autonomy availed by the PE
6. MDL	Yes. Monitoring of performance by Board and Administrative Ministry done periodically.	R&D efforts geared towards quality improvement in the areas of design, manufacture, and assembly erection.	Not availed	Since 1991-92 with approval of Board, company has been on MOU in which targets on various activities and performance parameters are laid down.	-do-
7. REIL	—	—	—	—	Operational autonomy given to a less extent. PE has not availed operational autonomy.
8. PCIL	Performance of Corporation is primarily monitored by Powergrid Board and thereby Group of Secretaries of GOI.	Powergrid has adopted new technologies like FACTS, series computerisation.	—	To some extent autonomy was availed.	—

(contd.)

Table 1.6 (contd.)

Name of PE	*Operational autonomy given and availed by the PE*				
	Monitoring of Performance by the Board	*Technology and R&D*	*Product Mix*	*Fixation of Performance targets*	*Remarks*
9. RCF	—	—	—	—	In view of there being no non-official Directors on Board, RCF cannot exercise the authority.
10. IMPCL	—	—	—	—	—
11. NMDC	—	—	—	It is arrived after discussion with ATF Members of DPE.	As per DPE's order in general.
12. KRL	—	—	—	—	As per DPE's order in general
13. BRPL	—	—	—	—	As per DPE's order in general.
14. STC	Quarterly performance is put to the Board for information.	Not Applicable	Free to deal in any item permitted to be exported/imported.	The corporation does not enjoy much autonomy with regard to the same.	—
15. CCIL	—	—	—	—	Autonomy is given to a moderate extent.
16. NFDC	The performance is evaluated by the Board	Decisions are taken by the Board and	Being a service sector diversifica-	MoU targets are finalised after due	—

(contd.)

Table 1.6 (contd.)

Name of PE	*Operational autonomy given and availed by the PE*				
	Monitoring of Performance by the Board	*Technology and R&D*	*Product Mix*	*Fixation of Performance targets*	*Remarks*
	itself.	implemented.	tion of activities to other medias like electronic media was carried out. The company is active in TV programmes and marketing in addition to the production and financing of Films.	negotiation between the Company and government keeping the realities in mind and without imposing views on each other.	
17. WPCSL	Quarterly performance is put to the Board for information.	Board level technical committees were constituted and the experience and expertise of Board members are used.	Diversified in taking up turnkey assignments in "small Hydros" and "Water Harvesting" to serve the national cause and also increase the turnover.	The MoU is based on Financial and Dynamic indicators to monitor the performance of the company.	—
18. HSCCL	Yes	N.A.	Yes	Yes	—

(contd.)

Table 1.6 (contd.)

Name of PE	*Operational autonomy given and availed by the PE*				
	Monitoring of Performance by the Board	*Technology and R&D*	*Product Mix*	*Fixation of Performance targets*	*Remarks*
19. HPC	—	No changes effected	No changes effected	No changes effected	—
20. PFCL	N.A.	N.A.	N.A.	N.A.	—
21. TCIL	—	—	—	—	Nothing added than what we are doing earlier

Source: Mishra, R.K., A Study of Operational and Financial Autonomy to Navaratna and Miniratna PEs, Ministry of Heavy Industry and Public Enterprises, Government of India, New Delhi—Planning Commission—Institute of Public Enterprise, Hyderabad, 2003.

Table 1.7 : Freedom to be given to incur Capital Expenditure

Name of the PE	*Views on the Freedom to be given on Capital Expenditure*
1. HPCL	He is of the view that: "the ceiling on investments in JVCs be made in line with Section 372A of the Companies Act wherein aggregate of intercorporate loans and investments made by the company in all other bodies corporate cannot exceed 60% of net worth or 100% free reserves, whichever is higher of investing company.The ceiling of 15% of net worth of the PE in all joint ventures / subsidiaries put together should not be made applicable to investments already made in the projects as this has been done after obtaining all government approvals.
2. ONGC	The Navaratnas have been empowered to incur capital expenditure on purchase of new items or for replacement without any monetary limit.
3. NTPC	Full power should be given for entering into Joint Ventures. Further, the power to incur capital expenditure on Projects financed through government guaranteed loan should also be provided to the Board.
4. SAIL	The current level of freedom is adequate.
5. REIL	Currently no freedom is given to incur capital expenditure. All capital expenditure requires prior budgetary approval of the Board. To begin with, a limit of Rs. 20 lakh may be considered.
6. RCFL	Although RCFL has been selected as Miniratna, since non-official Directors are yet to be appointed, the requisite autonomy has not been given to RCF.
7. PCIL	The corporation is availing the autonomy given to it and it may require enhancement in existing limits in future.
8. IMPCL	Keeping in view the present status, no more freedom is required than the existing one.
9. NMDC	The works or programmes to be undertaken should be the guiding factor rather than the monetary ceilings.
10. KRL	It is meeting capital expenditure through internal resources and OIDB loans. It has not used any budgetary support or government guarantee.
11. STC	The freedom to incur capital expenditure as granted to Miniratnas is subject to a number of stipulations ultimately requiring the PEs to seek approval of the administrative ministry. However, by virtue of STC's nature of operations, there are not many proposals involving huge capital expenditure.
12. CCIL	Requires complete freedom. All decisions taken by the management are reviewed by the CAG. Why should there be any restriction?

(contd.)

Table 1.7 *(contd.)*

Name of the PE	*Views on the Freedom to be given on Capital Expenditure*
13. NFDC	The present delegation of powers accorded by the government seems to be adequate.
14. WPCCL	The company can have autonomy to incur capital expenditure without any limit if the amount proposed to be spent is from its own sources and the company is not resorting to any financial assistance to the extent of provisions of Miniratna.
15. HPC	Board may be empowered to sanction capital expenditure of new projects /modernisation etc., upto a ceiling of Rs. 100 crore.
16. TCIL	Due to strategic requirements we have to invest in JV's and are limited by 15% of networth. We requested at all forums to allow us capital expenditure plus 15% of new investment in JV through Board.

Source: Mishra, R.K., A Study of Operational and Financial Autonomy to Navaratna and Miniratna PEs, Ministry of Heavy Industry and Public Enterprises, Government of India, New Delhi, Planning Commission, Institute of Public Enterprise, Hyderabad, 2003.

The respondents suggested more operational and financial autonomy to make PE perform in a natural and effective way. The suggestions given by some of the PEs are given below:

Water and Power Consultancy Services (India) Ltd. (WPCSL)

(a) Opening offices abroad to facilitate quick response to potential consultancy assignments and to develop effective liaisoning with clients.
(b) Networking with financial institutions to secure loans on behalf of the clients.
(c) Financial powers for capital investment.
(d) Opening of Subsidiary or Joint Venture company.
(e) Social obligation of the Government should be discontinued.
(f) Appointment of Functional and Non-Functional Directors in the specific fields of operation of the company.
(g) Grant or Aid for securing projects in developing countries.
(h) Autonomy to CEO to travel abroad as per exigencies of work and requirement for business development.

National Film Development Corporation Ltd. (NFDC)

Though financial autonomy has been granted to PEs to a significant extent, since the granting of Miniratna status, it is felt that the performance of each of the PEs and the roles governing its operation should be independent and need not necessarily be common. More delegation of powers would be advisable/desirable regarding deputation of Board level executives abroad on Business visits. The Chairman and Managing Director of the concerned PE should be the approving authority for such delegations depending upon the cost effectiveness. The delegation of powers in other spheres appears to be reasonably adequate for carrying out the company's operation in an effective way.

Telecommunications Consultants (India) Ltd. (TCIL)

(a) Creation of posts below Board level by CMD.
(b) For investment in J.V in India and abroad limit should be Rs. 300 crore plus 15 per cent of networth.
(c) Tendering process should be replaced by 'Request for Proposals', as in any private company.

State Trading Corporation of India Ltd. (STC)

(a) The Corporation should be allowed to formulate and implement its own reward and punishment schemes.
(b) The performance targets proposed by the Corporation under MOU should be accepted by the DPE if the same are agreed to by the DOC.

In general it is found that the status of Navaratna/Miniratna has changed the styles of management in PEs. They are becoming more commercial and market-oriented. Now, PEs are managed with management and professional-orientation and they are concerned about customers. However, the CMDs of IPCL, STC, CCIL, NMDC, PFCL, TCIL and HPC mentioned that there is no change in the styles of management in their respective organisations. Table 1.8 gives the details of styles of management followed by the PEs in a rating scale:

Table 1.8 : Degree of Changes in Styles of Management

Styles of Management	*Completely changed*	*Significantly changed*	*Moderately changed*	*Slightly changed*	*Remarks*
1. Commercial-orientation	—	3	1	2	—
2. Market-orientation	—	2	1	2	In the case of Power-grid corporation it is not applicable.
3. Management-orientation	—	3	—	3	—
4. Professional-orientation	—	4	1	1	HFCL management style has grown towards more of professional-orientation
5. Customer-orientation	—	2	1	1	In the case of Powergrid corporation it is not applicable.

Source: Mishra, R.K, A Study of Operational and Financial Autonomy to Navaratna and Miniratna PEs, Ministry of Heavy Industry and Public Enterprises, Government of India, New Delhi, Planning Commission, Institute of Public Enterprise, Hyderabad, 2003.

In general, all PE Boards under reference are availing the delegated authorities to a moderate extent and in some PEs it is availed to a great extent. They are implementing schemes relating to personnel and human resource management, wage negotiations, raising debt, training and voluntary schemes etc. The details given by some PEs are given below:

Organisational Restructuring

The following enterprises underwent some organisational restructuring after being accorded the status of Navaratna/Miniratna:

Oil and Natural Gas Corporation (ONGC)

(a) It has upgraded its communication network in the area of Finance, E&P, MM&HR.

(b) 12 major development projects costing a total of nearly Rs.1800 crore approved by ONGC Board subsequent to issue of government orders on Navaratna dispensation and upto 1-4-2000.

(c) Technology gaps identified and initiatives being taken by the respective R&D Institutes to acquire new technology through training of in-house personnel, collaboration and purchase.

(d) Six deep-water exploration blocks identified for strategic alliance with international companies with the requisite technology and expertise.

(e) Joint Venture for LNG, namely Petronet LNG, incorporated on 2.4.98 of which ONGC is a partner.

(f) Organisational restructuring initiated in 1997 and implemented in one region with effect from 1.4.1999.

(g) Revised pay scales for officers and staff as per DPE guidelines finalised in the year 2000.

National Thermal Power Corporation (NTPC)

(a) VRS was introduced to employees of NTPC upto level of E7 (DGM) in 1999 which was valid upto 30.4.2000.

(b) NTPC has already formed three joint venture companies:

1. NTPC ABB Alstom Power Services Ltd.
2. Power Trading Corporation.
3. SAIL Power Supply Co. Ltd.

Hindustan Petroleum Corporation Ltd. (HPCL)

(a) HPCL Board was restructured in January 1999 subsequent to which these decision-making authorities are being availed of from time to time as per requirements.

(b) HPCL has created strategic business units, profit centres and revised work practices. It has also revamped its information technology.

Steel Authority of India Ltd. (SAIL)

(a) The Board has availed considerable delegation of authority given under Navaratna-package in respect of capital expenditure on new projects, enter into technology joint venture, effect organizational restructuring and structure and implement schemes relating to personal and human resources.

State Trading Corporation of India Ltd. (STC)

Enjoys full delegation of authority in respect of:

(a) Organisation restructuring.
(b) Creation and winding up of all posts including and up to those of non-Board level directors.
(c) Voluntary Retirement Scheme (VRS) for the employees of the Corporation was formulated and implemented.
(d) Full autonomy in respect of raising debt from the domestic capital markets and borrowings from International Markets to the extent needed.

National Film Development Corporation Ltd. (NFDC)

(a) The Board avails the delegation of decision-making authority given by the government in all respects.
(b) As far as raising debts from the domestic capital markets and borrowing from international market is concerned it has not raised debts so far.
(c) Introduced VRS.

Water and Power Consultancy Services (India) Ltd. (WPCSL)

(a) Joint ventures/strategic alliances are made with national/international consultants on project to project basis for securing business in India and abroad.
(b) Technology and know-how is developed by way of on job assignments with international organisations, IITs and R&D institutions within the country.
(c) Schemes relating to personnel and human resource management, training etc., are being taken up.
(d) Marginal structural changes in working were brought to ensure accountability, reliability, speedy implementation and suitability of jobs vis-à-vis expertise and quality output.

Hospital Services Consultancy Corp. (India) Ltd. (HSCCL)

(a) To enter into technology Joint Venture or Strategic Alliances.
(b) To effect organisational restructuring.
(c) Creation and winding up of all posts including and upto those of non-board level of Directors, Functional Directors.
(d) Wage negotiation.

Telecommunications Consultants (India) Ltd. (TCIL)

It availed delegation of decision-making authority in respect of:

(a) Strategic alliance.
(b) Organisation restructuring.
(c) Creation and winding up of all posts except two levels below board.
(d) Implement schemes relating to personal and human resource management and training.
(e) Wage negotiations.
(f) Borrowing from international markets.

There is an impact of the Navaratna/Miniratna package on autonomy of the Board. The Table 1.9 shows the responses of the CMDs on the impact of the package on their enterprise.

From the Table 1.9, it is found that majority of the respondents are of the view that there is an impact of Navaratna/Miniratna package in their enterprise. There is gradual deregulation and debureaucratisation. There is enhanced delegation of powers to the Board, and Boards are given a free hand in taking decisions. Autonomy of the PE Boards has increased and at the same time accountability has also increased. Monitoring of the performance of PEs is primarily done by the Board and overall performance of PEs has improved. Employees at all levels are encouraged or actively involved in the areas of quality improvement, productivity, marketing and performance upgradation.

Table 1.9 : Navaratna/Miniratna Package and its Impact

Details	*No. of Respondents*				
	Strongly agree	*Agree*	*Neutral*	*Disagree*	*Stongly Disagree*
(a) There is deregulation, depoliticalisation and debureaucratisation	—	4	1	9	—
(b) Decision-making powers vested in various government agencies has reduced (or altered)	—	4	3	7	—
(c) There is enhanced delegation of powers to the Board now	—	8	2	3	1
(d) Board is given a free hand in taking policy decisions	—	6	4	4	—
(e) There are now transparent and effective systems of decision-making and internal monitoring	—	8	2	3	1
(f) Monitoring the performance of the PE is done primarily by the Board	1	10	2	1	—
(g) Autonomy of the PE has increased	—	4	4	5	1
(h) Accountability of the Management has increased	2	5	5	2	—
(i) Overall performance of the PE has improved	1	8	2	2	1
(j) Employees at all levels are encouraged or actively involved in the areas of quality improvement, productivity, marketing and performance upgradation	2	8	2	1	1

Source: Mishra, R.K., A Study of Operational and Financial Autonomy to Navaratna and Miniratna PEs, Ministry of Heavy Industry and Public Enterprises, Government of India, New Delhi, Planning Commission, Institute of Public Enterprise, Hyderabad, 2003.

There is an impact on board dynamics especially in the case of Restructured Boards of Navaratna/Miniratna PEs. The boards are broad-based and there is greater transparency in the functioning of the Board. The boards have been delegated more authority and have become more strategic and dynamic in their functioning as depicted in Table 1.10.

Table 1.10 : Navaratna/Miniratna Package and its Impact on Board Dynamics

Name of the PE	*Impact on Board dynamics*
1. HPCL	Board is broad-based by induction of 4 additional part-time non-official Directors with different background and experience. The Board has been given further delegation of power including in the capital expenditure, forming joint venture and other administrative areas. Matters concerning corporate strategy, future plans are deliberated in the Board for guidance/direction/approval as the case may be.
2. ONGC	The Board now consists of three main groups, the Functional Directors, Government nominees and Independent (non-official part-time) Directors. Deliberations hence are more broad-based covering the concern of the Government, the needs of the organisation and independent opinion.
3. SAIL	The Board has become more broad-based with outside expertise and professional Directors were inducted. There is greater transparency in the functioning of the Board.
4. NTPC	Inclusion of non-official Directors has brought outside intelligence into decision-making. Board is taking investment decisions hitherto reserved to Government. For participation in Joint-Venture within the limit prescribed in the guidelines the approval of MOP is not required, hence such proposals are also being approved by the Board.
5. PCIL	Induction of 3 Part-Time non-official Directors. This has added to the professionalisation of Board. Many committees of the Board are formed. Board became more strategic and dynamic in decision-making.
6. NMDC	Diversification into new areas as "Joint Ventures" or moving on own has become a reality. It has become feasible to easily open up overseas offices, subsidiaries since only the concurrence of Administrative Ministry is required.
7. KRL	Miniratna status is yet to become effective for KRL. However, the delegation of enhanced authority to the Board would enable expeditious implementation/action on various proposals in the areas of capital expenditure, joint ventures/subsidiaries /overseas offices, technology joint venture and strategic alliances and schemes for HRD.
8. STC	Moderate impact.

(contd.)

Table 1.10 *(contd.)*

Name of the PE	*Impact on Board dynamics*
9. CCIL	The introduction of external members has made the management more responsive.
10. NFDC	Policy decisions were expected. Financial performance got focussed. Professionalism at the functional level of executives improved. HRD matters/problems got resolved more effectively.
11. WPCSL	• Strong linkage with good financial powers have not been confirmed as yet. • For foreign tour, CMD has to depend much on the Power Ministry.
12. HSCCL	Moderate impact.
13. HPC	No impact.
14. PFCL	No impact.
15. TCIL	Discussions are lively and successful. Board Audit Committee has been formed.

Source: Mishra, R.K., A Study of Operational and Financial Autonomy to Navaratna and Miniratna PEs, Ministry of Heavy Industry and Public Enterprises, Government of India, New Delhi, Planning Commission, Institute of Public Enterprise, Hyderabad, 2003.

PE Boards

This section contains a survey of 38 PE Boards with regard to their composition and interest representation. As noted earlier, a board-led enterprise is an essential prerequisite for the success of working of an enterprise.

Composition and Strength of the Board

The institution of Board of Directors in PEs frequently reveal the need for making PEs as board-led organisations. The composition and strength PE boards should be such that it may improve their performance. The government should restrict the number of government directors on the enterprises and appoint independent directors and enhance the number of independent directors.

The maximum strength of PE Boards differs from PE to PE and ranges between 7 and 21. In most of the PEs, the maximum strength of the Board is not maintained and there are number of vacancies to be filled. Against the optimal number of 12 members suggested for effective corporate governance, the average size over the 6 years period turned to be 7 in the PEs. That the government lacked the understandings of the role that Boards could play in public enterprises is seen from the fact that 10 enterprises (of the sample enterprises) had vacancies on their Boards to the tune of more than 50 per cent. Table 1.11 shows that 19 enterprises had vacancies in the zone of 20-50 per cent.

On an average, there were three internal Directors in all the PEs. Only 12 PEs had representation from Financial Institutions. It is further observed that none of the respondent PEs had workers' representation on their Board. GAIL had one representative from INTUC.

Table 1.11 : Vacant Position in the Board

% Vacancy	*No. of Enterprises*	*Name of the Enterprises*
0-25	9	BDL (20), BEL (0), CMC (0), EIL (0), NTPC (7), MTNL (9), SCIL (14), NCIC (14), GSYL (0)
20-50	19	ANTRIX (41), CMPDL (41) ECL (42), GRSE (27), HAL (33), HFCL (33), ITI (27), MDL (33), MFL (35) NALCO (42), NHPC (33), NPCL (36), NSC (31), SIIL (25), NPC (36), STC (43), WPCS (25) ONGC (48), GAIL (35)
Above 50	10	BPCL (52), HLL (52), HPCL (58), HOVC (55), MAPL (52), MECL (58), RCFL (50), TCIL (65), VSNL (58), NEPA (56)

Source: Mishra, R.K., Boards of Directors in Public Enterprises, Institute of Public Enterprise, Hyderabad, 2003.

It is seen from Table 1.12 that the number of government nominees in most of the enterprises is high. Such a high representation make government's hold on PEs greater and deprive PEs of full functional autonomy. In the changed economic scenario, it is desirable to reduce the nominees from government and induct more internal and external professionals and expert members in the Board to make it function in a commercial manner.

Table 1.12 : Average Composition of the Board

Composition of the Board	*No. of Directors*
1. Internal Directors	3
2. Government Nominees	3
3. Nominees from Financial Institutions	1
4. Ex-officio Members	0
5. External Professionals/Expert Members	1
6. Workers' Representatives	0
7. Others	0

Source: Mishra R.K., Boards of Directors in Public Enterprises, Institute of Public Enterprise, Hyderabad, 2003

Table 1.13 shows that 10 enterprises (26%) had government nominees exceeding 50 per cent of the board strength, whereas 28 (74%) had government nominees turning out to be 50 per cent or less.

Table 1.13 : Composition of Internal vs. Government Nominees

Composition (% of the present size of the Board)	*No. of Enterprises (% of total)*
Internal Members	
0-50%	26 (68%)
> 50	12 (32%)
Government Nominees	
0-50%	28 (74%)
> 50%	10 (26%)

Source: Mishra, R.K., Boards of Directors in Public Enterprises, Institute of Public Enterprise, Hyderabad.

A majority of the respondents require internal experts in the areas of Technology and Production Management, followed by Finance, Marketing and HRM. In general the respondents were of the view that atleast one-third of the Directors should be professionals with adequate experience in the fields of economics, industry, finance etc.

External Board Members

Some PE Chiefs stated that they needed professionals in the areas of Personnel and Marketing. They also needed technocrats, practising managers, management consultants, industrialists and consumer representatives in their Board. There is a trend now to have more independent directors. According to Naresh Chandra Committee,[8] there is a need to have 50 per cent of the Board strength coming from independent directors.

Tables 1.14 and 1.15 point to lack of adequate representation of professionalism in the PE Boards. The technocrats did not get their due share in the composition of the Boards. The CMDs expressed their strong preference for the technocrats as members of PE Boards. The CMDs also suggested to limit the number of one government nominees to 1 which in exceptional cases could go to 2. This in their view ensures the continuation of the linkage with the government, on

Table 1.14 : Additional Internal Directors Required with Specialisation

Areas of Specialisation	*No. of Respondents*
Finance	8
Human Resource	8
Technical/Production Management	14
Marketing/Commercial	11
Research and Development	3
Workers Representative	1
MIS and Computer Network	1
Miscellaneous	1

Source: Mishra R.K., Boards of Directors in Public Enterprises, Institute of Public Enterprise, Hyderabad.

Table 1.15 : External Members required with Areas of Specialisation

Areas of Specialisation	*No. of Respondents*
1. Technocrats	14
2. Management Consultants and Practising Managers from Public and Private Sector	10
3. Retired and Experienced Government officials/Board Members, etc.	4
4. Industrialist(s)	7
5. Consumer Representative(s)	3
6. Trade Union Leaders	Nil

Source: Mishra R.K., Boards of Directors in Public Enterprises, Institute of Public Enterprise, Hyderabad.

the one hand, and thwart the domination of the government nominees on account of sheer numerical strength, on the other.

Investment-worthiness of PEs

Should we stop investing in PEs? Often, a suggestion is made that PEs should be closed down lock, stock and barrel as investment therein do not hold the potential to generate profits. Table 1.16 details the results of regression equation showing the degree of explanation of profitability by size is 58 per cent and 63 per cent respectively. The

Table 1.16 : Size and Profitability – Regression Results (a) PR $=b_0+b_1$ log size (b) PR $=b_0 + b_1$ log sales

	Steel Industry					
	Constant	*Co-efficient*	*R^2*	*Adj. R^2*	*F-Value*	*DW*
(a)	-10.243	2.94	0.36	0.32	9.91	1.50
(b)		(3.15)** (3.85)***				
	Minerals and Metals					
	Constant	*Co-efficient*	*R^2*	*Adj. R^2*	*F-Value*	*DW*
(a)	-52.09	14.64 (5.69)**	0.64	0.62	32.4	1.54
(b)	-30.444	10.58 (9.62)	0.84	0.83	92.62	1.66
	Coal and Lignite					
	Constant	*Co-efficient*	*R^2*	*Adj. R^2*	*F-Value*	*DW*
(a)	-26.241	7.23 (4.25)**	0.50	0.47	18.05	1.01
(b)	-25.520	7.76 (5.07)**	0.59	0.57	25.75	1.09
	Power					
	Constant	*Co-efficient*	*R^2*	*Adj. R^2*	*F-Value*	*DW*
(a)	-13.613	4.51 (4.86)**	0.58	0.56	23.62	0.40
(b)	-4.974	3.16 (5.36)**	0.63	0.61	28.69	0.40
	Petroleum Industry					
	Constant	*Co-efficient*	*R^2*	*Adj. R^2*	*F-Value*	*DW*
(a)	43.635	-6.60 (-3.62)**	0.42	0.39	13.11	0.31
(b)	36.883	-5.09 (2.00)*	0.18	0.14	4.01	0.26
	Chemicals and Pharmaceuticals					
	Constant	*Co-efficient*	*R^2*	*Adj. R^2*	*F-Value*	*DW*
(a)	-20.449	6.71 (2.05)*	0.19	0.14	4.21	0.97
(b)	-25.985	9.07 (2.98)**	0.33	0.29	8.87	0.99

Source: Vijayakumar, A. and Kadrivelu, S., "Firm Size and Profitability: An Empirical Testing-Indian Public Sector Manufacturing Industries, 1981-2001", The *Journal of Institute of Public Enterprise,* Vol. 25, July-September to Oct.—Dec. 2002, Hyderabad, p. 52.

* Figures within parentheses indicate 't' values.

** Significant at 1% level.

results also show the positive relationship between the size and profitability. It is evident from the results that one unit increase in assets has resulted in 4.51 unit increase in profitability and this is significant at one per cent level of significance. Similarly, one unit increase in sales leads 3.16 unit increase in profitability which is significant at 1 per cent level. of significance.

Conclusion

To conclude, there is a strong case for the government to reformulate its PE policy. The institution of Navaratna/Miniratna PEs deserves a further impetus in the form of a continuous upward revision in the managerial and operational autonomy. The Navaratna/Miniratna experience very clearly brings out the relationship between their improved performance and autonomy. The Board-led PEs possess potential to grow as organic business entities. Against the prevailing perception in the Government, it has been noted that the Government has to empower PE Boards with enhanced authority and limit the number of its nominee directors to one or two. The entire exercise of disinvestment needs to be conducted in a different way. 'PE' has to be made the focal point of disinvestment exercise. IPOs need to be preferred to the strategic sale.

NOTES

1. Department of Public Enterprises (Government of India, New Delhi), *Public Enterprises Survey:* Vol. 1, 2001-2002, pp. 3-4.
2. *Economic Survey: February 2003* (Government of India, New Delhi) p. 150.
3. Mohnot S.R., 'Rejuvenating the Public Sector', *Rajiv Gandhi Institute for Contemporary Studies,* New Delhi, 2003, p. 33.
4. *Economic Times,* Hyderabad Edition, June 27, 2003, p. 1.
5. Mahnot S.R., *Op. Cit.,* p. 33.
6. *Economic Times,* Hyderabad Edition, June 21, 2005, p. 1.
7. Sharma, Sheela 'Disinvestment: Accepting the ground realities of workers', *Kaleido Scope,* New Delhi, April, 2003, pp. 12-13.
8. Natarajan S., 'Independent Directors Emerging as Peer Group', *Chartered Secretary,* New Delhi, May 2003, pp. 577-584.

2

NAVARATNA AND MINIRATNA PUBLIC ENTERPRISES

A Critical Analysis

Conceptual Background

The Navaratna concept originated in the Common Minimum Programme of June 5, 1996 of the United Front Government which promised identification of PEs having comparative advantages, to be supported in their drive to become global giants. On July 4, 1997, the Government decided to confer wide powers on nine PEs, christened Navaratnas. Two more were added to the list later (Annexure 2.1).

Under the Navaratna package, PEs were given the following financial and operational autonomy:

(a) to incur capital expenditure on purchase of new items or for replacement;
(b) to enter into technology Joint Ventures or Strategic Alliances;
(c) to obtain, by purchase or other arrangements, technology and know-how;
(d) to effect organisational restructuring including establishment of profit centres, opening of offices in India and abroad, creating new activity centres;
(e) to create scrap posts including and upto those of non-Board level Directors;
(f) to structure and implement schemes relating to personnel and human resource management, training, voluntary or compulsory retirement schemes;
(g) to raise debt from the domestic capital markets and borrowings from the international market, subject to the normal clearance

of the Reserve Bank of India and the Department of Economic Affairs.

(h) to establish financial joint ventures and wholly-owned subsidiaries in India or abroad subject to a ceiling of Rs. 200 crore in any one project, 5 per cent of the net worth of the PE in any one project, and 15 per cent of the net worth of the PE in all joint ventures/subsidiaries put together.

On October 8, 1997, a package for 97 consistently profit-making PEs called Miniratnas was announced. These PEs were put in two categories. The first category covered enterprises (i) making profits continuously for the last three years, with a pre-tax profit of at least Rs. 30 crore in at least one of the three years, (ii) having a positive net worth, (iii) not having defaulted on government loans, and (iv) not receiving any budgetary support. The second category comprised PEs with pre-tax profits (no amount mentioned) during the last three years; (ii), (iii) and (iv) being the same, as for category-I (Annexure 2.2).

Category I, PEs were empowered to: (i) Incur capital expenditure upto Rs. 300 crore or equal to their net worth, whichever is lower, (ii) Establish Joint Ventures and Subsidiaries in India, and if abroad with the concurrence of the administrative ministry, with an equity limit of Rs. 100 crore or 5 per cent of the net worth in any one case, and 15 per cent of the net worth for all joint ventures and subsidiaries put together, and (iii) Enter into technology Joint Ventures and Strategic Alliances subject to government guidelines.

For category II, the figures under various heads were restricted to:

(i) Rs. 150 crore or 50 per cent of the net worth, (ii) Rs. 50 crore, the two percentages and the power under (iii) being the same as for category-I. According to the Navaratna/Miniratna package, the Boards of these companies, should be professionalised by inducting a minimum of 4 non-official directors in the case of Navaratnas and 3 non-official directors in the case of Miniratnas before the Board exercise the enhanced powers. Adequate number of non-official directors have been appointed in all the Navaratna PEs and 17 of the Miniratnas. In respect of the remaining Miniratnas it is in the process.

Impact Analysis

The impact analysis has been done on the basis of a structured questionnaire (enclosed) which was initially pilot tested on one Navaratna PE and one Miniratna PE. In all 3 Navaratnas and 9 Miniratnas responded to the questionnaire.

Criteria

On being asked as to why the enterprise was selected as Navaratna/ Miniratna, it was pointed out that consistent profit making, growth, investment and infrastructure acted as the main considerations for their selection. According to one respondent, Oil and Natural Gas Company Ltd. (ONGC), the Navaratna status was accorded to it as it is one of the largest and consistently very high profit making PE, it is in the business of hydrocarbon exploration and production which is considered to be of strategic importance and capacity of the company to finance large capital projects from internally generated resources. Similar views were reflected in the response by the Navaratna, Steel Authority of India Ltd. (SAIL). Another Navaratna PE, Hindustan Petroleum Corporation Ltd. (HPCL), disclosed that Navaratna status was granted to it as it has been able to achieve consistent growth and development. National Mineral Development Corporation (NMDC) was given the Miniratna status in view of its consistently good financial performance and technical and personnel attributes. Power Grid Corporation of India Ltd. (PGCIL) has been recognised as a Miniratna due to it consistent profit making, doubling of the net worth and consistency in dividend payment. Kudremukh Iron Ore Ltd. (KIOL) received the Miniratna status due to its outstanding performance as a 100 per cent Export Oriented Unit, achievement in production and export targets and all-round development. Rajasthan Electronics and Instruments Ltd. (REIL) obtained the Miniratna status owing to wealth accumulation for shareholders and meeting its business objectives while maintaining financial health through internal accruals, short term market borrowings and timely servicing of debts.

Autonomy

The respondents identified autonomy as the basic prerequisite for effective functioning.

According to HPCL, autonomy to an enterprise should be full freedom to the CEO and his senior management team to manage an enterprise to achieve the overall objectives of development and growth of the enterprise, but functioning within highest norms of ethics and corporate governance. The CEO should be accountable to the Board. Board intervention should be limited to overall reviews and control and guidance on policy-related matters.

ONGC's response was that currently, public enterprises are additionally subject to approvals and guidelines of the administrative ministry and DPE and also answerable to various Parliamentary and Government bodies.

KIOL responded that PE Management should be allowed to take decisions on expansion works, acquiring additional business investment in new projects without any financial limits as long as there is no budgetary support from Government.

REIL emphasised the authority to take quick decisions in response to market conditions, especially on the front of product design and manufacturing modification. It felt the need for a level playing field vis-à-vis the competitive forces, especially to take recourse to mobilisation from means other than internal accruals or budgetary support from Government. This would be meaningful especially for raising long-term capital loans from the free market, collaborations, Joint Ventures, overseas operations, national operations, etc. Employee participation in organisation's growth and profits through stock options, policy for rewards and growth was also recommended.

RCF stressed on absolutely no interference from bureaucrats in general and other frivolous rules applicable to the PSU should be coming in the way of total freedom of management. NMDC felt that the company should be Board-managed.

Impact on Operational/Financial Autonomy

From the responses to the questionnaire, it is found that most of the respondents agreed that there is operational/financial autonomy to a moderate extent. Table 2.1 provides the views of the respondents on operational autonomy.

Table 2.1 : Operational autonomy given and availed by the PEs

Name of PE	*Operational autonomy given and availed by the PEs*				
	Monitoring of performance by the Board	*Technology and R&D*	*Product Mix*	*Fixation of performance targets*	*Remarks*
1. HPCL	—	—	—	—	Under Navaratna package only "decision making authority accorded and no special operational autonomy.
2. ONGC	Overall performance monitored by Board on quarterly basis.	Initiatives being taken by various R&D institutes in ONGC to acquire new technology. Except for the guidelines issued by Government in January 2000 for technology joint ventures, no other change and existing tendering procedures have to be followed.	No change. Crude oil, natural gas and value-added products continue to be primary revenue earners.	Financial targets carrying 60% of weight are still as per existing directive of DPE. Physical targets and dynamic efficiency parameters modified to reflect organisation's focus on production, reserves accretion, HR, IT and R&D etc.	
3. KIOL	Yes	Yes	Yes	Yes	Operational autonomy availed by the PE

(contd.)

Table 2.1 (contd.)

Name of PE	*Operational autonomy given and availed by the PEs*				
	Monitoring of performance by the Board	*Technology and R&D*	*Product Mix*	*Fixation of performance targets*	*Remarks*
4. MDL	Yes. Monitoring of performance by Board and Administrative Ministry done periodically.	R&D efforts geared towards quality improvement in the areas of design, manufacture, and assembly erection.	Not availed	Since 1991-92 with approval of Board, company has been on MOU in which targets on various activities and performance parameters are laid down.	Operational autonomy availed by the PE
5. REIL	—	—	—	—	Operational autonomy given to a less extent. PE has not availed operational autonomy.
6.. PCIL	Yes. Performance of Corporation is primarily monitored by Powergrid Board and thereby Group of Secretaries of GOI.	Powergrid has adopted new technologies like FACTS, series computerisation, GIS retch.	—	To some extent autonomy was availed.	
7. RCF	—	—	—	—	In view of there being no non-official Directors on Board, RCF cannot exercise the authority.

(contd.)

Table 2.1 (contd.)

Name of PE	*Operational autonomy given and availed by the PEs*				*Remarks*
	Monitoring of performance by the Board	*Technology and R&D*	*Product Mix*	*Fixation of performance targets*	
8. IMPCL	—	—	—	—	As per DPE's order in general
9. NMDC	—	—	—	It is arrived after discussion with ATF Members of DPE.	—
10. KRL	—	—	—	—	As per DPE's order in general.
11. BRPL	—	—	—	—	As per DPE's order in general.
12. SAIL	Yes	Yes	No	Yes	—

Source : Compiled from responses to questionnaire.

Styles of Management

From the responses received to the questionnaire, it is found that the status of Navaratna/Miniratna has changed the styles of management in the PEs and they are becoming more commercial and market-oriented. Now the PEs are managed with management and professional-orientation and they are concerned about customers. However, the CMDs of IMPCL and NMDC, mentioned that there is no change in the styles of management in their respective organisations. The Table 2.2 gives the details of styles of management followed by the PEs:

Table 2.2 : Styles of Management

Styles of Management	*Completely changed*	*Significantly changed*	*Moderately changed*	*Slightly changed*	*Remarks*
1. Commercial-orientation	—	2	1	2	—
2. Market-orientation	—	1	1	2	In the case of Powergrid corporation it is not applicable.
3. Management-orientation	—	2	—	3	—
4. Professional-orientation	—	3	1	—	HPCL management style has grown towards more of professional-orientation.
5. Customer-orientation	—	1	1	1	In the case of Powergrid corporation it is not applicable.

Source: Compiled from responses to questionnaire.

Navaratna/Miniratna Package and its Impact

The CMDs were asked certain questions on the impact of Navaratna/Miniratna package on their enterprise in a rated scale, which is given in Table 2.3. The questions and their responses are given in tabular form.

Table 2.3 : Navaratna/Miniratna Package and its Impact

Details	*No. of Respondents*			
	Strongly agree	*Agree*	*Neutral*	*Dis-agree*
(a) There is deregulation, depoliticalisation and debureaucratisation	—	3	2	4
(b) Decision-making powers vested in various government agencies has reduced (or altered)	—	5	2	2
(c) There is enhanced delegation of powers to the Board now	—	8	—	2
(d) Board is given a free hand in taking policy decisions	—	5	2	1
(e) There are now transparent and effective systems of decision-making and internal monitoring	—	6	1	1
(f) Monitoring the performance of the PE is done primarily by the Board	—	6	1	1
(g) Autonomy of the PE has increased	—	4	1	3
(h) Accountability of the Management has increased	2	3	2	1
(i) Overall performance of the PE has improved	1	5	1	1
(j) Employees at all levels are encouraged or actively involved in the areas of quality improvement, productivity, marketing and performance upgradation	2	4	1	1

Source: Compiled from responses to questionnaire.

Composition of the Board

From the responses we observe that the strength of the Boards ranges between 9 to 21. Further, it is observed that in eight of the PEs, maximum strength is not maintained. On an average, three to six vacancies are there. Only in the case of Kudremukh Iron Ore Co., the full strength is maintained.

Table 2.4 : Composition of the Board

S. No.	*Name of the PE*	*Board size as per Articles of Association*	*Present size of the Boards*	*Details of Directors*	
1.	HPCL	15	12	CMD	- 1
				Internal Directors	- 4
				Government Nominees	- 3
				Non-official Directors	- 4
2.	ONGC	21	15	CMD	- 1
				Functional Directors	- 6
				Government Nominees	- 3
				Non-official/Directors	-5
3.	KIOCL	9	9	CMD	- 1
				Full-time Directors	- 3
				Non-official Directors	- 4
				Government Nominee	- 1
4.	MDL	15	10	CMD	- 1
				Full Time Directors	- 4
				Govt. Nominees	- 2
				Non-official Directors	- 3
5.	REIL	12	8	Chairman	- 1
				Managing Director	- 1
				Directors	- 5
				Government Nominee	- 1
6.	PCIL	12	8	CMD	-1
				Full-time Directors	- 3
				Govt. Nominees	- 2
				Non-official Directors	- 2
7.	RCFL	12	7	Details were not given	
8.	IMPCL	10	7	Details were not given	
9.	NMDC	12	10	CMD	- 1
				Full-Time Directors	- 4
				Govt. Nominees	- 2
				Non-official Directors	- 3
10.	KRL			Board has not been restructured by induction of non-official Directors and it is in process.	
11.	BRPL			Board has not been restructured by induction of non-official Directors and it is in process.	
12.	SAIL			Functional Directors	-9
				Government Nominees	-2
				Non-Official Part Time Directors	-8

Source: Compiled from responses to questionnaire.

Audit Committees and Board Members

Out of 11 PEs, six are having Audit Committees and there are non-official Board Members in the Audit Committees. Five PEs are not having Audit Committees. They are: (1) MDL, (2) REIL, (3) IMPCL (4) BRPL, and (5) KRL.

In all the Audit Committees three to six Board Members are there and out of these members one to three are non-official Board Members. The details are given in Table 2.5.

Table 2.5 : Audit Committees and Number of Board Members

Name of the PE	*No. of Directors*	*Details*
Hindustan Petroleum Corporation Ltd.	3	CMD Two Non-official and a Part-Time Directors
Oil and Natural Gas Corporation Ltd.	6	Two Functional Directors, One Govt. Nominee Director, Three Non-official Directors
Kudremukh Iron Ore Co. Ltd.	3	All are non-official Part-Time Directors
Power Grid Corporation of India Ltd.	4	Two Functional Directors, One Part-Time Govt. Director, One Non-official Director
Rashtriya Chemicals and Fertilizers Ltd.	3	Details are not given
National Mineral Development Corporation	3	CMD, MMTC Professor from IIMA Social Economist

Source: Compiled from responses to questionnaire.

Most Important Issue faced by the Enterprise

The respondents were asked to the state the single-most important issue faced by their concerned PEs. Their statements are recorded in the Table 2.6.

Challenges to Navaratna and Miniratna PEs

From the above discussions on the impact of Navaratna/Miniratna Package on PEs, the research findings can be summed up as follows:

There is no budgetary support to PEs, they are self-financed and are raising debts from domestic and international markets Boards are given sufficient operational and financial autonomy in taking decisions

Table 2.6 : Most Important Issue Faced by the Enterprises

Name of the PE	*Single-most important issue faced*
1. Hindustan Petroleum Corporation Ltd.	After the process of disinvestment during 1992 and public issue in 1995 that has resulted in GoI holding coming down t) a level of 51.01%; the need to balance between efforts to manage the company on commercial lines to enhance productivity and value addition while adhering to PSU norms.
2. Oil and Natural Gas Corporation Ltd.	There is an urgent and pressing need to significantly enhance domestic production of crude oil and natural gas. The main contributing basins are already in the mature phase and potential of frontier areas is still uncertain. It is a challenging situation even for the best of companies. Government support and internal reforms embracing new technology and new methods of working are essential for ONGC to succeed under these conditions.
3. Kudremukh Iron Ore Ltd.	Mining lease given to KIOCL over an area of 4605 which expired in 1999. On expiry of regular mining lease, KIOCL was given a work permit to mine only broken area for a year. This was an important issue by this PE.
4. Mazagon Dock Ltd.	"Wage Revision of Employees of MDL" pending in various counts since March 1976. This pending dispute often resulted in agitation at crucial times. This was finally solved by the signing of two separate Memoranda of Settlements with the Unions on the Bargaining Council.
5. Rajasthan Electronics and Instruments Ltd.	Shortage of working capital is the most important issue, as higher turnovers are needed to attain economies of scale necessary for viable profitability levels, in the face of increased competition.
6. Powergrid Corporation of India Ltd.	Realisation of "wheeling charges from SEBs, POWERGRID has formulated the recovery mechanism. Insistence is now on signing of "Bulk Power Transmission Agreement" with provision for "Escrow" and "Letter of Credit" for every new project. To liquidate the arrears of Government of India to assist POWERGRID through Central Plan Assistance (CPA).
7. Rashtriya Chemicals and Fertilizers Ltd.	The shortage of gas supply by ONGC, which affects the overall performance of the Company because all the plants of the Company are basically gas based plants. To meet the gas requirement, the Company has already initiated action to

(contd.)

Table 2.6 (contd.)

Name of the PE	*Single-most important issue faced*
	finalise the contract with M/s METGAS Co and M/s TATA TOTAL, for supply of the required gas. In the meantime, the Company is using naptha as the alternative feedstock to overcome the difficulties, which the PE was facing due to shortage of gas.
8. Indian Medicines Pharmaceutical Corpn. Ltd.	Since our organisation's main assumption in the project report is to supply mainly to CGHS, etc, besides in open market, keeping in view the quality of medicines of the company it is felt that share in the open market be increased so that overall masses be benefited.
9. National Mineral Development Corporation	The main problem is autonomy of Corporation. The issues regarding growth, expansion and new strategies for development all get stinted due to approvals needed from Ministry even when no financial help is sought. The board decisions are again scrutinised afresh by bureaucratic chain in the Ministries.

Source: Compiled from responses to questionnaire.

in investment in new projects, capital expenditure, monitoring the performance of the PEs, technology and R&D and product-mix, and entering into agreements for joint ventures.

Composition of the Board has changed in respect of Navaratna PEs and there is an induction of non-official Directors in PE Boards and Audit Committees and PE Boards have become more professionalised. The Government has given sufficient delegation and decision-making authority to the Navaratna/Miniratna PEs. Government interference has come down to the minimum. The Boards are functioning with dynamism and with business culture. Autonomy and accountability of the Boards has considerably increased. It is acknowledged that this measure has helped in more objective decision-making while the inducted Directors have brought in fresh thinking. It will also help in injecting an enhanced dose of autonomy into the public sector.

The Boards are conducting more meetings than prescribed in the Articles of Association and devoting extra time in the Board Meetings. Majority of the Board members are attending and decisions are taken after detailed discussions with the members. Decisions are taken unanimously. This has resulted in the reduction of time span in getting clearances from one to two years, which used to cause substantial delays and escalations. The autonomy for investment approvals now available cut down this time to about eight to ten months. The styles of management have changed and PEs have become more commercial and market-oriented. There is professionalisation at the Board and management level. The overall performance of PEs has improved. There is restructuring of organisations in certain PEs and in others it is in process. They are implementing schemes relating to personnel and human resource management, training and voluntary retirement schemes.

ANNEXURE 2.1

LIST OF NAVARATNAS

1. Bharat Heavy Electricals Ltd. (BHEL)
2. Bharat Petroleum Corporation Ltd. (BPCL)
3. Hindustan Petroleum Corporation Ltd. (HPCL)
4. Indian Oil Corporation (IOC)
5. Indian Petrochemicals Ltd. (IPCL)
6. National Thermal Power Corporation (NTPC)
7. Oil and Natural Gas Corporation (ONGC)
8. Steel Authority of India Ltd. (SAIL)
9. Videsh Sanchar Nigam Ltd. (VSNL)
10. Gas Authority of India Ltd. (GAIL)
11. Mahanagar Telephone Nigam Ltd. (MTNL)

ANNEXURE 2.2

LIST OF MINIRATNAS

Category 1

1. Bharat Aluminium Co. Ltd. (BALCO)
2. Bongaigaon Refinery and Petrochemicals Ltd. (BRPL)
3. Central Warehousing Corporation (CWC)
4. Cochin Refineries Ltd. (CRL)
5. Container Corporation of India Ltd. (CCIL)
6. Dredging Corporation of India Ltd. (DCIL)
7. Engineers India Ltd. (EIL)
8. Fertilizers and Chemicals (Travancore) Ltd. (FCTL)
9. Hindustan Newsprints Ltd. (HNL)
10. Hindustan Organic Chemicals Ltd. (HOCL)
11. Hindustan Zinc Ltd. (HZL)
12. IBP Co. Ltd. (IBPCL)
13. India Tourism Development Corporation Ltd. (ITDCL)
14. IRCON International Ltd. (IRCON)
15. Kudremukh Iron Ore Co. Ltd. (KIOCL)
16. Lubrizol India Ltd. (LIL)
17. MMTC Ltd. (MMTC)
18. Madras Refineries Ltd. (MRL)
19. National Aluminium Co. Ltd. (NALCO)
20. National Fertilizers Ltd. (NFL)
21. National Mineral Development Corporation Ltd. (NMDC)
22. Oil India Ltd. (OIL)
23. Power Finance Corporation (PFC)
24. Power Grid Corporation of India Ltd. (PGCIL)
25. Rashtriya Chemicals and Fertilizers Ltd. (RCFL)
26. State Trading Corporation of India Ltd. (STC)
27. Telecommunications Consultants (India) Ltd. (TCIL)

Category 2

28. Educational Consultants (India) Ltd. (ECIL)
29. Ferro Scrap Nigam Ltd. (FSNL)

30. HMT (International) Ltd. (HMTIL)
31. Hospital Services Consultancy Corp. (India) Ltd. (HSCCIL)
32. Indian Medicines Pharmaceutical Corpn. Ltd. (IMPCL)
33. MSTC Ltd. (MSTC)
34. Manganese Ore (India) Ltd. (MOIL)
35. Metallurgical and Engineering Consultants (India) Ltd. (MECIL)
36. National Film Development Corporation Ltd. (NFDC)
37. PEC Ltd. (PECL)
38. Rajasthan Electronics and Instruments Ltd. (REIL)
39. Water and Power Consultancy Services (India) Ltd. (WPCSL)

3

PRIVATISATION OF PUBLIC ENTERPRISES IN INDIA

Challenges Ahead

Logic of Privatisation

Privatisation is emerging as a new economic technique for development. Among a number of reasons argued out in favour of privatisation, the relatively more important ones are as follows:

- Releasing huge amounts of scarce public resources locked up in non-strategic public enterprises (PEs) for deployment in areas much higher on social priority such as economic and social infrastructure.
- Reducing the public debt of unmanageable proportions.
- Transferring the commercial risk as related to investments in PEs to the private sector.
- Releasing other tangible and intangible resources such as manpower currently locked up in areas that are much higher on social priority but are short of such resources.
- Exposing the privatised companies to market disciplines and thereby forcing them to become more efficient.
- Promoting wider distribution of wealth through offering of shares of privatised companies to small investors and employees.
- Creating a beneficial impact on the capital market through the increase in floating stock resulting in greater depth and liquidity in market, establishing more accurate benchmarks for valuation and pricing and facilitating raising of funds by the privatised companies.
- Increasing employment and tax revenues.

- Bringing relief to consumers by way of ending public sector monopoly leading to more choices, and cheaper and better quality products and services.

Privatisation Policy

The privatisation policy was initiated in the Interim Budget,[1] 1991-92 of the Government of India. Since then, the policy has gone through a number of motions and is still in the process of attaining depth, maturity and unassailable continuity. The evolution of privatisation policy from its state of infancy to the state of puberty could be traced as follows.

During 1991-92, the Government of India in its Interim Budget decided to divest upto 20 per cent of the Government's equity in selected PEs in favour of public sector institutional investors. The objective of such divestment was to broad base equity, improve management, enhance availability of resources for PEs and yield resources for the exchequer. The Industrial Policy Statement of July 24, 1991, advocated for divesting part of government holdings in selected PEs to provide further market discipline to the performance of such PEs. The final Budget speech, 1991-92 of the Government of India, announced to offer upto 20 per cent of Government equity in select PEs to mutual funds and investment institutions in the public sector, as also to workers in such firms to raise resources, encourage wider public participation and promote greater accountability. The Rangarajan Committee Report (Report of the Committee on the Disinvestment of Shares in Public Sector Enterprises), 1993 emphasised the need for substantial disinvestment and stated that while the percentage of equity to be divested should be not more than 49 per cent for industries explicitly reserved for the public sector, it should be either 74 per cent or 100 per cent for others. As per the Rangarajan Committee, the government could hold 51 per cent or more equity in 6 industries viz., coal and lignite; mineral oils; arms, ammunition and defence equipment; atomic energy; radioactive minerals; and railway transport. The Common Minimum Programme of the United Front Government, 1996, laid down the withdrawal of PEs from non-core strategic areas, setting up a Divestment

Commission, implementation of decisions to disinvest in a transparent manner and ensure job security, opportunities for retraining and redeployment for the labour force. The Disinvestment Commission set up in 1996 as an advisory agency in its 12 Reports submitted between February 1997 and October 1999, suggested divestment in 58 out of 72 PEs referred to it. The Commission accorded priority to strategic/trade sales, with transfer of management, instead of public offerings, as was recommended by the Rangarajan Committee in 1993. The Disinvestment Commission recommended strategic sale in 29 PEs and trade sale in 8. It identified 5 enterprises for offer of shares and suggested deferring disinvestment in 11 enterprises. The Commission suggested closure/sale of assets in 4 enterprises and no disinvestment in one enterprise. The Budget Speech 1998-99 of the Government of India brought out the Government's determination to bring down the Government's shareholdings in PEs to 26 per cent in the generality of cases, retain majority of holdings in PEs involving strategic considerations and protect the interests of workers in all cases. The Budget Speech 1999-2000 of the Government of India resolved to strengthen strategic PEs, privatise non-strategic PEs through gradual disinvestment or strategic sale and devise viable rehabilitation strategies for weak units. The Central Cabinet in its meeting of March 1999, identified strategic PEs as those related to defence, atomic energy and railway transport. The remaining PEs were classified as non-strategic. The Cabinet decided to reduce the government stake in such PEs to 26 per cent on a case to case basis on two considerations: (1) whether the PE is required as a countervailing force to prevent concentration of power in private hands; and (2) whether the PE is required to give in way for setting up a proper regulatory mechanism to protect the consumer interests.

The Budget Speech 2000-2001 of the Government of India suggested disinvestment of PEs to put in place mechanisms to raise resources from the market against the security of their assets for providing an adequate safety net to workers and employees, establish a systematic policy approach to disinvestment and privatisation by setting up a new Department of Disinvestment and use the entire receipt from disinvestment and privatisation for meeting expenditure in social sectors, restructuring of PEs and retiring public debt. The address by the President in the Parliament in the Budget Session, February 2001, mentioned a four-fold objective of privatisation policy: revival of potentially viable enterprises, closing down of those PEs which cannot be revived, bringing down government equity in non-strategic PEs to 26 per cent or less and protecting the interests of workers through attractive VRS and other measures.[2]

Privatisation Process

Initially the responsibility for carrying out disinvestment rested with the Department of Public Enterprise which had to report to the group of empowered secretaries whose decisions were vetted by the Cabinet Committee on Economic Affairs. Later a Disinvestment Commission was set up in 1996 under executive order. The recommendations of the Commission had to pass through the Department of Public Enterprise to the Empowered Group whose recommendations were vetted by the Cabinet Committee on Economic Affairs. In November 1999, the Disinvestment Commission ceased to exist.

A new Department was created to deal with disinvestment headed by a Minister for State supported by a Secretary to the Government of India. Initially the Department's recommendations were referred to the Department of Public Enterprises to pass through the Empowered Group. However, this process was modified and the reference to the Department of Public Enterprise was deleted. The Department of Disinvestment consequently brought the enterprise to be disinvested and the connected Ministry in the picture. This was done to obviate the criticism of bypassing the concerned Ministry and the enterprise. Vexed with the innumerable problems slowing down the tempo of disinvestment, very recently the Department of Disinvestment has suggested the creation of a full fledged Ministry for privatisation to be put in complete charge of the enterprises slated for disinvestments. The Administrative Ministry, the Department of Public Enterprises and all other related agencies will cease to exercise any control once an enterprise is transferred for privatisation to the proposed Ministry. The fragmentation of machinery has obstructed the speed and the quality of disinvestment.

Once the Department of Disinvestment identifies an enterprise for privatisation/disinvestment, it appoints advisors to chart out the disinvestment path for the enterprise under reference (See Annexure 3.1 for detailed list). Earlier, the department could appoint only Indian advisors but later the Central Cabinet permitted the Department to appoint even Foreign Advisors. The Advisors carry out the due diligence including valuation of assets, acquiring bids, scouting for strategic investors and the completion of the business deal. However, the finality of their task depends on the Department which moves at a snail's pace as its recommendations go to the Cabinet Committee on Economic Affairs and finally to the whole Cabinet. The various Ministers and the Secretaries opposing privatisation/disinvestment of enterprises under their control put cold water on the proposal. The opposition to privatisation of petroleum and telecom sector enterprises are cases in point.

Privatisation Scenario and Challenges

Privatisation scenario includes in its ambit disinvestment and privatisation in the central PEs and the State level PEs. Table 3.1 provides details about actual disinvestment/ privatisation effected in central PEs during April 1991 to March 2001.

Table 3.2 shows the approximate number of State level PEs in 17 States of the Indian Union and the State level PEs identified for disinvestment/restructuring /winding up in each of the States and the process initiated in the number of enterprises in this regard.

An overview of privatisation scenario points out the following:

1. Privatisation is spreading far and wide at the central level. In the case of the central PEs, even in the case of the strategic PEs, the cold privatisation has made inroads which includes contracting out, franchising, leasing, amalgamations and mergers and management restructuring through reorganisation in the form of strategic business units, strengthening the internal audit and adjustment of labour force. The joint ventures are being promoted by financially successful PEs to overcome the limitations of the State-ownership. Such joint ventures have become very popular with the petroleum sector enterprises.

Table 3.1 : Actual Disinvestment from April 1999 to March 2001

Year	*No. of Companies in which equity sold*	*Target Receipt for the Year (Rs. in crore)*	*Actual Receipts (Rs. in crore)*	*Methodology*
1991-92	47 (31 in one tranche and 16 in other)	2500	3038	Minority shares sold by auction method in bundles of "very good", "good" and "average" companies.
1992-93	35 (in 3 tranches)	2500	1913	Bundling of shares abandoned. Shares sold separately for each company by auction method.
1993-94		3500	Nil	Equity of 7 companies sold by open auction but proceeds received in 1994-95
1994-95	13	4000	4843	Sale through auction method, in which NRIs and other persons legally permitted to buy, hold or sell equity, allowed to participate.
1995-96	5	7000	362	Equities of 4 companies auctioned and Government piggy backed in the IDBI fixed price offering for the fifth company.
1996-97	1	5000	380	GDR (VSNL) in international market
1997-98	1	4800	902	GDR (MTNL) in the international market
1998-99	5	5000	5371	GDR (VSNL)/Domestic offerings with the participation of FIIs (CONCOR), Cross purchase by 3 Oil sector companies i.e., GAIL, ONGC and IOC
1999-00	2	10000	1829	GDR (GAIL) in international market, MFIL's strategic sale & some other disinvestments
2000-01	1	10000	551#	Strategic sale of BALCO shares
Total	41*	54300	19189#	

Source: Government of India, Department of Disinvestment, New Delhi, April 2001.

* Total number of companies in which disinvestment has taken place so far.

\# Provisional Figures.

Table 3.2 : Disinvestment in States

S. No.	*Name of the State*	*Approximate number of State Level Public Enterprises (SLPEs)*	*Estimated total investment in SLPEs (Rs. in crore)*	*SLPEs identified for disinvestment/ restructuring/winding up*	*No. of SLPEs in which process initiated*	*No. of SLPEs Privatised/Disinvested*
1.	Andhra Pradesh	51	4444	21	10	
2.	Assam	42	3676	1	—	
3.	Goa	12	4869	1	—	
4.	Gujarat	49	23438	11	5	
5.	Haryana	27	4746	8	2	
6.	HimachalPradesh	21	3143	15	—	
7.	Jammu & Kashmir	N/A	N/A	7	2	
8.	Karnataka	77	16641	17	9	
9.	Madhya Pradesh	34	8561	27	2	
10.	Maharashtra	65	19186	6	3	
11.	Manipur	14	N/A	10	—	
12.	Orissa	72	8544	N/A	N/A	
13.	Punjab	53	12425	9	2	
14.	Rajasthan	24	10838	11	—	
15.	Tamil Nadu	84	10158	13	3	
16.	Uttar Pradesh	50	17313	25	6	
17.	West Bengal	80	14081	2	2	

Source: Mishra and Navin, *State Level Public Enterprises in India,* Anmol, New Delhi.

2. In the case of the retained central PEs, the concept of *Navaratna* and *Miniratnas* was introduced in 1997[3] to provide them adequate autonomy to become globally competitive. The concept has resulted in internal liberalisation of operations and a new control and accountability model determining the government-enterprise interface. Table 3.3 sums up the views of some Navaratnas/Miniratnas based on a research study conducted by Mishra and Navin (2001).

Table 3.3 : Navaratna/Miniratna Package and its Impact

Details	*No. of Respondents*			
	Strongly agree	*Agree*	*Neutral*	*Dis-agree*
1. There is deregulation, depoliticalisation and debureaucratisation	—	3	2	4
2. Decision-making powers vested in various government agencies has reduced (or altered)	—	5	2	2
3. There is enhanced delegation of powers to the Board now	—	8	—	2
4. Board is given a free hand in taking policy decisions	—	5	2	1
5. There are now transparent and effective systems of decision-making and internal monitoring	—	6	1	1
6. Monitoring the performance of the PE is done primarily by the Board	—	6	1	1
7. Autonomy of the PE has increased	—	4	1	3
8. Accountability of the Management has increased	2	3	2	1
9. Overall performance of the PE has improved	1	5	1	1
10. Employees at all levels are encouraged or actively involved in the areas of quality improvement, productivity, marketing and performance upgradation	2	4	1	1

Source: Mishra and Navin (2001), Navaratna and Miniratna Public Enterprises: A Critical Analysis, Working Paper 4, Institute of Public Enterprise, Hyderabad.

3. The privatisation moves in the central PEs have made forays into public sector banks and bureaucratic set-up. The public sector banks have reduced their staff by around 20 per cent from 3,00,000 to 2,40,000. The Central Government proposes to reduce employment in Central Government departments by 10 per cent by 2005.

4. The manufacturing, service and financial enterprises are being targetted for disinvestment/privatisation at the State level. In the case of promotional enterprises, the commercial activities have been identified for privatisation. The utility enterprises such as the power sector enterprises and the road transport corporations are undergoing the process of restructuring. The State electricity boards have been trifurcated with the separate establishment of transmission, generation and distribution enterprises. Whereas generation and distribution are intended to be widely privatised, the transmission is yet to be privatised. The central electricity regulatory authority and the State electricity regulatory authorities have been set up to regulate the electricity industry. The State road transport corporations are either being privatised or restructured to function as self supporting organisations.

5. Between the Central and the State Governments, privatisation and disinvestment has made a greater headway in the case of the latter due to the size of the units, area of their operation and private sector's keenness to own such units. The State governments have been more successful due to quick decision making, dominance of ruling parties in State legislatures and pressing need to reduce fiscal deficit. The nature of privatisation has also been diverse in the case of State level PEs as compared to the central PEs. The enterprises privatised/ disinvested ranging from State tanneries corporation to State fertiliser units. The State governments have taken up the privatisation of State level PEs as a part and parcel of the economic restructuring programme of the State. The Government of Andhra Pradesh has been the privatisation leader in India. The State Governments of Maharashtra, Rajasthan, Madhya Pradesh, Gujarat have launched privatisation programmes.[4]

6. The Government of India has been avoiding to set up an independent privatisation commission and divest itself of divestments. It has politicised the privatisation process by creating an independent department whereas the State governments have been proposing to enact a separate law to introduce a great deal of objectivity.

7. The State governments have been more clear about the guidelines for effecting privatisation which has helped them in speeding up the process and mobilising resources.

8. The guidelines issued by the Government of India on July 13, 2001 have made privatisation a complicated task. The clauses that bidders can be disqualified if they are charge sheeted on security related matters or indicted or convicted by either a court or a regulator on non-security issues can preclude many of the top firms from the process. Nothing would ever be bought if the government starts nit-picking. The research shows that half of the 20 Indian companies might easily turnout to be borderline cases. Hindustan Lever Limited (HLL) cannot bid for any PE since some of its Directors have been indicted for insider trading. HLL was also recently charged with the violation of environmental laws. ITC was penalised heavily for excise evasion and cannot be expected to inspire public confidence. Adani Exports have been issued show cause notice by the customs authorities. SPIC has run into several controversies with the Tamil Nadu State Government. GRASIM, managed by Kumar Mangalam Birla was forced to shut its Mavoor Plant in 1998 by the Kerala State Pollution Control Board. Videocon International has been indicted by SEBI for insider trading and BPL Communications Ltd. also gets excluded on account of this charge. Sterlite Industries cannot raise money in capital markets as SEBI indicted the group for insider trading. Wipro does not inspire public confidence as it has also been investigated for insider trading. Reliance Industries is surrounded by controversies, allegations, show cause notices *et al.* Reliance Petroleum, it is alleged, siphoned off money raised through the company's public issue into closely held investment companies.

9. The State level PEs preferred privatisation through trade sale, leasing and closure. The Central Government relied initially on the partial privatisation model and later shifted the emphasis to the strategic sale. However, the sale of Modern Foods Limited and the Bharat Aluminium Company Ltd. has been done on the basis of disinvestment of majority stake.

10. The valuation decisions have earned disreputation both in the case of central PEs and the State level PEs.[5] The initial inexperience and the continued absence of database on the various methods of valuation have resulted in under recovery of investments.

11. The multiplicity of institutions tackling privatisation/ disinvestment at the Central level have obstructed the speed and quality of privatisation. The continuous feud between the Ministry of Industry and the Disinvestment Commission, created distrust between

the two and hampered the working of the latter. This does not inspire any hope about the success of the newly constituted Disinvestment Commission.

12. Both the Central and the State governments have shunned the path of restructuring PEs for disinvestments which has led to the distress sale. The P/E ratio of selected Oil and Telecom Majors show that restructuring and readying appropriately the Indian Oil and Telecom Majors could result in a windfall.

Table 3.4 : P/E (Price/ Earnings Per Share) Ratios—Global and Asian Giants Comparable

(A) Selected Oil Majors	*P/E Ratio*
Petronas Gas (KL)	11.5
Seoul Gas(SK)	10.2
British Gas (UK)	13.8
Centrika (UK)	12.0
Gas Natural (ESP)	13.5
Petron Corp (PS)	09.6
BP Amoco (UK)	25.4
Exxon -Mobile (US)	23.7
Royal Dutch (Neth)	22.8
IOC (IN)	4.9
BPCL (IN)	5.7
HPCL (IN)	5.9
GAIL (IN) [13.5 million shares @ Rs.70.00 per share]	4.4
(B) Selected Telecom Majors	
British Telecom	43.0
Vodaphone Aritouch	75.0
NT & T (Nippon Telegraph & Telephone)	48.0
France Telecom	55.0
Telecom Malaysia	46.0
VSNL (10 million shares @ Rs. 785 per share)	**6.0**

Source: Government of India, Department of Disinvestment, New Delhi, April 2001.

The examples of some strategic deals within the Indian private sector (Table 3.5) reflects that high premiums were paid for regaining control.

Table 3.5 : Examples of Strategic Deals within India (Private Sector) Reflecting Premium Paid for Control

Industry	*Target Co.*	*Bidder*	*Equity Stake acquired*	*Market price (6 months average)*	*Offer Price*	*Premium (Rounded Off)*
IT	Silverline	Subra Holding	51%	22	30	37%
IT	IIS Infotech	FI Group	100%	46	101	120%
Auto Comps.	Sahney Paris	Delco	57%	71	117	65%
FMCG	Wimco	Swedish Mach	20%	20	35	74%
Aluminium	Indian Aluminium	Alcan	20%	93	200	116%
Gas Marketing	Gujarat Gas Co.	British Gas	64.3%	125	270	117%
Industrial Gases	Bombay Oxygen	Grieshiem GMBH	50%	1238	3000	142%
Cement	ACC	GACL	7%	215	370	72%
Tea	Rossell	Hindustan Levers	100%	43	173	298%
Pharma-ceuticals	American Remedies	Dr. Reddy's Lab	64.9%	89	175	97%
					Mean	**114%**

Source: Government of India, Department of Disinvestment, New Delhi, April 2001.

13. Restructuring is certain to increase the sheen of the PE shares. A comparison of cost structure between public and private sector shows that PE operations were four times more expensive with regard to power and fuel and wages while on interest front public sector costs were three times as compared to the private sector. The financial, manpower, organisational and product restructuring could bring these costs in line with the private sector.

14. Privatisation initially results in surplus manpower. The institution of social safety net provision is a pre-condition for effecting any privatisation. The Government of India set up a National Renewal Fund in 1992 to provide funds for voluntary retirement, redeployment and employment insurance. These provisions benefited only the

textile workers. Huge funds are required for a successful implementation of the social safety net scheme. Despite the recommendation of the Disinvestment Commission to set up a disinvestment fund which could contribute to social safety net provisions and turnaround of sick PEs among other things, through their technological upgradation, the Government of India sidelined this recommendation. No such National/State Renewal Fund was set up for the State level PEs.

15. The due diligence has erred on a number of vital grounds in the case of the central PEs. The Singapore-Tata Airlines Consortium, the only bidder for Air India had strongly objected to the government's move of nominating four directors on their Board. They have also strongly objected to the government's intention to seek the government's permission on taking any decision to raise debt, declare dividends or embark on any long term plans without the official nod as they are not in a monopoly situation where delays do not cost much and they being a part of competitive service industry. The disinvestment agreements have run into rough weather also on account of lock-in period issue. The government has shown its bias in favour of a five-year lock-in period. Both the Modern Foods and Bharat Aluminium Ltd. have found fault with this condition since in a dynamic business world, the business entities should tend to make entry and exit decisions fairly rapidly. As per the latest reports, the Singapore Airlines have lost interest in joint bidding for Air India. The GoI has asked Tatas to indicate whether they would like to have another bidder in place of Singapore Airlines.

Both the Central and the State governments have assigned a very low importance to the communication aspect of privatisation. They have not established an interface with the labour at various levels, consumers, media etc. As a result, they have faced a hostile reaction and lost political patronage barring Andhra Pradesh and Orissa.

Cases in Privatisation

This section presents cases in privatisation, one each from the central PEs and the State level PEs. Incidentally, these happen to be the trend setters for privatisation for the Central and the State level PEs. It may be mentioned that at the Central level, only one more privatisation relating to Bharat Aluminium Company Ltd. (BALCO) has taken place in 2001. In the case of State level PEs, there have been around two dozen cases of privatisation covering Andhra Pradesh, Tamil Nadu, Karnataka, Pondicherry, Maharashtra, Punjab, Haryana, Rajasthan, Madhya Pradesh, Bihar, Uttar Pradesh, Assam, and Orissa.

Modern Food Industries (India) Ltd. (MFIL)

MFIL was set up in 1965 to popularise wheat consumption and set up model bread production facilities with emphasis on hygiene and nutrition. The company commenced its commercial operations from 1968 and set up manufacturing facilities in four metros and seven other cities in India between 1968 and 1977. During 1977, the bread industry was reserved for small scale industries. Meanwhile, the company set up three more units at Jaipur, Indore and Delhi. The company diversified its operations by setting up Maize mill/roller flour mill at Faridabad, solvent extraction plant at Ujjain, fruit juice bottling plant at Delhi, pineapple processing plant at Silchar and fruit pulping facilities at Bhagalpur. The company also started supplying energy foods, processed ready-to-eat foods and this line of business accounted for 43 per cent of MFIL's revenues in 1997-98. The response to small scale industry reservation was met with by outsourcing, franchises and setting up ancillaries. However, the company had to restructure its business. It closed down its Ujjain plant but continued to pay its workers due to court stay. The Silchar facility was also closed down and the Bhagalpur facility reorganised to produce nutrient foods. The sales trend of the company showed a marginal increase from Rs. 137.69 crore in 1995-96 to Rs. 166.53 crore in 1998-99. The sales in the area of energy food and breads, bars and cakes declined over this period. The profit before tax, for the company as a whole, declined from Rs. 11.13 crore to (–) Rs. 7.20 crore during the above period. The bread and bakery industry in the private sector earned profits during the same period. The Government, therefore, referred the case to the Disinvestment Commission in 1996. The Commission in its very first report (April 1987) recommended full-fledged privatisation of MFIL, in stages, in view of the company being in the core sector. The company had wide presence in the form of its manufacturing units in various parts of India. It had a fairly well established national brand and a strong distribution network. It had a large market share and potential for growth. However, it had vast underutilised facilities, large workforce and low productivity, limited flexibility to respond to changing market needs and poor synergies resulting from past government decisions. It faced threats such as removal of subsidised wheat allocation by the Government of India, reduction of budgetary support to supplementary nutritional products and highly fragmented and intensely competitive market. The Disinvestment Commission suggested 74 per cent immediate disinvestment to a strategic partner and a divestment of the remaining 26 per cent shareholdings subsequently. The Commission suggested the divestment of all the units in one go for better price realisation. The concerned administrative ministry rejected the recommendation of the Disinvestment Commission in May 1997. However, the Cabinet approved disinvestment of 50 per cent of shareholdings based on recommendation of the Committee of Secretaries. Between October 1997 and June 1998, the process of the appointment of a global advisor was completed. During October 1998, the Government of India appointed ANZ Grindlays as the global advisor. Since the appointment of global advisor, the proposal for disinvestment was revised up to 74 per cent of shareholdings to facilitate control by the strategic buyer and better valuation. In January 1999, the Central Cabinet approved disinvestment upto 74 per cent. Between January 1999 and February 1999, all the issues raised by the global advisor were resolved by the Government. On April 15, 1999, the global advisors invited Expression of Interest (EoI). 10 companies expresses their interest in MFIL. Only 4 companies qualified for due diligence. HLL and Brittania Biscuits Ltd. turned out to be serious bidders. In July 1999, M/s Pathak and Associates were appointed legal advisors. By October 15, 1999, only one bid from HLL was received. By October 22, 1999, the Bid Evaluation Committee completed its task and the HLL emerged as the successful bidder. The Bid Evaluation Committee was an Inter-Ministerial Committee comprising Joint Secretary, Department of Economic Affairs, Joint Secretary, Department of Public Enterprise, Joint Secretary, FPI, Representative of Global Advisor and Additional Secretary and Financial Advisor as Chairman. On December 6, 1999, the Government created the Department of Disinvestment (DoD) and later during this month the

Ministry of Agriculture and the DoD approved the disinvestment in favour of HLL. On January 27, 2000, the extraordinary general meeting of MFIL approved the induction of HLL as the strategic partner. On January 31, 2000, the deal between the government and the HLL was completed through share purchase/shareholder agreements and payment of purchase price by the HLL to the Government.

The Global Advisors valued the shareholdings of MFIL for Rs. 78.55 crore by using four valuation models viz., discounted cash flow, transaction multiple, balance sheet value and asset valuation. A Government valuer valued the assets of MFIL for Rs. 109 crore based on market value of land and buildings without taking into considerations restrictions on sale/conditions regarding use of land. The HLL offered Rs. 125.45 crore for 74 per cent shareholdings of MFIL and valued the total shareholdings for Rs. 150 crore. The HLL was finally selected in view of their strategic intent and fit, technical plans, plans regarding employees, management depth and track record in turning around and MFIL's inability to attract managerial talent and overdue investment of Rs. 80 crore. The valuation of the company posed a number of issues such as how to value 'Modern' brand, Brand Strength Multiple—low/ fast fading and losses/ declining profit in recent years. It was being found difficult to isolate superior earnings attributable to the brand and estimating brand strength multiple based on a variety of factors such as leadership, stability, trend, support, scope, etc. The valuation of real estate posed another serious problem. Only 5 out of 14 bakery units had freehold land and others had leasehold land. 3 out of 7 Supplementary Nutritional Foods (SNF) had freehold land. The Government of India has its own perspective of valuation. It was concerned about decline in the core business and high volatility of SNF. It was not ready to inject fresh funds to finance losses/overdue investment in facilities. Further it was not ready to support any brand building exercise which is characteristic of private enterprises such as HLL which spends about Rs. 1500 crore (15 per cent of turnover) on advertisement. The Government was not prepared to carry out decisive restructuring and expressed its inability to unlock value by selling surplus land.

A tripartite agreement was carried out among Government of India (GoI), MFIL and Strategic Partner (SP). HLL agreed to pay

Rs. 11,490 for a Rs. 1000 share. HLL agreed to pay Rs. 125.45 crore to MFIL for 1,09,187 shares which were 74 per cent of the total 1,47,550 shares. The GoI agreed to discharge the previous potential liabilities. It was agreed that the estate could be transferred at Rs. 5 crore. The agreement took into consideration the audited figures of the company as on January 31, 2000 which were different from March 31, 1999. The key features of the agreement indicated payment by HLL to GoI 74 per cent of the difference if Net Working Capital (NWC) on January 31, 2000 was more than Rs. 25.48 crore. If NWC was less than Rs. 25.48 crore, GoI was to pay HLL 74 per cent of the difference. If debt as on January 31, 2000 is more than Rs. 15.96 crore, GoI was to pay HLL 74 per cent of the difference. In case the debt was less than Rs. 15.96 crore GoI was to pay HLL 74 per cent of the difference. A three-year lock-in period for shares was agreed by all the three parties. The size of the Board was agreed to be of 7 persons composed of Chairman and a Board Member to be nominated by the GoI and the Managing Director and the rest of the Members were to be nominated by HLL. The agreement contained an important clause of put option of GoI to sell all its shares to HLL after one year and call option of HLL to buy all of GoI holdings after three years. This was to be done on the basis of fair market value, being the highest of the book value, DCF value and P/E multiples. In any case the valuation was to be not less than Rs.11,489.56. The agreement also laid down a provision for resolving the Fair Market Value (FMV) dispute. In the event of default, the GoI reserved the right to buy strategic partner share at the rate of 25 per cent discount or sell its shares to the SP on a premium of 25 per cent. The agreement ensured protection of the then existing terms and conditions of the services of employees. It also barred retrenchment during the first year without paying at least the maximum benefit.

The post-disinvestment scenario has seen a break on decline in volumes of business in MFIL. HLL's initiative for the turnaround of MFIL include synergising wheat/*atta* (wheat flour) procurement with HLL's branded *atta* business, introducing additional ingredients/new formulations, training on quality initiatives, overhaul of equipment, aggressive promotions, negotiating cheaper debt, improving cash management systems, introduction of strong MIS and monitoring system and widespread computerisation across all units and head office.

Allwyn Nissan

Allwyn Nissan Ltd. was promoted as a joint venture by Hyderabad Allwyn Ltd. in collaboration with Nissan Ltd. for the manufacture of Light Commercial Vehicles (LCVs) with pay load upto 3 MT. The estimated project cost was Rs. 52 crore, to be implemented in two phases. The first phase was implemented at a cost of Rs. 24.10 crore. The commercial production of LCVs commenced in April 1985.The licensed capacity has been increased from 10,000 units to 50,000 units. The installed capacity was 5,000 numbers per year.

Ownership

Out of the total equity of Rs. 16.70 crore holding is as follows:

	No. of Shares	*Percentage*
Hyderabad Allwyn Ltd.	5,999,948	35.93
Nissan Motor Company	2,500,000	14.97
NRIs and Indian Public	8,200,052	49.10

The first-two years of operations resulted in losses and continued to do so mainly due to the stagnant LCV market and 'Yen' appreciation. Due to continuation of low sales and production volume the workings in 1987-88 also resulted in loss of Rs. 404 lakh. As of June, 1998 accumulated losses amounted to Rs.1110.98 lakh. Other reasons for such losses are: (1) The market of LCV has not grown as expected and the demand has stagnated. (2) Yen fluctuations could not be countered with a faster rates of indigenisation. The indigenisation process was slow due to low volume and heavy tooling costs. (3) Sale prices had to be increased in view of the Yen appreciation, which adversely affected the demand which was already weak.

As per normal practice, the Management and Industries Department of Government of AP formulated a rehabilitation plan or what has been termed as 'turn around strategy'. This strategy comprises of short term, mid term and long term measures; reduction process; plan break even and covered marketing production, indigenisation plans and other economic measures. The proposal was under consideration for one year since April 1987 with *ad hoc* measures of "reserved procurement" of these vehicles for Government use irrespective of the price. The proposal in 1998 sought the following from the Government:

- Rs. 200 lakh financing for certain basic infrastructure facilities and the funding expenditure by way of outright sale.
- Support for marketing such as directing the Government Departments to buy LCVs subsidising promotional expenses etc.
- Support for faster indigenisation which were essential to counter the 'Yen' appreciation and reduce imports. A suggestion was to provide investment as an interest free loan.
- Support for concessional sales tax facilitating the financers and bankers for financing the purchase of the LCVs with suitable amendments to Motor Vehicles Act, exempting for power cuts etc.
- Equity support of Rs. 5 crore.
- Interest on Loans at 11.5 per cent was assured.

The Government considered further budgetary support and decided that the activity did not warrant any further financial flows from the exchequer. There was no formal decision to privatise but options available included it (though by implication), when a Committee was appointed for the purpose. Subsequently tenders were placed and the process of closure was completed after selection of the bidder by the Committee. Allwyn Nissan is the first case of privatisation in India through divestiture. Ownership was transferred to Mahindra & Mahindra, an automobile manufacturing company in the private sector. The Government held a very small portion of equity to ensure that the interests of labour was protected. Towards this end, an agreement was signed with Mahindra & Mahindra ensuring non-retrenchment of existing labour force. The privatisation was successful as it provided the technological and financial advantage to Mahindra & Mahindra whereas the Government benefited from immediate cash yields and ensuring itself from financing any future outgoes.

Following conclusions emerge from the two case studies. Non-core PEs are more amenable to privatisation. The clarity in objectives facilitates a faster privatisation. PEs, having market interface are easier to be privatised. The threat of increased loss making and making it good by public exchequer paves the way for privatisation of

Central and State level PEs. A professional global advisor helps in the requisite due diligence and successful completion of privatisation exercise. The selection of strategic partner alone is no guarantee of successful privatisation unless the management control by way of majority stake in shareholdings is also passed on to the strategic partner. The agreement on privatisation should be tripartite involving enterprise, government and strategic partner. Such an agreement should not provide for indirect control of the Government on vital issues such as lock-in period, access to capital markets, revision of tariffs etc.

Some Pointers

Privatisation/disinvestment is an important component of business strategy. The only thing that needs to be assured is to constantly disinvest/privatise and enhance the tempo to attain the critical mass. Table 3.6, depicts the budgetary support to central PEs.

Table 3.6 : Budgetary Support to Public Sector Enterprises (Excluding provisions for Voluntary Retirement Scheme)

Year	*Plan*		*Non-Plan*	*Total*	*Dividend*
	Equity	*Loan*	*Loans*	*Support*	*Paid*
1990-91 (RE)	3531	2477	1067	7075	413
1991-92 (RE)	2491	2735	759	5985	687
1992-93 (RE)	2238	2403	600	5241	792
1993-94 (RE)	2419	4072	780	7271	1028
1994-95 (RE)	3442	3613	911	7966	1436
1995-96 (RE)	2050	3218	1184	6452	2205
1996-97 (RE)	2439	2956	1459	6854	2836
1997-98 (RE)	3004	2550	1583	7137	3609
1998-99 (RE)	3215	2161	1854	7230	4932
Total	24829	26185	10197	61211	17938

Paid-up capital of all CPSUs as on 31.3.90	About 40000
Paid-up capital of all CPSUs as on 31.3.99 (as per DPE Survey 1998-99)	77066

Source: Government of India, Department of Disinvestment, New Delhi, April 2001.

It is clear from Table 3.6 that Rs. 36,611 crore were advanced to central PEs as budgetary support for the period 1991-92 to 1998-99. During this period, Rs.16,809 crore was raised through disinvestment as shown in Table 3.1. Thus it is clear that Rs. 19,802 crore was committed as fresh investments in these PEs pointing out clearly to the fact that disinvestments did not provide any resources to the Government. The situation of the State level PEs should have been very akin to that of the central PEs. This indicates the need for initiating suitable steps to make the privatisation/disinvestment exercise meaningful.

As a first measure, both the Central and the State governments should admit the need for setting up independent machinery clothed with the requisite powers and staffed by professionals and researchers. The machinery should draw a transparent programme of action to be implemented in conjunction with the domestic and international capital markets. The politicisation and bureaucratisation of disinvestment will be nullified by such a move. The corporate governance mechanisms and procedures should be put in place before any exercise of privatisation/disinvestment. The need for restructuring must be considered and it appears very difficult to privatise/disinvest enterprises without restructuring them to obtain the best value and avoid social travails arising out of labour and consumers. Divestiture policies should match the level of complementary reforms. The interest rate, credit policies, bank appraisals, external sector policies, trade policies and legal and institutional frameworks should perfectly align with the divestiture policy. Often times privatisation exercise at both the Central and the State levels has been alleged to smack corruption. On the other hand, the bureaucrats involved in privatisation have demanded a shield for their protection against false charges of corruption. There is need to study the world experience to prevent corruption in privatisation. The UK/US models appear to be ideal in this regard. Any privatisation exercise has to leave strategic PEs out of its scope. In India, for the leftover enterprises it is advisable to pursue more vigorously the application and extension of the *Navaratna/Miniratna* models. These models could be further strengthened by delinking PEs from the Government.

To make the privatised PEs work smoothly in the post-privatisation era, regulatory mechanisms should be put in place which must ensure a competitive functioning of such entities, among other things through competition law and related initiatives. A stock taking of international experiences must be done to understand the political economy of privatisation and the conditions which led to the success/failure of the move.

REFERENCES

1. Government of India, "Presentation on Disinvestment", Department of Disinvestment, April 2001, New Delhi.
2. Kurian N. J. and Hajela J.D., "Indian Economy: Liberalisation, Globalisation and Privatisation", *The Journal of the Institute of Public Enterprise,* Vol. 24, 1 and 2, Jan-Mar; April-June, 2001, IPE, Hyderabad, p.12.
3. Mishra R.K., "Disinvestment: 1992-2001", *The Chartered Accountant,* June 2001, New Delhi, p. 13.
4. Mishra R.K. and Navin B., *State Level Public Enterprises in India,* Anmol Publications, New Delhi.
5. Mishra R.K. and Navin B. (2001), "Navaratna and Miniratna Public Enterprises: A Critical Analysis", *Working Paper 4,* Institute of Public Enterprise, Hyderabad, p. 8.

ANNEXURE 3.1

List of PEs Approved for Disinvestment and Names of the Advisors Appointed

Company	Advisor (nature of entity)
1. Air India	JM Morgan Stanley (Indian-foreign Joint venture)
2. CMC Ltd.	KPMG India Private Limited (Indian subsidiary of foreign investment bank)
3. Hindustan Copper Ltd.	IDBI (Indian)—Sumitomo Bank (foreign)
4. Hind. Insecticide Ltd.	A.F.Ferguson (Indian subsidiary of foreign investment bank)
5. Hind. Org. Chem. Ltd.	A.F. Ferguson (Indian subsidiary of foreign investment bank)
6. HTL	KPMG India Private Ltd. (Indian subsidiary of foreign investment bank)
7. Hindustan Zinc Ltd.	BNP Paribas (foreign)
8. Indian Airlines	IDBI (Indian)—ANZ Grindlays Bank (Indian subsidiary of foreign investment bank)—Speedwing (Foreign)
9. IBP Ltd.	HSBC Securities and Capital Markets (I) Ltd. (Indian subsidiary of foreign investment bank)
10. IPCL	Warburg Dillon Read (foreign investment bank)
11. ITDC	Lazard India Ltd. (Indian subsidiary of foreign investment bank)
12. Madras Fertilizer Ltd.	ICICI Securities (Indian)—Bank of America (foreign)
13. Maruti Udyog Ltd.	To be appointed
14. Metal Scrap Trd. Corpn	Disinvestment process yet to begin.
15. Mines and Metals Trd. Corpn.	Disinvestment process yet to begin
16. National Fertilizers Ltd.	Rabo Finance Private Ltd. (Indian subsidiary of foreign investment bank)
17. Paradeep Phospht. Ltd.	Deloitte Touche Tohmatsu India Pvt. Ltd.
18. Sponge Iron India Ltd.	A.F. Ferguson (Indian subsidiary of foreign investment bank)
19. State Trading Corpn.	Disinvestment process yet to begin
20. VSNL	SBI Capital Markets Limited (Indian) and CS First Boston (Foreign)
21. Bh. Hvy. Plts. and Vessels	S.B. Billimoria (Indian Co.)
22. Bharat Pumps and Comp	SBI Capital Markets Ltd. (Indian Co.)
23. Hindustan Cables Ltd.	ICICI Securities (Indian Co.)
24. Hindustan Salts	SBI Capital Markets Ltd. (Indian Co.)

25. Instrumentation Ltd.	IDBI (Indian Co.)
26. Jessop & Co.	A.F. Fergusan (Indian subsidiary of foreign investment bank)
27. NEPA Ltd.	SBI Capital Markets Ltd. (Indian Co)
28. Praga Tools	None
29. Scooters India Ltd	Price Waterhouse Coopers (Indian subsidiary of foreign investment bank)
30. Tungabhadra Steels	IDBI (Indian Co.)

Source: Government of India, Department of Disinvestment, New Delhi, April 2001.

4

INSOLVENCY PROCEDURE AND CORPORATE RESTRUCTURING

The Case of State Public Sector Undertakings in Orissa

The corporate restructuring of the SPSUs in India has assumed vital dimensions in the context of the fiscal crisis faced by the various States of the Indian Union. The losses incurred by these enterprises are about 1.5 per cent of the nation's GDP. The closure/retention of these enterprises is subjected to a number of provisions imposed by the various Acts relating to the functioning and control of these enterprises such as Companies Act, Industrial Laws, Monopolies and Restrictive Trade Practices Act, Insolvency Act, Securities and Exchange Board of India Act, Sick Industrial Companies Act, State Financial Corporations Act, State Road Transport Corporations Act, Employees State Insurance Act and Article 12 of the Indian Constitution to mention a few. Whereas insolvency procedures stress the technical aspects of the closure of the company, there are several other non-technical (socio-economic and political) aspects that need to be imparted careful consideration while winding up an enterprise or deciding about its restructuring. These range from size, compulsion of using the local resource base, retaining the human face and warding off the dangers of destabilisation. The purpose of this Chapter is to explain the insolvency procedure and corporate restructuring in the case of the State Public Sector Undertakings (SPSUs) through the case study of such SPSUs in the State of Orissa.

Backdrop

SPSUs in Orissa were set up to achieve the following objectives :

- To help in the rapid economic growth and industrialisation of the region and the country and create the necessary infrastructure for economic development;

- To earn return on investment and thus generate resources for development;
- To promote redistribution of income and wealth;
- To create employment opportunities;
- To promote balanced regional development;
- To assist the development of small-scale and ancillary industries; and
- To promote import substitutions, save and earn foreign exchange for the economy.

The State Government had 77 Government Companies including 24 subsidiaries, three companies governed by the provisions of Sec. 619-B of the Companies Act, 1956) and four Statutory corporations as on 31.03.1999. The total investment in these government undertakings was Rs. 8354.82 crore consisting of equity of Rs. 2328.43 crore and long-term loans of Rs. 6026.39 crore. Orissa at the time of formation as a State, was one among the least developed regions in the country. It lacked entrepreneurship, capital, infrastructure and innovation. The State Government had to come forward to fill up this gap.

The classification of the Government companies was as under:

Status of Companies	*Number of Companies*	*Investment (Rs. in Crore)*		*Number of Companies referred to BIFR*
		Paid-Up Capital	*Long Term Loan*	
Working Companies	40	2070.03	5431.43	06
Non-Working Companies				
(a) Under Liquidation	15	0.37	—	—
(b) Under Closure	19	26.56	13.25	02
(c) Under Merger	02	11.25	10.33	—
(d) Others	01	0.03	—	—
Total	77	2108.24	5455.01	08

The total investment in four statutory corporation as on 31st March, 1999 (provisional) are as under:

Sl. No.	*Name of the Corporation*	*Capital (Rs. in crore)*	*Loan (Rs. in crore)*
1.	Orissa Road Transport Corporation	129.43	23.04
2.	Orissa State Financial Corporation	87.57	511.59
3.	Orissa Warehousing Corporation	3.20	0.31
4.	Industrial Infrastructure Development Corporation	—	36.43
	Total		571.37

Source: Both the above tables are based on Prof. Mishra's Study of Orissa SPSUs as Member of the Study Group on Disinvestment and Restructuring of SPSUs in India appointed by the Planning Commission where the author had extensive interaction with several experts, policy makers and public enterprise managers in the course of writing this chapter.

The total capital employed in SPSUs amounted to Rs. 5229.95 crore. The power sector dominated the total capital employed maintaining its share in the range of 40-50 per cent. The term lending and promotional sector shared 20-25 per cent and manufacturing sector accounted for 10 per cent of the total capital employed. The overall asset utilisation ratio stood at 0.44 in 1985-86 and increased to 0.83 in 1994-95 and remained static thereafter. These enterprises incurred heavy losses as a result of which for all the enterprises taken together the overall net worth increased from (–)Rs. 507.36 crore in 1985-86 to Rs.(–)Rs. 852.67 crore in 1994-95. The implied subsidy to SPSUs skyrocketed from Rs. 98.43 crore in 1985-86 to Rs. 579.01 crore in 1994-95. The heavy loss making forced the Government to think in terms of closure of many of the SPSUs. The situation prevailing in the SPSUs sector created abnormal pressure on the State exchequer and the Government has to take alternative measures by curtailing its projected plan / non-plan expenditure every year due to ground realities. The proponents of the SPSUs have been vociferously suggesting for their continuation through non-privatisation reforms. However in recent years the State Government has taken a decision to overcome these problems by divesting its shares to mobilize its resources and divert the proceeds for other welfare purposes. Accordingly a Cabinet sub-committee was formed in thc year 1996 under the Chairmanship of Deputy Chief Minister, Government of Orissa went into the question of restructuring the SPSUs and to recommend the policy measures for the SPSUs.

Restructuring and Privatisation*

Judged on the basis of consistent losses, poor asset utilisation, negligible contribution to State exchequer, substantial erosion of net worth and presence of implied subsidy, it is suggested that the following enterprises be wound up/handed over to workers or to managers/leased out/partially privatised or sold out: Orissa State Textile Corporation Ltd.; S.N. Corporation Ltd.; Elcosmos Electronics Ltd.; Orissa State Financial Corporation Ltd.; General Engineering and Scientific Works Ltd.; Orissa Timber and Engineering Works Ltd.; ABS Spinning Orissa Ltd.; Orissa Bridge and Construction Systems Ltd.; Elcosmos Communications Systems Ltd.; Orissa State Handloom Development Corporation Ltd.; Electronics Development Corporation Ltd.; Orissa State Police Housing and Welfare Corporation Ltd.; Elimarc Ltd.; Orissa State Seeds Corporation Ltd.; Idcol Piping and Engineering Works Ltd.; Orissa State Leather Corporation Ltd.; Orissa Agro Industries Corporation Ltd.; Orissa Forest Development Corporation Ltd. and Orissa Instruments Company Ltd. The Orissa Textile Mills Ltd. will be merged with the Orissa State Textile Corporation Ltd. and the Orissa State Warehousing Corporation Ltd. will be merged with the Orissa State Civil Supplies Corporation. A Cabinet Sub-Committee under the then Deputy Chief Minister and Minister, Finance, Water Resources and Parliamentary Affairs suggested the closure of Orissa State Seeds Corporation, Orissa State Commercial Corporation, Orissa State Leather Corporation, Orissa Fish Seeds Development Corporation, New Mayurbhanj Textiles, Orissa State Handloom Development Corporation, Konark Television, Orissa Instruments Company, and Orissa Textile Mills. It proposed the following enterprises for restructuring: Orissa Bridge and Constructions Corporation, Orissa Constructions Corporation, Orissa Tourism Development Corporation, Orissa State Cashew Development Corporation, Orissa Maritime and Chilka Area Development

* *Please refer to Annexure 1 for Status and Options of Restructuring of SPSUs in Orissa.*

Corporation, Industrial Promotion and Investment Corporation, Orissa Forest Development Corporation and Orissa Police Housing and Welfare Corporation.

The Report has suggested the modalities and techniques that could be followed for privatisation and restructuring. The State Industrial Policy of 1996 stated that the SPSUs should undertake rationalisation of the existing manpower and seek more commercial borrowing instead of depending on the budgetary support from the State Government. The Government's general policy is to continue with the promotion of SPSUs and to strengthen them to lay their role effectively and privatise commercial undertakings. The profit making commercial undertakings could undergo partial disinvestment while shares of loss making SPSUs could be disinvested to the extent of 51 per cent or more in order to infuse private management and capital for revival. Some SPSUs having similar activity could be merged to derive complementary benefits and avoid duplication of functions. While setting up a broad policy for the SPSUs the Government of Orissa is now guided by the following framework:

* Promotional SPSUs will have to continue if their promotional role has relevance in the present day context.
* Commercial SPSUs which are making profit should continue but, the State Government could consider divestment of minority shareholdings to the Public Financial Institutions or divest them to private parties in order to raise resources to meet the needs of their expansion/modernization/diversification programmes.
* Commercial SPSUs, which are making loss, should be privatized either partially or fully and in the event of such privatization not succeeding, should go in for liquidation.
* Co-operative commercial enterprises should be privatized at least to the extent of 51 per cent so that the private management could bring in greater efficiency in management, greater economy of operation and infuse fresh funds for rehabilitation and modernization.
* Co-operative Powerloom Units and other small Co-operative Enterprises should be totally privatized.
* Some of the SPSUs with similar activities could be merged to derive complementary benefits and avoid duplication of functions.

* Present Status of Restructurization of the SPSUs as per the Cabinet Decision basing on the Recommendation of the Cabinet Sub-Committee.

Industrial Development Corporation of Orissa Limited (IDCOL)

Re-rolling Mill. Final proposal to hive off the Unit in favour of OSIL after being approved by Ministerial Level Committee has been submitted to Industries Department for Government approval. Meanwhile, VRS Scheme is in operation, after which advertisement will be issued.

Hira Cables and Hirakud Industrial Works (HIW)

As per the decision of Government both the Units have been merged with effect from February 1997. Due to requirement of additional funds by the Unit and present liquidity crisis of IDCOL steps are being taken to divest 51 per cent of its share holding to a private party who can bring in the required finance to the Company. Three offers have been received by IDCOL in the mean time and negotiation process is in progress with the highest bidder and it will be finalized after Government communicates its approval in principle for divestment of the required share holding.

IDCOL Piping and Engineering Works Ltd.

The Task Force formed for ICL will look after the affairs of privatization of the Unit. This Unit was under BIFR as a sick company and a rehabilitation package was submitted by the company to IFCA (OA). IFCI has forwarded the draft rehabilitation scheme based on one time settlement of the dues of FIs and Banks to BIFR. However, due to super cyclone, at the instance of State Government, IDCOL has requested BIFR to allow at least six months time for the above repayment. Meanwhile, at the instance of BIFR, IFCI has released an advertisement seeking offer for change in management. As no offer was received, BIFR has now issued show cause notice for winding up.

ABS Spinning Mills

BIFR has issued winding up orders.

ORICHEM Limited

Closed under ID Act. After payment of the dues of the Financial Institutions and reduction in manpower fresh attempt will be taken for disinvestment.

SN Corporation

The Corporation has been closed under ID Act w.e.f. 06.07.1998 and approval of Government is awaited for transferring the Unit to the highest bidder as per the recommendation of the Restructuring Committee subject to final orders of BIFR. Advertisement issued for Disinvestment.

Konark Jute Limited

Offers received against the recent advertisement made by IDCOL for privatization of the Mill was not acceptable, as the amount offered was very low. The Board of IDCOL discussed the matter and decided for fresh advertisement. In response to the fresh advertisement 4 Parties have made enquiries and information memorandum have been forwarded to them for making their offer. In the mean time Government have been moved for conversion of the loan of Rs. 877.00 lakh into equity to facilitate the divestment process as decided in the joint review meeting taken by Ministers PE, Finance and Industries. Fresh advertisement has been issued for Disinvestment.

IDCOL Cement Limited (ICL)

IDCOL is in contact with M/s LAFARGE, France for take over of the Unit. Simultaneously, the Unit has been referred to BIFR for revival and the IDBI is the Operating Agency. The company is under BIFR. BIFR advised to go for disinvestment after the net worth becomes positive.

Kalinga Iron Works (KIW) and Ferro Chrome Plant (FCP)

TISCO has made an offer to take over both Mines and the Plant.

Konark Television Limited (KTV)

The company is now passing through extremely financial difficulties due to heavy loss and total erosion of its capital base. Out of 553 employees, 212 have left the organization on VR Scheme for which Government have provided financial support to the extent of Rs. 2.77 crore. But considering its present position, future prospects and viability, the liquidation of the Company is under active consideration of the Government.

Orissa Small Industries Corporation (OSIC)

The share capital of Rs. 25.00 lakh has been transferred to Shri Mahesh Kumar Agarwal, a private entrepreneur at a consideration of Rs. 33.82 lakh being the Net Asset Value of the Unit as evaluated by OSFC and the agreement for transfer of shares was concluded on 21.10.98. The Management was transferred on 01.11.98. The private entrepreneur has acquired 51 per cent stake in the Unit at present and the balance shall be taken over within a period of one year. OSIC now holds a minority shares in the Company.

General Engineering and Scientific Works (GESW), Berhampur

The Unit has been closed since 11.06.98 and all the employees have been paid closure compensation amounting to Rs. 36.30 lakh as per ID Act. Earlier efforts to privatize the Unit could not attract any encouraging offers. It has been decided to make all out efforts to sell the assets of the Unit and salvage whatever possible.

K.S. Refractories Limited, Jharsuguda

The Unit has been closed under ID Act w.e.f. 04.12.98 and closure compensation to the tune of Rs. 1.00 crore need to be provided by the Government for payment to the workers. The dues of FIs to the tune of Rs. 1.00 crore need also to be settled and the revaluation of the assets need also to be undertaken to decide the selling price of the Unit. The dues of the FIs need be settled under OTS and steps are being taken to sell the Unit immediately.

Orissa Timber and Engineering Works (OTEW), Sunabeda

No offer was received against the advertisement for privatization of the Unit even with the efforts of OSFC. Presently, the Unit is doing well and has earned a net profit of Rs. 8.52 lakh in FY 1998-99 against the turnover of Rs. 102.75 lakh. In the recent joint review meeting taken by Ministers, PE, Finance and Industries it has been decided to make the Unit independent and privatize the Unit by offering to HAL along with its existing land of about Rs. 22.00 crore, if possible.

Orissa State Leather Corporation

The Corporation along with its 18 number of units has been closed with effect from 18.06.98 under Section 25 (o) of ID Act. Government has provided a sum of Rs. 1.75 crore for meeting the expenditure toward payment of arrears salaries and statutory dues of all the employees and compensation benefit only to the workmen as per the provisions of ID Act. Similarly, sanction of Rs. 24.50 lakh is required for payment of compensation for closure of Orissa Leather Industries Ltd. The number of workmen whose services have been terminated on account of closure of the Undertaking is 182.

Orissa Instruments Company

The company has been closed under ID Act with effect from 20.03.98 and accordingly Government have provided Rs. 46.86 lakh for payment of arrears salary, closure compensation and other statutory dues of the workmen.

Orissa State Electronics Development Corporation

IPITRON Times, ELCOSMOS Electronics and ELCO Communication System, the subsidiary companies of the Corporation have been closed under ID Act w.e.f. 25.03.98, 20.02.98 and 10.08.98 respectively. All the employees of these 3 companies have been paid notice period pay, closure compensation, gratuity, bonus, arrears wages and other essential expenses to the extent of Rs. 3.99 crore. The companies have already filed liquidation petitions before the Hon'ble High Court. The total number of workman disengaged on account of closure of these 3 companies is 276.

Orissa Film Development Corporation

In order to implement the decision of the Government to convert the

Kalinga Studio into a Joint Venture for better performance its assets has been revalued at Rs. 7.57 crore and action is being taken to find a suitable Joint Venture partner.

Orissa Fish Seeds Development Corporation

Both the above corporations have been merged and a new corporation has been incorporated in the name of M/s Orissa Pisciculture Development Corporation w.e.f. 05.05.1998.

Orissa State Seeds Corporation

As a measure of restructurization the corporation has taken up steps for privatization of its retail sales network and has appointed 207 dealers during FY 1997-98, 301 number of dealers during FY 1998-99 (up to 30.06.1998) in the undivided 13 districts covering 193 number of blocks.

Orissa Agro Industries Corporation

As per the decision of the Government for privatization/Joint Venture of agricultural implement units of the corporation advertisements were made in the leading national and local dailies. But, only one response has been received from a party who subsequently did not show any interest. Hence, the corporation has taken steps to run these factories effectively. The cattle feed unit is also being restructured within the available resources of the corporation. Besides, installation and energisation programmes such as bore wells, dug wells and tube wells has been taken up effectively to compete with the private parties.

But subsequently, the Agricultural Department has asked the Corporation to take immediate steps to privatise agricultural implements factories located at Remed, Sambalpur and Bhograi and accordingly, action has been taken by the Corporation to issue advertisement inviting offers from private entrepreneurs to take over the Units either on lease basis or to manage the Units under Joint Venture.

Orissa State Handloom Development Corporation

As the efforts of locating a suitable Joint Venture partner could not materialize, the Government have decided to close the Corporation under ID Act. It has been advised to update its accounts immediately so as to ascertain the correct position of its assets and liabilities. Meanwhile, the Employees Union have filed a writ petition before the Hon'ble High Court challenging the decisions of the Government for closure of the Corporation and the case is under subjudice. In the mean time Government have provided Rs. 6.00 crore to SBI and PNB in March 1999 as OTS of their loan dues against the Corporation.

Orissa State Textile Corporation (BTM)

Action for privatization has been held up as the acquisition of BTM has been challenged by the erstwhile owner. The AG, Orissa has advised that there can be no transfer/lease without leave of the court and advised to await the judgment of the case.

Orissa State Textile Mills (OTM)

The Mill is under rehabilitation package as approved by BIFR commencing from FYs 1997-98 to 2000-2001. The total rehabilitation package comes to Rs. 3722.88 lakh. Out of this amount the State Government contribution is Rs. 2912.88 lakh and that of OTM Rs. 810.00 lakh. By FY 1998-99, Government have already released Rs. 22.52 crore in favour of OTM against its share of contribution and the balance amount will be provided in the subsequent two years i.e., FY 1999-2000 and FY 2000-2001. The entire equity base of the Mill amounting to Rs. 26.79 crore has been eroded and its net worth has become negative to the tune of Rs. 35.22 crore as on 31.12.98. Despite release of the required funds by the State Government the Mill has incurred a net loss of Rs. 21.44 crore in these two years and even after implementation of the total rehabilitation package the Mill may sustain further cash loss to the extent of not less than Rs. 12.00 crore per annum.

Due to non-viability position of the Mill and pending decision on either privatization or closure it has been decided to keep the Mill running and accordingly an amount of Rs.3.05 crore has been released to OTM in the month of May 1999.

Cooperative Enterprises

SBI CAPS and OSFC have been entrusted for valuation work of Co-operative Sugar Mills and the Spinning Mills. The Co-operative Act has since been amended to facilitate privatization of unviable units.

Orissa Lift Irrigation Corporation (OLIC)

The Government have taken a decision to have over the LI points to User's Co-operatives. But there is little progress in this regard because the cultivators are not coming forward to take over the projects from OLIC for operation and maintenance. The field officers have been instructed to persuade the cultivators for the above purposes. OLIC has also taken steps to abolish 11 divisions out of its total 29 divisions as a measure to reduce its establishment expenditure. The Corporation is also introducing VR Scheme to get rid of its surplus staff and proposes to retrench 974 employees with a financial outflow of Rs. 2.00 crore to be provided by the Government. Nearly, 1200 Government employees who are continuing on deputation in the Corporation will retire within a period of 2 years and retirement vacancies would not be filled up as a measure of austerity.

Orissa Tourism Development Corporation (OTDC)

The following progress has been made by OTDC in accordance with the decisions of the Cabinet Sub-Committee. All the units of OTDC have been treated as Strategic Business Unit (SBU) and MoUs have been signed with the Managers of the concerned units for achievement of financial as well as physical targets. The performance of each unit is evaluated separately. Steps have been taken to revitalize Rourkela and Rambha Panthanivas, which have shown sign of improvement after effective management and cost curtailment. Mega projects like Phantom House, Convention Hall, Revolving Restaurant and other Hi-tech Projects were placed before the Board of OTDC and Board decided that such Projects should not be taken up by OTDC. However, it was reported that OTDC has proposed to take up an Aquarium Project in near future for which necessary funding would be provided by Forest and Tourism Departments. OTDC is also taking up wayside amenities centre on the highways, which offer fast food counter and other facilities to the highways tourists.

New Mayurbhanj Textiles (NMT)

The process for privatization of the company has been held up as there is dispute regarding the ownership of the land under possession of the company. The land is yet to be mutated in favour of the company to effect privatization.

Orissa Forest Development Corporation (OFDC)

Commercial Plantation: There are legal lacunae in harvesting of commercial plantations. Once these obstacles are over, OFDC will take up commercial plantations over 2500 Ha. during 1999-2000. However, preparation of the same will commence during current year.

Tissue Culture etc. in Joint Venture

No action has been taken for tissue culture and plantation of medical species. However, joint venture plantations with paper mills is under process.

Reduction in Surplus Staff

TATA consultancy service has reported 3,000 staff as excess. In the meanwhile 666 numbers of staff were repatriated to the department and out of 776 numbers of staff who were illegally appointed from 1.1.90 to 1.1.95, 552 numbers of staff have been retrenched and 224 numbers of staff have brought stay order from court and retrenchment is under process. 186 numbers of staff have been redeployed in O.C.B. and 376 numbers in bamboo cutting works done for raw materials procurers.

Orissa State Commercial Transport Corporation (OSCTC)

The Corporation has been closed under ID Act, with effect from 30.05.1998 and 325 employees have been retrenched on account of the closure. An amount of Rs. 507.33 lakh has been paid to the employees towards arrears salary, closure compensation and statutory dues.

Orissa Mining Corporation (OMC)

Proposal for placing the Chrome Ore Beneficiation Plant and the China Clay Plant under Joint Venture Management is under consideration.

Orissa State Export Development Corporation

As the Corporation has been established in 1990 and has been continuing in preoperative stage and the Directorate of EPM is looking after the export promotion activities of the State, it has been decided to wind up the Corporation.

Experience with Disinvestment and Restructuring

The State of Orissa has taken some very meaningful measures in the direction of privatisation. It has made a detailed review of its SPSUs for identification of such units. The whole affair has been discussed a couple of times at the Cabinet-level and the inputs for such discussion were prepared intensively by the State Bureau of Public Enterprises. The SPSUs have been transferred to the private sector on the basis of outright sale, lease and management contract. The Charge Chrome division of Orissa Mining Corporation was sold to Tata Iron & Steel Company (TISCO) in 1991. The Baramba Cooperative Sugar Mill was handed over to Shakti Sugar Management of Tamil Nadu on management contract in 1991. The Nayagarh Sugar Mill was taken over by Dharni Sugars and Chemicals. The Baragarh Cooperative was handed over to Ponni Sugar Management Industries on a management contract in 1991. The East Coast Breweries was leased to United Breweries in 1993.

The Baminipal Charge Chrome Plant of the Orissa Mining Corporation was handed over to the Tatas. Privatisation of this plant became the talk of the day as it created tornado of public and legal controversies resulting into a public interest litigation (PIL) in the Orissa State High Court. The plant initially started as a State Government project with a cost estimation of Rs. 28.62 crore which escalated to Rs. 59.08 crore in 1991. Its installed capacity was 50,000 tonnes and it had 100 acres of land. The project started making losses right from the first day. By 1991, it had accumulated a loss of Rs. 50 crore. The State Government was no more in a position to fund further losses and, therefore, decided to privatise the plant. On the basis of the report by concerned departments, the Government privatised the plants on September 23, 1991. It is alleged that the State Government lost Rs. 57.71 crore due to faulty valuation and inappropriate transfer procedures. However, the productivity of the labour has gone up fourfold, the plant has wiped out accumulated losses and the labour harmony has been restored. The Government of Orissa have sought the services of the Adam Smith Institute to restructure and privatise its ailing SPSUs.

Case Studies on Power and Transport Sector Public Corporations

Orissa has been the first State to privatise the power sector and has emerged as the pioneering State in power sector reforms in the country. The reforms process initiated in 1992 with the proposed financial assistance from the World Bank unbundled the Orissa State Electricity Board into two entities viz., the Orissa Grid Corporation and the Orissa Hydel Power Corporation, the former to take over the transmission and bulk supply assets whereas the latter was to take over the hydro power generation assets. The thermal generating assets had been earlier formed into a government corporation called the Orissa Power Generation Corporation. A Regulatory Commission was set up in 1995 consequent to the enactment of Orissa Electricity Reforms Act, 1995 to regulate the transmission and distribution business. The Orissa State Electricity Board was found to be unequal to match the demand for power. It incurred huge losses. It suffered from heavy overstaffing. Its tariff policies were found to be irrational and the energy losses were unparalleled. The Government, therefore, restructured the Board and unbundled it into Transmission, Generation and Distribution Companies. Whereas the Government has made commendable progress with regard to the privatisation of generation and distribution, it is making all efforts to enlist private participation even with regard to transmission. One of the advantages of the unbundling of the power sector is the initiation of a regime of transparency which for the first time revealed that 50 per cent of the power consumed in the capital city of Bhubaneswar was not metered and that the existing tariffs have to provide for the transmission and distribution losses. The Commission pegged the loss figures at 35 per cent for the determination of tariff for the year 2000. During the course of reform the transmission and distribution losses have come down from 15 per cent to about 43 per cent. In Orissa, entire distribution system concerning power has been privatised with the formation of five companies viz., Western Supply Corporation (WESCO), North-Eastern Supply Corporation (NESCO), Southern Supply Corporation (SOUTHCO), Central Supply Corporation (CESCO). The WESCO, NESCO and SOUTHCO have been taken over by BSES whereas the CESCO has been taken over by AES-JYOTI. in terms of 51 per cent equity holdings. The 51 per cent equity offered for sale was estimated to give Rs. 1147.19 crore. However the money yielded was Rs. 1590.09 crore. The offered price per share on an average yielded Rs. 13.86 against the face value of Rs. 10 per share.

The regulator as a surrogate to the market mechanism claims that it has effectively ensured efficient working of the industry by issuing license, codes, standards and practice directions. The Commission claims to have rationalised the tariff structure which has moved towards a cost based tariff giving due regard to performance of the licensee, cost conditions, growth of State and per capita incomes, inflationary situation, ability to pay the personnel, fuel price hikes, economic use of energy, gradual reduction of cross subsidy and near elimination of general subsidy. The Commission has successfully hiked tariffs in 1996 (17%), 1997 (10.33%), 1998 (9.3%) and 1-2-2000 (4-5%). The Commission formulates supply regulations and publicises consumer rights statements which play a vital role in safeguarding consumer interests. However the Commission has not been able to achieve reduction in unacceptably high level of transmission and distribution losses, improve commercial practices and the consumer service of distribution companies and elimination of accumulated losses of more than Rs. 900 crore creating a situation of high debt, unusually high interest liability, cash crunch an impending bankruptcy. Some of the bottlenecks encountered by the Commission include lack of financial support. The Orissa model is being implemented by several States. The PWC have done the entire restructuring of the power sector. The power sector reforms have resulted in improving quality of service, upgradation of system performance, optimal use of energy, rational tariff for customers, increased realisation of revenue and greater private sector involvement, inadequacy of inter-State grid to allow export of power and long term and rigid allocations of power from Central stations without reference to demand and capability to pay. The Government has not ploughed back money received through disinvestment in the power sector. Finally, the different departments of the government are not moving in tandem. The silver lining is provided by the disinvestment in Orissa Power Generation Corporation Limited (OPGC) which was a 420 MW coal fired power station having a lean employee structure with only 839 regular employees. The divestment was affected by an empowered committee constituted by the Government of Orissa. The committee comprised officials from the energy, finance and public enterprises departments and the Managing Director and Director Finance of the OPGC. Its decisions were cleared by the project appraisal committee and wherever required by the cabinet. The DSP Meryl Lynch, the merchant banker invited global tenders for divestments of 26 per cent of share holdings. After due diligence with regard to the bids submitted by six parties from India and abroad, the share holdings were unloaded to AES (India) for Rs. 603.40 crore. The existing shareholdings reflects 51 per cent of the total share holdings with the Government of Orissa and the rest 49 per cent with AES (Mauritius and India). The World Bank in its mid term review (March 31, 2000) observed that power sector reforms in Orissa need to be applauded particularly the reforms with regard to regulation which have set a precedent of independent functioning, efficient performance and transparency for other regulatory agencies now being established in the power sector at the Central and State level. however, the fact of matter is that privatisation of power could become a complete success only when the generation is privatised fully which requires a considerable financial accommodation on the part of the Government of Orissa. However, power being a public good, the Government of Orissa should continue to retain the ownership of enterprise in this sector which will balance the welfare consequences in favour of people of Orissa.

The Orissa Road Transport Corporation is another major enterprise awaiting privatisation. The Corporation as on March 31, 2000 accumulated losses of Rs. 232.41 crore against the paid-up capital of Rs. 130.37 crore. Its bus fleet has come down to a mere 500 buses of which about 250 always remain off the roads.

Despite the recommendations of the Cabinet Sub-Committee (1996) for its rejuvenation the situation has not improved. The bus-staff ratio is 1 : 16. As money for the VRS is not available this ratio cannot be brought in line with the general ratio of 1 : 6 for the country as a whole. The Chief Minister reviewed the position of the Corporation on July 5, 2000 and has appointed a Committee under the Chairmanship of the Additional Chief Secretary to recommend suitable strategies. The general opinion of the management of the Corporation and the policy makers is to wind up the Corporation. The DFID is being approached for extending financial support to provide VRS. There is no denying the fact that public transport is an important public good. It may be difficult for private operators to operate transport services to villages and hamlets. In such an event, privatisation of public transport in Orissa cannot be justified although there is need to restructure the public transport operations in terms of scheduling of services, selection of routes and improving performance with regard to operational and financial parameters.

Conclusion

At the time of its inception as a State, Orissa was one among the least developed regions in the country lacking in entrepreneurship, capital, infrastructure and innovation. The State Government had to come forward to fill up this gap by creating a large number of SPSUs, however, over the years, the heavy loss making forced the Government to think in terms of closure of many of the SPSUs. The situation prevailing in the SPSUs sector created abnormal pressure on the State exchequer and the Government has to take alternative measures by curtailing its projected plan / non-plan expenditure every year due to ground realities. The SPSUs in Orissa need to be privatised and restructured at a brisk pace. There is a considerable unanimity among political parties and the bureaucracy to hasten the face of reforms in SPSUs. The Department of Public Enterprises, Government of Orissa has already created the basic framework. The appointment of an expert agency is expected to provide a fillip to this task. The insolvency procedures in the case of the SPSUs are radically different from the procedures existing in relation to the private corporates in as much as the fact that the SPSUs have to comply not only with the legal framework concerning the insolvency and restructuring equally applicable to their counterparts in private sector but also have to adhere to the compulsions of the social regulation in terms of which appropriate institutional structures and machinery are created for the formulation and implementation of the ideas in this realm. Some implementation issues such as insolvency and corporate restructuring with a human face, the nature of the enterprise in terms of its providing public/non-public good and use of local resources need to be provided a special attention. There is a need to redraw the line between public and private with respect to electricity and power reform.

ANNEXURE 4.1

STATUS AND OPTIONS OF RESTRUCTURING OF SPSUs IN ORISSA

Name	*Status & Options of Restructuring*	*Total Assets (Rs. Crore)*	*Total Sales (Rs. Crore)*
General Engineering & Scientific Works	Closed in June 1998	0.63	0.12
Ipitron Times Ltd.	Under Liquidation	—	—
Idcol Piping & Engineering Work Ltd.	Agreement Signed by a Private Party for Takeover	65.99	1.43
Orissa Instruments Corporation Ltd.	Wound Up	2.97	1.07
Orissa State Leather Corporation Ltd.	Closed since June 1998	6.68	2.75
Iptron Registors Ltd.	Closed in August 1994	—	—
Elcosmos Electronics Ltd.	Under Liquidation	8.34	0.13
Orissa State Commercial Transport Corporation Ltd.	Closed in May 1998	—	—

S*ource:* Based on Prof. Mishra's Study of Orissa SPSUs as Member of the Study Group on Disinvestment and Restructuring of SPSUs in India appointed by the Planning Commission where the author had extensive interaction with several experts, policy makers and public enterprise managers in the course of writing this chapter.

5

PERFORMANCE OF ANDHRA PRADESH STATE WAREHOUSING CORPORATION

A Multi-Dimensional Analysis

The Andhra Pradesh State Warehousing Corporation (APSWC) is a statutory body established in the year 1958. The Corporation was set up to provide storage space to farmers for the purpose of warehousing of agricultural produce. Andhra Pradesh is predominantly an agrarian economy. The Vision 2020 accords a priority place to agriculture in the plan to develop the State Economy. APSWC is in 45th year of its operation. There is a need to conduct a multi-dimensional assessment of the performance of the Corporation to chart out a sound path for its functioning in future.

Performance analysis means in the present context the analysis of both the financial and physical aspects of the working of APSWC. A multi-dimensional assessment has been attempted to inculcate a holistic view. For absolute analysis, APSWC's performance has been measured on certain key parameters. The comparative analysis maps APSWC's functioning with select SLPEs in Andhra Pradesh. 23 parameters have been selected to carry out such comparison. Five State warehousing corporations have been selected to benchmark the performance of APSWC. The horizontal analysis of APSWC's performance has been conducted by comparing its working with five top counterparts in the other States of the country.

Absolute Analysis

Table 5.1 depicts the performance of APSWC during 1998-99 to 2001-02. Whereas average surplus rose to 770 per cent during this period, average expenses registered a decline of 20 per cent. The net worth became fourfold. The capital employed also surged to fourfold. The profit performance was outstanding in that not only the three profit indicators, i.e., Gross Profit to Turnover, Net Profit to Net Worth and Net Profit to Capital Employed, showed a highly appreciable increase but they enjoyed an unrivalled status to the generally laid down standards. The productivity of the personnel in terms of turnover per employee increased during this period to 460 per cent and the average utilization of capacity increased from 67 per cent in 1998-99 to 93 per cent during 2001-02. The use of Capital Employed increased from 57.98 per cent in 1998-99 to 69.32 per cent in 2000-01 but slightly declined to 67.45 per cent in 2001-02 owing to the construction of new godowns. To sum up, the financial and physical performance of APSWC was quite robust.

Table 5.1 : Performance Indicators for APSWC

Performance Indicators	*1998-1999*	*1999-2000*	*2000-2001*	*2001-2002*
Average Revenue Per Tonne*	19.52	22.69	24.97	31.25
Average Expenses Per Tonne*	17.17	14.30	13.70	13.15
Average Surplus Per Tonne*	2.35	8.39	11.27	18.10
Turnover per employee*	1.62	2.68	4.87	7.38
Net Worth* (Paid-Up Capital + Reserves + Subsidy + P&L Appropriation)	1476.79	2282.12	3481.51	5794.97
Capital Employed* (Net Block + Working Capital)	1470.50	2284.82	3500.91	5665.78
Total Turnover on Capital Employed (%)	57.98	60.29	69.32	67.45
Gross Profit to Capital Employed (%)	11.20	24.85	33.38	41.26
Gross Profit to Turnover (%)	19.32	41.22	48.16	61.17
Net Profit to Net Worth %	6.77	35.46	34.98	41.92
Net Profit to Capital Employed (%)	6.80	35.42	34.79	42.87
Average Utilization of Capacity (%)	67	80	94.00	93.00

Source: Published Financial Statements of APSWC.

* Indicates Rs. in lakhs.

Performance Indicators for APSWC

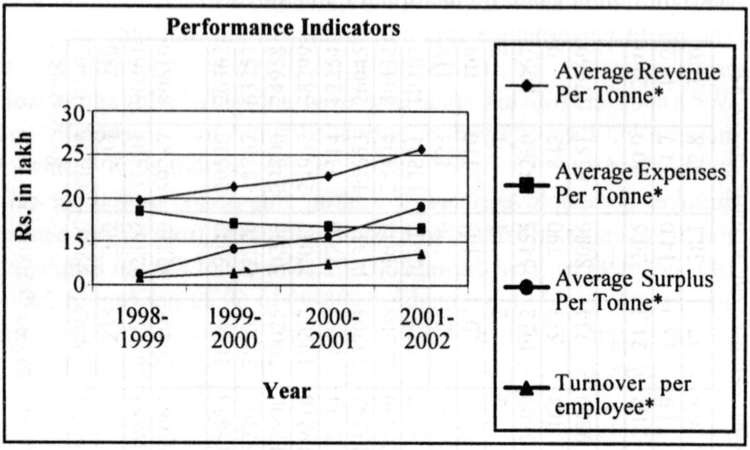

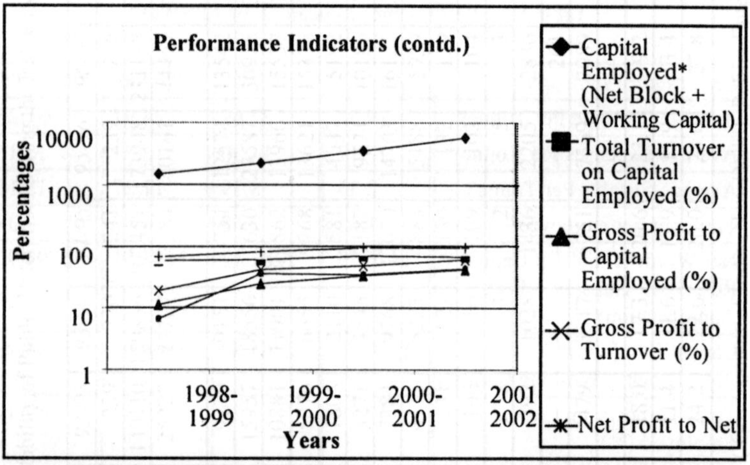

Capital Employed is Rs in lakhs

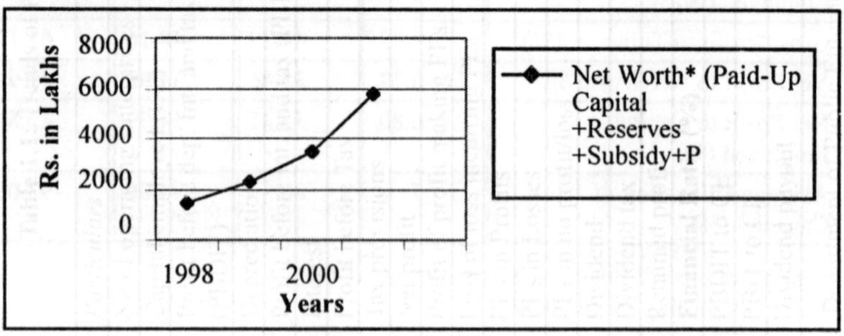

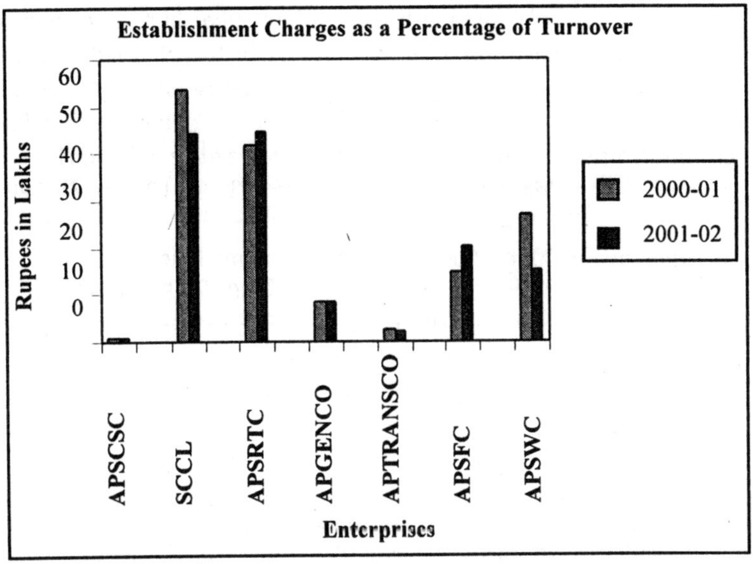

Comparative Performance Analysis

A mix of 23 parameters have been selected for the comparative performance analysis. Six SLPEs have been chosen for the purpose of comparing the trends and performance which are given in Table 5.2. The select SLPEs include the AP State Civil Supplies Corporation, Singareni Collieries Company Limited, Andhra Pradesh State Road Transport Corporation, Andhra Pradesh Power Generation Corporation, Andhra Pradesh Power Transmission Corporation and Andhra Pradesh State Financial Corporation. These enterprises are engaged in providing services, undertaking mining operations and generating power.

The highlights of the comparative performance analysis are as follows:

1. APSWC is a zero debt Company. It could also be called as a debt free Company. This implies that the company has no financial risk. It also signifies the potential created for the further growth of the Company. The Company should be able to raise resources for this purpose without seeking the Government guarantees. The SCCL and APSRTC have a low Debt-Equity

mix. The APSCSC, APGENCO, APTRANSCO and APSFC are highly levered and characterised by high degree of risk. (See Table 5.3)

2. The Net Worth in APSWC was higher than investment by seven times in 2001-02 pointing out to the fact that effective corporate governance was in place in the Corporation. APSCSC, SCCL and APGENCO do not share this distinction. APSRTC and APSFC have negative Net Worth. (See Table 5.3)
3. APSWC financed both its fixed assets and working capital from its own sources whereas none of the other sample SLPEs achieved this distinction. (See Table 5.3)
4. APSWC had no accumulated losses. Excepting APSCSC, the remaining sample enterprises had accumulated losses.
5. APSWC had a comfortable cash flow position. APTRANSCO, APSRTC, APSFC have negative Cash Flows. APSCSC and APGENCO have positive but inadequate cash flows.
6. APSWC has positive gross profits, operating profits and net profits. APSFC, APTRANCO, APGENCO and APSRTC are deep in the red. APCSC earned net profits but they turned out to be very low as compared to those of the APSWC.
7. The Establishment Charges declined to 15.02 per cent in 2001-02 from 26.91 per cent in 2000-01 in the case of APSWC. The establishment charges were almost three times higher than this benchmark in the case of SCCL and APSRTC. In the case of APSFC, the establishment charges were higher as compared to those incurred by the APSWC. APSCSC, APGENCO and APTRANCO had a smaller percentage of establishment charges incurred to their turnover.
8. None of the enterprises under the study declared dividends. APSWC could take lead in this regard. APSWC declared dividends for the years 2001-2002 and for 1998-1999, 1999-2000 and 2000-2001, the Corporation ploughed back the dividends equivalent into equity as per the Memorandum of Understanding (MoU).
9. The per capita turnover of employees increased by 65 per cent in 2001-02 over 2000-01 in the case of APSWC. None of the other enterprises could achieve this benchmark.

Table 5.2 : Performance of Select SLPEs in Andhra Pradesh during 2001-2002

(Rs. in Crore)

Enterprises / Parameters	APSCSC		SCCL		APSRTC		APGENCO		APTRANSCO		APSFC		APSWC	
	2000-01	*2001-02*	*2000-01*	*2001-02*	*2000-01*	*2001-02*	*2000-01*	*2001-02*	*2000-01*	*2001-02*	*2000-01*	*2001-02*	*2000-01*	*2001-02*
Equity	3.00	3.00	1733.20	1733.20	140.20	140.20	2106.80	2106.80	1434.34	1448.75	87.76	87.42	7.62	7.62
Debt	337.31	346.92	1227.54	1377.11	61.07	61.07	8469.75	9176.86	3767.21	5504.69	894.64	982.61	—	—
Total Investment	340.31	349.92	2960.74	3110.31	201.27	201.27	10576.55	11283.66	5201.55	6953.44	982.40	1070.33	7.62	7.62
Net Worth	54.25	55.58	1154.79	1361.13	-315.61	-587.71	1725.11	1660.17	1478.73	1487.48	(-)43.03	(-)56.21	34.82	57.95
Capital Employed (NFA + WC)	89.35	402.66	1350.81	2435.08	624.65	498.65	10022.46	10444.54	(-)102.75	257.23	(-)6.93	(-)13.36	35.00	56.65
Accumulated Losses	Nil	Nil	565.94	260.77	523.07	795.13	321.69	446.63	1281.02	317.50	147.18	160.30	Nil	Nil
Turnover	2481.30	2034.25	2741.32	2949.02	2540.00	2575.65	3828.65	3934.82	6490.81	7663.12	126.28	147.80	24.26	38.21
Cash Flow	3.47	2.13	420.62	343.78	—	—	370.69	370.27	(-)1028.63	(-)265.82	Nil	Nil	13.05	25.84
Gross Profit	2.57	1.31	420.00	695.17	(-)209.95	(-)272.06	962.86	1045.51	(-)767.66	48.99	2.68	1.13	11.69	23.38
PBIT/Operating Profit	2.57	1.31	221.72	326.30	260.78	401.32	(-)116.03	(-)124.94	(-)1281.08	(-)370.51	2.68	1.13	11.69	23.38
Establishment Charges	18.80	20.24	1470.90	1304.91	1067.47	1151.67	327.55	328.51	175.24	148.01	18.43	29.82	6.53	5.74
Establishment Charges as a % of Turnover	0.76	0.99	53.65	44.24	42.02	44.71	8.55	8.34	2.69	1.93	14.59	20.17	26.91	15.02
Net Profit	2.57	1.31	81.82	308.43	(-)209.95	(-)272.07	Nil	Nil	(-)1281.08	(-)370.51	(-)11.66	(-)13.12	12.17	24.29
Dividends	Nil	Nil	Nil	Nil	Nil	Nil	Nil	Nil	Nil	Nil	Nil	Nil	Nil	Nil
Total No. of employees	1478	1472	105627	99442	128796	126418	14000	14000	4924	4924	730	587	499	518
Per capita Turnover (in lakh)	167.88	138.19	2.595	2.96	0.019	2.03	27.34	28.10	131.81	155.62	17.29	25.17	4.86	7.31
Capacity Utilization	NA	NA	76%	76%	63%	70%	85.09%	86.30%	Purchasing Power		—	—	94%	93%
Expansion of Capacity	Nil	Nil	Nil	Nil	Negble	Negble	1MW	300M	No	No	Nil	Nil	5000 tonnes	4000 tonnes
Status of ISO	Nil	Nil	Nil	Nil	Nil	Nil	—	—	NO	No	ISO9002	ISO9001	Wholly	Wholly
Computerization	Partly	Partly	Partly	Partly	90%	90%	Partly	Partly	Partly	Partly	In Progress		Yes	Yes
Diversification	Gruhamitra Scheme		—	—	—	—	—	—	Entering into Telecom		Yes	Yes	Yes	Yes
Status of Accounts	F	NF	F	NF	F	NF	NF	NF	F	NF	F	F	F	F
Business Plan	Nil	NIl	No	No	No	No	No	No	No	No	Yes	Yes	Yes	Yes

Source: Data collected from the files of select enterprises.

Table 5.3 : Performance Ratios for Select SLPEs

Parameters / *SLPEs*	*GP to Turnover*		*PBIT to CE*		*NP to NW*		*NW to CE*		*NW to TI*		*D-E Ratio*	
	2000-01	*2001-02*	*2000-01*	*2001-02*	*2000-01*	*2001-02*	*2000-01*	*2001-02*	*2000-01*	*2001-02*	*2000-01*	*2001-02*
APSCSC	0.10	0.0d6	2.87	0.32	4.73	2.35	60.71	13.80	15.94	15.88	∞	∞
SCCL	15.32	23.57	16.41	13.39	7.08	22.65	85.48	55.89	39.00	43.76	0.70:1	0.79:1
APSRTC	-8.26	-10.56	41.74	80.48	66.52	46.29	-50.52	Nil	Nil	Nil	0.44:1	0.44:1
APGENCO	25.14	26.57	-1.15	-1.19	Nil	Nil	17.21	15.89	16.31	14.71	4.02:1	2.62:1
APTRANSC	-11.82	0.63	Nil	-143.89	-86.63	-24.90	Nil	57.87	28.42	21.39	2.62:1	3.79:1
APSFC	2.12	0.76	38.67	8.45	Nil	Nil	Nil	Nil	-4.38	-5.25	10.1:1	11.2:1
APSWHC	48.18	61.18	33.40	41.27	34.95	41.91	99.48	102.2	42.52	70.42	Nil	Nil

Source: Computations based on data provided in Table 5.2.
GP = Gross Profit; PBIT = Profit Before Interest and Tax; NP = Net Profit; NW = Net Worth; TI = Total Income; D E = Debt Equity

10. APSWC maintained a very high level of capacity utilization as compared to the other enterprises.
11. APSWC fared well in terms of non-financial indicators. Not only that it has finalized its annual report and annual accounts and is diversifying its business, it has initiated business modelling, is in advanced stages of receiving quality certification and is commencing on-line-warehousing. Excepting APCSC, the other corporations have yet to finalize their reports and annual accounts for 2001-02. APSFC is the only enterprise which has obtained ISO 9002 and 9001. Computerization was partly in progress in the various enterprises and the concept of business planning eludes them. Only APCSC and APTRANSCO are considering seriously to diversify their businesses. APSWC has engaged KPMG for preparing Business Model and strategy mapping. The Corporation has already initiated action for diversifying into ICD/ Container Freight Stations (CFS) and bulk storage.

To sum up, the comparative analysis of the financial and non-financial performance of the select SLPEs points out that APSWC was leading the pack.

Horizontal Analysis

A number of States have set up State warehousing corporations. It would be appropriate to relate the performance of APSWC to some other State warehousing corporations. Table 5.4 depicts the financial and physical performance of the APSWC, Maharashtra State Warehousing Corporation (MSWC), Haryana State Warehousing Corporation (HSWC), Tamilnadu State Warehousing Corporation (TSWC), Rajasthan State Warehousing Corporation (RSWC) and Uttar Pradesh State Warehousing Corporation (UPSWC).

Table 5.4 reveals the following features:

1. The Total Income in APSWC registered a Compound Average Growth Rate (CAGR) of 36.28 per cent as compared to 5.46 per cent in MSWC, 24.09 per cent in HSWC, 16.56 in TNSWC, 21.9 per cent in RSWC, 50.63 per cent in UPSWC.

Table 5.4 : Comparative Performance of Andhra Pradesh State Warehousing Corporation

Financial Performance *(Rs. in Lakh)*

	Andhra Pradesh State Warehousing Corporation						*Maharashtra State Warehousing Corporation*					
Particulars	*1996-97*	*1997-98*	*1998-99*	*1999-00*	*2000-01*	*2001-02*	*1996-97*	*1997-98*	*1998-99*	*1999-2000*	*2000-01*	*2001-02*
Total Income	689.87	796.29	852.65	1377.52	2426.90	3821.65 (36.28)	4261.35	4461.85	4783.48	5486.87	5525.91 (5.46)	—
Expenditure	670.33	741.23	749.82	868.46	1331.85	2604.0 (29.4)	2859.21	2975.86	3269.16	3876.82	4155.20 (7.93)	—
Profit	19.54	55.06	102.83	509.06	1095.05	2217.85 (114.9)	1402.14	1485.99	1514.32	1610.05	1370.71 (0.13)	—
Storage Charges	632.89	735.42	740.64	1257.54	2256.52	3510.5 (25.76)	3146.34	2990.22	2789.75	3225.85	3720.65 (3.86)	—
Opening Sundry Debtors	418.64	463.22	473.49	440.56	966.41	14.52 (34.97)	1051.15	1085.85	1130.85	1097.16	1969.02 (16.78)	—
Closing Sundry Debtors	463.22	473.49	440.56	966.41	1451.82	25.48 (8.62)	1085.85	1130.85	1097.16	1969.02	1625.68 (12.64)	—
Est. Charges	373.12	419.78	440.72	460.00	653.84	574.0 (24.31)	816.09	1064.70	1115.16	1336.24	1226.33 (9.36)	—

Physical Performance

Total Storage Capacity	5.64	5.46	5.42	6.31	8.58	10.19	8.89	8.88	9.14	9.55	19.26	—
Occupancy	3.85	3.93	3.64	5.06	8.1	7.58	7.02	6.22	6.59	9.16	8.15	—
% Occupancy	68	72	67	80	94	93%	79	70	72	96	79	—
Construction of new godowns	—	—	—	—	0.06	0.40	0.08	0.21	0.22	0.2	0.57	—

Financial Performance

Table 5.4 (contd.)

(Rs. in lakh)

	Haryana State Warehousing Corporation						Tamil Nadu State Warehousing Corporation					
Particulars	*1996-97*	*1997-98*	*1998-99*	*1999-00*	*2000-01*	*2001-02*	*1996-97*	*1997-98*	*1998-99*	*1999-2000*	*2000-01*	*2001-02*
Total Income	2008.93	3546.12	3515.68	2977.94	3856.78 (24.09)	—	839.66	990.86	1154.60	1384.16	1777.47 (16.56)	—
Expenditure	1110.90	1360.12	1285.75	1672.02	1944.87 (12.66)	—	606.67	854.44	957.26	1033.59	1323.02 (17.76)	—
Profit	898.03	2186.00	2229.93	1305.92	1911.91 (30.07)	—	232.99	136.42	197.34	350.57	454.45 (22.09)	—
Storage Charges	1043.58	1114.37	1575.85	1758.03	2549.87 (68.75)	—	790.14	927.92	1082.83	1260.24	1656.60 (16.39)	—
Opening Sundry Debtors	445.67	541.06	710.39	782.21	830.08 (13.78)	—	162.78	168.68	212.06	298.56	322.66 (27.04)	—
Closing Sundry Debtors	541.06	710.39	782.21	830.08	1256.36 (19.77)	—	168.68	212.06	298.56	322.66	499.94 (25.89)	—
Est. Charges	518.51	561.33	620.17	761.54	804.92 (9.44)	—	380.45	490.88	584.68	672.11	680.60 (12.86)	—
Physical Performance												
Total Storage Capacity	9.81	9.79	10.7	10.49	12.45	—	6.21	6.24	6.23	6.27	6.95	—
Occupancy	4.16	5.09	8.65	7.2	11.91	—	5.34	7.34	4.91	6	6.77	—
% Occupancy	42	52	81	69	96	—	86	92	79	96	97	—
Construction of new godowns	0.15	0.03	—	0.26	0.65	—	—	—	—	—	—	—

Table 5.4 (contd.)

	Rajasthan State Warehousing Corporation						*Uttar Pradesh State Warehousing Corporation*					
Particulars	*1996-97*	*1997-98*	*1998-99*	*1999-2000*	*2000-01*	*2001-02*	*1996-97*	*1997-98*	*1998-99*	*1999-2000*	*2000-01*	*2001-02*
Total Income	902.34	1050.26	1419.87	1629.47	2332.77 (21.9)	—	2055.13	2146.03	6163.09	9959.04	9959.04 (50.63)	—
Expenditure	677.66	857.58	912.39	987.12	1108.73 (10.68)	—	1849.09	1921.35	5276.16	8302.91	7460.02 (45.14)	—
Profit	224.68	192.68	507.48	642.35	1224.04 (58.94)	—	206.04	224.68	886.93	1656.13	2499.02 (88.16)	—
Storage Charges	759.01	870.06	1163.91	1407.54	2052.54 (23.03)	—	1550.88	1764.98	2553.47	3378.09	5338.23 (29.75)	—
Outstanding												
Opening	86.20	58.13	86.82	152.48	144.36 (23.93)	—	—	942.79	1403.50	1503.43	2142.40 (19.69)	—
Closing	58.13	86.82	152.48	144.36	170.10 (27.5)	—	—	942.79	1403.50	1503.43	2142.40 (32.43)	3506.93
Estt.Charges	471.05	562.81	649.90	670.59	679.10 (7.87)	—	—	1083.51	1217.00	1275.59	1638.54 (13.72)	2015.93
Capacity (Mts)	NA	NA	NA	928.00	1090.00 (17.45)	—	—	686.00	682.00	718.00	794.00 (3.05)	NA
Physical Performance												
Total Storage Capt	5.05	5.39	5.77	6.13	6.75	—	12.86	12.84	13.53	17.61	23.65	—
Occupancy	2.41	3.5	3.69	4.03	4.01	—	9.47	10.41	11.91	17.81	24.38	—
% Occupancy	48	65	64	66	59	—	74	81	88	101	103	—
Construction of new godowns	0.36	0.15	0.42	0.32	0.24	—	—	—	—	0.14	0.96	—

Source: Compiled from Planning Commission Data Base on SLPEs set up by Prof. R.K. Mishra *et al.*
Note: Figures in parentheses indicate CAGR.

2. The Expenditure in APSWC registered a CAGR of 29.4 per cent as compared to 7.93 per cent in MSWC, 12.66 per cent in HSWC, 17.76 per cent in TSWC, 10.68 per cent in RSWC, 45.14 per cent in UPSWC. In case of APSWC, it is because of leveraged growth strategy followed by APSWC. Instead of creating assets themselves, APSWC has chosen to make profit out of the assets of others. However, it has to be noted that in doing so they incur rent expense which accounts for substantial percentage of expenditure.
3. The Profits in APSWC registered a CAGR of 114.98 per cent as compared to 0.13 per cent in MSWC, 30.07 per cent in HSWC, 22.09 per cent in TSWC, 58.94 per cent in RSWC, and 88.16 per cent in UPSWC.
4. The Storage Charges in APSWC registered a CAGR of 25.96 per cent as compared to 3.86 per cent in MSWC, 68.75 per cent in HSWC, 16.39 per cent in TSWC, 23.0 per cent in RSWC, and 29.75 per cent in UPSWC.
5. The Establishment Charges registered a CAGR of 8.62 per cent in case of APSWC as compared to 9.36 per cent in MSWC, 9.44 per cent in HSWC, 12.86 per cent in TNSWC, 7.87 per cent in RSWC, and 13.72 per cent in UPSWC.
6. The Closing Outstandings registered a CAGR of 34.97 per cent in APSWC as compared to 12.64 per cent in MSWC, 19.77 per cent in HSWC, 25.89 per cent in TSWC, 27.5 per cent in RSWC and 32.43 per cent in UPSWC. Receivables management should be emphasised.
7. In terms of productivity, APWC is the best because in 2001-02 the earning per employee was Rs.7.38 lakh and per employee handling increased to more than 2000 tonnes.
8. Despite more than four times the capacity, UPSWC's profit is proportionately less than that of APSWC. The same applies vis-à-vis HSWC and MSWC.

Taken as a whole only UPSWC emerged as a rival to APSWC in physical and financial performance. However between the two APSWC fared better in case of CAGR related to Profit, Expenditure and Establishment Charges. In the area of receivables management, APSWC was closely following the UPSWC.

Suggestions

A few comments could be offered in the nature of suggestions as follows:

1. APSWC should continue to take measures to increase its income. The diversification efforts are appreciable and need to be further enhanced.
2. The growth of Establishment Cost is showing a southward trend as a percentage of earning. The Corporation should consolidate this trend.
3. The present profitability trend should be strengthened.
4. A modicum of dividends to owners could be considered by the corporation.
5. The corporation could increase the business by employing prudent volume of debt. This would also boost the EPS and enhance the shareholder value creation. Currently, APSWC is a debt free company.
6. The State of corporate governance is heartening. Necessary measures should be taken for its greater permeation.

6

MEMORANDUM OF UNDERSTANDING AND PUBLIC ENTERPRISES IN INDIA

Backdrop

Introduction

Public Enterprises (PEs) in India are the result of planned economic development. The policy makers of independent India wanted to provide equal employment opportunities through the establishment of PEs and the State took up the issue of 'social justice' and 'public good'. Contrary to this design, the PEs over the years have become overextended and a number of problems have cropped up in these enterprises and they are unable to make return on the investments made on them. Various reform measures have been taken from time to time by the GoI to improve the performance of the enterprises.

As a part of the reform measure, Memorandum of Understanding (MoU) was introduced into the Central Public enterprises (CPEs) in 1987. The objective of the MoU system as per the Public Enterprise Survey 1996-97 is to:

- Introduce a performance improvement system that would simultaneously increase autonomy and accountability in the public sector.
- Remove the fuzziness in the goals and objectives of the enterprises.
- Set up an objective performance evaluation system and introduce a performance incentive system.

Problems and Issues of PEs

The study discusses the problems and issues in PEs, which are

directly, or indirectly affecting the performance of the enterprises. The following observations have been made:

- *The problem of entry of PEs into non-core sectors:* PEs were initially set up in the infrastructure area (core sectors). But in the due course of time they entered into areas which did not suit them. Heavy investments have gone into sectors where PEs have failed to perform and which are now difficult to retrieve.
- *Uncertain tenure of the Chief Executives:* The common problems, which the PEs face, is that their chief executives are hardly given a tenure of 1-2 years with each enterprises. By the time the officer sets the tone and tunes himself to the environment he is shifted to another enterprise. This has created a general apathy among the officers, and the officers in turn see that their involvement with the enterprise is not a serious one.
- *Varying interests of the Chiefs:* There is a tendency of the chief executives of the enterprises to pursue certain ideas, which they believe are very important for the growth of the particular enterprise. They pursue them with great interest, generate a lot of interest in their staff too, for the particular idea. Lot of investments is made for pursuing the policy. When the chief leaves the organization, and another one replaces him he comes with a new set of priorities for the enterprise. The investment in both ways i.e. resources and manpower goes waste as there is change in idea at the management level.
- *Political interventions and interests:* PEs are known to be hot beds for political combats. The political parties have their interests going high in appointing the top management. For example the senior member who could not be given a ministerial berth is accommodated as the Chairman of a public enterprise. Thus the political parties have always found the PEs as areas of vested interests. Of late there is growing awareness regarding this issue and the PEs themselves have ceased to be lucrative and the political chiefs have found better pastures and now are talking about their privatization.
- *Lack of operational autonomy and accountability:* The major problem that the PEs face is lack of operational autonomy for them. Number of efforts have been done in order to overcome

this problem. The Navaratna package was announced for the blue chip companies and it gave them the necessary operational freedom to work for a better performance. The MoU is also a similar exercise, which was undertaken by the Government in 1987-88 in order to induce professionalism into the PEs working.

- *Cyclic performance of enterprises:* Another major problem with the PEs enterprises is that there is a cyclic pattern of performance in these enterprises. They work successfully for a certain period of time and then there is a gradual decline in their performance. The insiders as well as researchers have observed this trend.
- *Lack of flexibility and adaptability:* The PEs are lagging behind in all the major areas of changes i.e. technology, novel management techniques, advanced information system. At the same time the private enterprises make the best use of these developments. The PEs are stuck with outdated technology and techniques, which forces them to show bad performance and end up with a sense of defeat.
- *Changing role of the State:* The State had initially taken up the role of a Welfare State with an agenda to provide equal opportunity to all. With the changes in the socio-political and economic conditions, the State decided to pull out of its responsibilities and restrict itself to activities in a select few sectors where it could give a better performance. The State realizes that it is no more competent to give profitable results in many areas, which are otherwise taken over by the private sector. Almost all the countries with large PEs have opted for privatization in the late 80s and early 90s. The initiation of MoU in India was also a step in this direction. The system of MoU was formally introduced in the year 1988-89 following the recommendations made by the Arjun Sengupta Committee report of 1985. Almost 110 CPEs have signed the MoU in the year 1996-97.

Government's Policy on Performance Evaluation

The Industrial Policy Resolutions of 1948 and 1956 broadly classified the role of Government vis-à-vis the private sector undertakings. The Government of India assured to take the responsibility for industrial and economic development of the country. Accordingly all strategic industries were to be set up, developed, strengthened and diversified under Government ownership. But nothing was discussed in these Policy Resolutions about the performance evaluation of PEs. Mostly *ad hoc* measures were introduced from time to time. Further, 1977 Industrial Policy Statement focused on its package of development of rural industries and strengthening the agrarian sector. But no attention was focused in regard to performance evaluation.

However, the 1980 Industrial Policy Statement did not pay much attention to the problem of performance evaluation of PSU's. Only *ad hocism* governed the performance evaluation and techniques of evaluation differed from enterprise to enterprise and ministry to ministry. Government did not go for any comprehensive package of performance evaluation for PSUs. A significant development that took place prior to the announcement of the New Economic Policy in 1991 was the appointment of Arjun Sengupta Committee in 1985. The Committee was entrusted with the task of suggesting suitable performance evaluation mechanism for the Indian PEs. Based on the experience of other developing countries with regard to performance evaluation of PEs, the Committee made detailed recommendations in regard to performance evaluation of PEs through the MoU system and the same was accepted by the Government and adopted to the PEs.

In 1991 Industrial Policy Statement (Public Enterprise Survey, 1996-97) aimed at improving the portfolio and performance of public sector. The salient features of the policy include,

- Portfolio of public sector investments will be reviewed with a view to focus the public sector on strategic, high-tech and essential infrastructure, whereas some reservations for the public sector are being retained, there would be no bar for areas of exclusivity to be opened up to the private sector selectively. Similarly, the public sector will also be allowed entry in areas not reserved for it.
- PEs which are chronically sick and which are unlikely to be turned around will for the formulation of revival or rehabilitation scheme be referred to the Board for Industrial and Financial Restructuring (BIFR), or other similar high level institutions created for the purpose. A social security mechanism will be

created to protect the interest of workers likely to be affected by such rehabilitation packages.

- In order to nurse resources and encourage public participation, a part of the government's share holding in the public sector would be offered to mutual funds, financial institutions, general public and workers.
- Boards of public sector companies would be made more professional and given greater powers.

Adoption of MoU System

Arjun Sengupta Committee Report in 1985 dealt with the issue of improving the performance of the CPEs. The contractual system, which India adopted for the PE performance, was named as the "Memorandum of Understanding". The MoUs have been in operation in Indian PEs since 1987, commencing in an experimental way with 4 PEs. The number of PEs, which signed the MoUs, has gone up to 109 in the year 1997-98. The system has remained so far confined to the CPEs and has not percolated to the State Level Public Enterprises (SLPEs).

The Industrial Policy Statement 1991 (Public Enterprise Survey, 1996-97) regarding the system of MoU clarified that,

(1) There will be greater thrust on autonomy through MoU systems through which manufacturers would be granted greater autonomy and will be held accountable. Technical expertise on the part of the Government would be upgraded to make the MoU negotiations and implementation more effective.

(2) To facilitate a fuller discussion on performance, the MoU signed between Government and the PE would be placed in Parliament. While focusing on major manufacturing issues, this would also help place matters of day to day operations of PEs in their correct perspective.

As per the Public Enterprise Survey, the following observations are made for the reason for implementing the system of MoU to CPEs:

1. Widely held perception that the PEs are less efficient than their private sector counterparts.

2. PEs are unable to perform because there are a variety of agencies that feel that they have a mandate to run the PEs. These organizations keep setting different objectives for the enterprises, which are often conflicting.
3. No one in the PEs is accountable for the performance of the enterprise.
4. PEs are handicapped in their operation due to absence of functional autonomy.

Contents of Performance Contracting

Ingredients of a Performance Contract

Performance contracts are adopted as tools by the PEs to improve their performance. Based on the contents, the contracts are broadly classified under two systems (a) the French based systems and (b) the Signalling system.

The main difference between the two types of contract is that the typical French Contract Plans don't allocate weights to the targets. This adds to a high degree of subjectivity to the evaluation process. This system is followed in France, Africa (Senegal, Benin and Morocco), and Latin America. In the signalling system signals are sent to the managers in order to monitor the results of the contacts. This system originated in Pakistan and Korea is popular in Asia (Pakistan, South Korea and Bangladesh), Africa (Ghana, Nigeria and Gambia) and Latin America. There are countries like India, which practice both the systems. Initially MoU in India was based on the French System, while those signed more recently follow the Signalling system.

The enterprises contracts essentially comprise of the mission of the enterprise, the objectives of the enterprise, the criteria selected, the weightages assigned to each criteria, the period of contract and the mode of evaluation.

Organizational Environment

Every organization has a number of different types of plans for improving its performance. They can be generally classified on the basis of the Purpose or Mission, Objectives of the enterprise, Strategies,

Policies, Procedures and Rules, which the organization must follow to reach the goals. The Programmes and budget would be the basis on which the enterprise would pursue to achieve the goals. In the same way, performance contracting of an enterprise comprises of a number of components, which can be arranged in a hierarchy.

The Hierarchy of Performance Contract

Mission

The mission or purpose identifies the basic function or task of an enterprise. Every kind or organized operation has, or at least should have if it is to be meaningful, a **purpose or a mission.** In every social system, enterprises have a basic function or task, which is assigned to them by the society. The purpose of a business is generally production and distribution of goods and services. This can be accomplished by fulfilling a mission of producing certain types of products. It is generally thought that the mission of an enterprise is to make surplus. This is absolutely necessary for the enterprise to survive and to perform the task that the society has entrusted to it. But this basic objective is achieved only by undertaking certain activities as per the clearly defined directions and accomplishing the mission.

All the PEs are presumed to serve the public. There is a tendency, therefore, to state the mission in very broad terms and in a way that anything that is considered good for the public is included.

There is also a tendency to describe the mission in grandiose terms. For example, the mission of a PE, which is in the consultancy business, is set out 'to be the most important international consultancy organization in the world.' It is not wrong to set out the mission of the enterprise somewhat ambitiously, but there is a need to make it realistic and achievable in the next 20-25 years. In writing a mission there should be a judicious balance between the great expectations on the one hand and the achievable results on the other hand.

The performance contracts in India open with the mission of the enterprise. The enterprises have a sector-wise distribution and each of the enterprise has a separate well-defined function. This individual function is brought out clearly in the mission of the enterprise. It has been observed that this is an approach adopted by all the public enterprises signing the performance contracts. The mission of the enterprise is clearly spelt out at the beginning of the contract. The mission is actually the long term planning for the enterprise. It highlights what the enterprise is aiming at in the long run and intends to achieve through undertaking certain activities.

Objectives

The objectives are the goals towards which the activity is aimed at. They represent not only the end point of the planning but also the end towards which organizing, staffing, leading, and controlling are aimed. While enterprise objectives are the basic plan for the firm, a department may also have its own objectives. These goals would certainly be congruent to the goals of the enterprise as a whole. Objectives state the end results and the overall objectives need to be supported by the sub-objectives. Thus objectives form a hierarchy as well as a network. Moreover organizations and managers have multiple goals which are sometimes incompatible and may lead to conflicts within an organization, within a group or between individuals.

As presented in the diagram below the objectives form a hierarchy ranging from the broad aim to specific individual objectives. In this hierarchy first there is the purpose of the society. It involves the organization to contribute to the welfare of the people by providing goods and services at reasonable costs. Second there is a purpose of the business, which might be to furnish convenient, low cost transportation for the average person. The next level of hierarchy contains more specific objectives, such as those in the key result areas. These areas are the ones in which the performance is essential for the success of the enterprise.

Hierarchy of Objectives

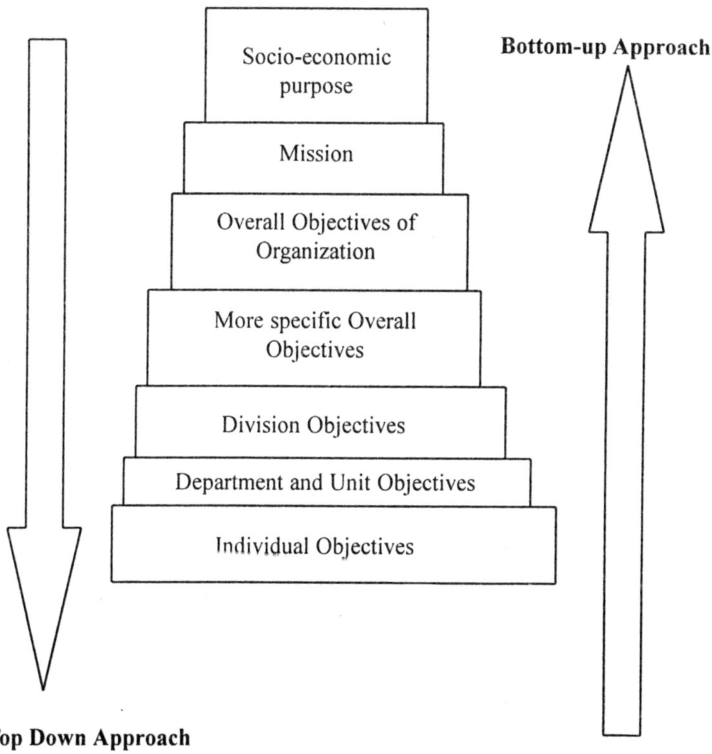

Management by Objectives

Management by Objectives is now practiced round the world. MBO in the words of George S. Odiorne is defined as, "Management by objectives is a comprehensive managerial system that integrates many key managerial activities in a systematic manner and that is consciously directed towards the effective and efficient achievement of organizational and individual objectives."

Fredrich V. Malek, a former special assistant to the President of United States, recognized the need for Management by Objectives (MBO) in Government. For any Government enterprise, in order to be managed efficiently, it clearly needs a system for setting priorities, pinpointing responsibilities requiring follow-through, and generating feedback that could be monitored and evaluated from the top.

As the PEs being Government run organizations were also made a part of the system of controls by objectives. Objectives of the enterprise are the major feature of the performance contract in India. The objective of the enterprise is actually the short-term reachable goals of the enterprise. It highlights what the enterprise wants to achieve in the nearest future (3-6 years). The objectives are an essential component of the contract process. Based on the objectives the other components are decided. The PEs in India are accountable to a number of different agencies like the Planning Commission, Finance Ministry, Administrative Ministry, aid givers like the WB, IMF, and are stretched on all directions by them. This was the reason for the setting up of Arjun Sengupta Committee in 1985. The committee was expected work out a method that would liberate the PEs from the pulls from all directions. The committee recommended the introduction of an MoU system, which would be an annual agreement between the public sector management and the Government.

For setting of objectives for any enterprise there is a need to follow certain guidelines. In the case of PEs the MoU is formulated on the basis of guidelines supplied by the Department of Public Enterprises. The specific guidelines are issued at the beginning of the financial year to all the enterprises and the contract is designed based on these guidelines.

There are a number of benefits of introducing a system of assessment based on the objectives set for the enterprises. With the introduction of this system there are possibilities of improving the management and clarification of organizational goals. It also enhances the encouragement of personal commitment to work and at the same time increases the effective controls over the system. The two features of autonomy and accountability are achieved at the same time with the introduction of MBO.

There are a few disadvantages with the system of MBO. It is generally seen that there are serious possibilities that the goal setters themselves might not be very clear about the ideas of the real objectives of the enterprise. This might lead to failure to give guidance to goal setters and difficulty in goal settings. The lack of clarity of goals is considered as one of the major reasons for the failure of the public sector, in India. With the introduction of objectives there is very little room for flexibility for the mangers. The objectives also have the drawback of emphasizing only the short-term benefits of the organization, as they seldom reflect the enterprises long term plans.

Criteria

The next major component of the contract is the performance criteria or indicators. Criteria are decided before entering into the contract and based on the criteria, weightages are assigned to them. The selection of proper criteria is considered to be as important as the selection of an appropriate measure. Prajapathi Trivedi (1988) spelt out certain prerequisites for selection of criteria. He says that regarding the performance criteria there are a few preconditions, which have to be fulfilled for the contracts to be a success. Performance criteria included in the contract must be clearly defined and understood. The mission of the enterprise, the objective of the enterprise, the criteria should be clearly spelt out. Only then will it be possible to decide whether the enterprise has covered the target, which it was expected at the end of the year.

Performance criteria should be 'fair' to the manager and it should encompass only areas within the control of the PE management. If the criteria decided is beyond the control of the enterprise manager it would be practically impossible for him to reach the targets that have been specified.

Performance criteria should be fair to the country. The performance criteria decided should be in accordance to the ideology of the nation. If the country is following a mixed economy pattern where it has not given itself to the commercial forces the assessment also should accordingly. At the same time if the country is totally a privately managed one it can opt for harsh financial targets and lead the enterprises towards achieving them. It is not sufficient that the contracts are made keeping in mind the criteria for measurement, it has to also look into the necessary institutional arrangements, which are available, for fulfilling the contract terms. The institutional arrangements need to be compatible with the purpose of the enterprise, which would ensure positive results.

Suresh Kumar in his observations on the Indian MoU system and particularly highlighting upon the selection of criteria has given the following as very desirable, Performance criteria , like Corporate Objectives should be limited. There should be congruence between the objectives and the performance criteria. There should not be any duplication in the selection of criteria. Selected performance criteria should be measurable and their evaluation method predetermined and laid down in the MoU.

The corporate objectives should sharply focus the ideology of the enterprise. There is a need for the objectives to be unambiguous and clear. Based on the goals of the enterprise, the criteria have to be selected. There has to be a complete congruence between the objectives of the enterprise and the performance criteria. The criteria selected must be clear and must not be overlapping, as this will hamper the results and the actual performance of the enterprise will not be highlighted. The criteria selected for the evaluation process must be verified and measurable. They should be properly laid down in the MoU. Pakistan signalling system aims at motivating management to maximize return on the capital. In order to attain this objective, attempt is made to evolve primary criteria of evaluation, which reflects the improvement in real productivity, which in turn leads to an increase in socially relevant profit. The Pakistani Signalling system has the important feature like the profit (real). This is a factor, which is not the basis for foundation of the PEs as their objective is achieving the social profitability. Public profits are private profits adjusted for those elements not deemed relevant to a public enterprise. Pakistani Signalling system is based on the principle that public enterprise management should be appropriately guided to aim at improving real productivity. Its efforts should be acknowledged and rewarded by an incentive system. Deciding on the performance criteria is a crucial exercise for the enterprises. The success of any contract depends on the type of criteria that has been selected. The true performance of an organization is reflected only when proper criteria are selected.

Target-Setting Process

Targets

Performance contracts set targets for all goals and indicators of a PE, and these may include targets in non-financial areas apart from the financial ones, such as personnel; marketing and technological development, which are covered by a corporate plan but not usually by a budget. Targets are based on what the enterprise can reasonably achieve, given the expected policy environment, market prices, planned capital expenditures, and the level of management autonomy where there is a performance variable. For each indicator a range of values is set so that performance can be graded, e.g. as excellent, good, fair, poor or bad.

Targets are individual to an enterprise and to a particular period. The same targets for profitability should not be applied to all PEs, or even to a group of similar enterprises. Targets, should be set which reflect each enterprise's exogenous conditions, such as inherited plant and equipment, labour force and local infrastructure.

A typical Indian performance contract will have the following elements in it; (approximate figures are given)

(1) Physical Factors—55
(2) Project Implementation—3
(3) Energy—5
(4) Environment—5
(5) MoU related—0
(6) Financial—25
(7) HRD—7

A typical Indian MoU would contain components like the physical factors which would include production, exploration, distribution, sales etc. It comprises the major part of the contract. The project implementation is also spelt out in the contract, as to how successful the enterprise has been in completing the projects assigned to them. Factors relating to energy consumption and its effect on the environmental conditions also figure out in the contract. The financial performance of the enterprise i.e., profitability, productivity etc. is brought in through these parameters. The financial factors spell out the real performance of the enterprise. There are other non-financial parameters like the HRD related issues and MoU related issues, which highlight in the MoU.

A typical Pakistani performance contract negotiates the three agreed criteria as shown below. The concerned parties may give relative priority to these criteria in terms of weights as:

Production	: 30%
Profit	: 50%
Project implementation	: 20%

The weights may be specified as percentages when they should add to 100. Alternately, the weights may be fractions adding up to one, like 0.03, 0.50, 0.20, which adds to 1.00.

Pakistan signalling system aims at motivating management to maximize return on the capital. In order to attain this objective, attempt is made to evolve primary criteria of evaluation, which reflects the improvement in real productivity. This in turn leads to an increase in socially relevant profit. The Pakistani Signalling system has the important feature like the profit (real). This is a factor, which is not the basis for foundation of the PEs as their objective is achieving the social profitability. Public profits are private profits adjusted for those elements not deemed relevant to a public enterprise. Pakistani Signalling system is based on the principle that public enterprise management should be appropriately guided to aim at improving real productivity and efforts acknowledged and rewarded by an Incentive System. Deciding on the performance criteria is a crucial exercise for the enterprises. The success of any contract depends on the type of criteria that has been selected. The true performance of an organization is reflected only when proper criteria are selected.

Target Level

Targets should be neither too low that they are achieved without effort nor so high that manager considers them as unachievable, resulting in a counter-productive effect. Managers often complain that if they achieve a target, it is raised the next year. The target-setters should distinguish between targets, which can be raised without limit, such as profitability, and targets, which have physical limits, such as capacity utilization. Otherwise this may lead to the tendency for the enterprises to set targets in such a way that it is very much within the reach of the enterprise. This distorted feature has been noticed in the enterprises during the study and this happens to be one of the reasons for the failure of the system. Asymmetry of information between an enterprise and target-setters (the information superiority of those who are to choose to the production process) allows the enterprise to get the targets it wants through selective disclosure of information.

For each indicator there should be a target value to motivate the managers. The Government has a great interest in each target because it represents the enterprise's intended contribution to a public goal. The Ministry of Finance, for instance, will be concerned with profit and how much of that it will receive as income tax, interest, dividend, etc. It is also concerned about what subsidy the enterprise will need. The Government is concerned that the targets are challenging and that they, as owners of the enterprise, get value of money spent. Larger and stronger PEs may be able to negotiate lower targets. Government negotiators should aim to be equally tough with all enterprises.

The targets should be set in such a way that they are compatible in the contracting system as a whole. It is generally observed that the target levels assigned to each criterion depends on the past performance on that particular criterion and the expectations of its performance on that particular criterion in the coming years. This process is greatly influenced by the information flow between the Government and the PE. There is a tendency to give lower targets and get away with better performance.

Efficient target setting should be carried out in a participatory process. Without this approach, targets tend to take the form of formal directives, which are often overtly accepted and covertly resisted. Targets should be clear-cut. Targets should neither be too low nor too high. This would give wrong signals to the managers. Each enterprise must be looked at in its own unique environment which must be taken into account. The targets must ensure that generation of surplus is significantly more than distribution by way of bonus. Targets must take into account the social tasks, which are taken up by the enterprises.

The target setting exercise in Pakistan is done by the Expert Advisory Cell. It ensures that the targets are clear cut and neither too high nor too low. The targets are set keeping in mind the environment in which the PE is working. It is ensured by the cell that the targets take care of the surplus factor which would go as a bonus at the same time consider the social accountability of the enterprise.

Fundamental for Target Setting

In principle, there are three possible bases for setting future enterprise targets.

Inter-firm comparison: The recent performance of comparable firms, adjusted for difference in circumstances and expected future exogenous change.

Inter-year comparison: Past performance of the enterprise, adjusted for exogenous change.

Inter-year method: The production engineering or work-study estimate, applying "reasonable" standards to each cost and revenue element in each activity and expected values of exogenous variables. A mixture of methods may be used, and the same mixture should then apply to all public enterprises in each period. Qualitative indicators are usually assessed retrospectively, using the inter-year method.

Comparison with other firms is not usually possible for monopoly enterprise, except where they are broken up regionally and the regional bodies can be compared. International comparisons of firms are rarely easy, because differences in cost condition, markets, and fiscal and regulatory requirements are not readily known as adjusted for.

Past performance is a poor indicator of potential performance. Nevertheless, trend analysis may still be used as a basis for assessing performance improvement, on which incentives can be based. If performance contracting is conceived as an instrument for progressive improvement of performance, then past performance adjusted for exogenous change is a sufficient standard.

The Korean performance contracts make extensive use of regression analyses of past data. Seven-year time series analysis is made for most of the quantitative indicators. From these it is possible to project the expected targets for the following years, and also the standard deviation. This method is said to simplify target setting and reduce controversy. However it rests on the assumption that the future will be a simple projection of the past.

Yardstick competition is applied by a target-setter knowing the unit costs in similar enterprises. In Bangladesh, for example, a detailed system of comparing cotton textile mills is used by the Bangladesh Textile Mills Corporation. The target is set by reference to the average enterprise, or the most efficient enterprise, taking the best performance on each activity. The United Kingdom Audit Commission has a tradition of "inter-firm" comparisons of local authority performance, which indicates that such comparisons may be valid and useful, despite disputes on their interpretation.

Work study and management audit is also used to set up targets, which represent reasonably efficient performance. Though this method is slow and costly. The United Kingdom Monopolies and Mergers Commission carries out indepth review of efficiency as required by the Department of Trade and Industry. The MMC examines the trend of performance indicators, such as unit costs and quality, and management processes. For want of valid international or intra-national comparisons of performance indicators, it tends to conform to widely accepted standards of management practices.

Management Participation

One technique that has been given strong support as the result of motivation theory is the increased awareness and use of participation. In addition to this most people in the centre of an operation have knowledge both of problems and of solutions to them. As a consequence, the right kind of participation yields both motivation and knowledge valuable for an enterprise success.

Targets should be negotiated between the Government and management and should not be imposed. Certainly, the Government is in a position to set whatever targets it likes and to apply sanctions. The principle of negotiation is the principle of participatory management under another name. PE managers are encouraged to participate in setting their targets so that they "internalize" them and are more committed. In fact, most contracting systems require initial targets to be proposed by the management. Korea is an exception where the Task Force sets targets in a top-down fashion. The mode of target setting is very much affected by the information of the parties.

The benefits of participation are not confined to the Government management interface. It is apparent that improvement of performance can arise only by changes in behaviour at the operating level. Therefore, there should be an internal dialogue through all levels of the enterprise extending the corporate goal and incentives to divisions and sections of the enterprise.

Period of Contract

The key to choosing the right planning period lies in logical planning. Planning encompasses a future period of time necessary to fulfil through a series of actions and commitments made. Since the capital which is the lifeline of an organization is normally limited in relation to the firm needs. Its expenditure must be accompanied by a reasonable possibility of recovering it, plus a return on investment, through operations.

Targets may be set for each year in a multi-year agreement or for a single year only. Irrespective of the period of agreement, it is better to set short-period targets. If targets are set for a number of years ahead, they are likely to be soon outdated by events. So they may be updated and revised each year as in a rolling plan. The performance contracts in Kenya provide examples of this.

Early French contracts were made to terminate with the National Plan. The Sixth Plan in 1975 and the Seventh Plan in 1980 were seen as instruments for the implementation of National Plan targets. In several countries, only the first year's targets are used for purposes of performance evaluation, and subsequent year's targets are reset on an Annual Rolling Plan basis.

In the case of India targets are made annually coinciding with the Annual Plans of the enterprises. During the survey of 109 MoU signing enterprises it was noted that the enterprises varied in their views on the period of the contract. While production companies accepted the time span of one year the companies which were in the construction and exploration business were of the view that the contracts should be for a longer period. They suggested that the period should be at least for 24-36 months, which is minimum time period for completion of a project.

Pakistani contracts made under the signalling system were initially for one year. However, this reflected the lack of corporate plans at that time, and it was anticipated that longer time horizons would be adopted with the development of corporate planning by enterprises.

In Gambia, for instance, performance contracts have been for four years. They spell out the goals of the enterprise, and autonomy for the management. The targets are separately negotiated each year and signed at the technical level. These are the basis on which annual performance is evaluated and rewarded or penalized.

Ideally targets may be set for each year only. Irrespective of the period of the agreement, it is better to set short-period targets within a medium-term-planning framework. If targets are set for a number of years ahead, they are likely to be soon outdated by events, so they may be updated and revised each year.

Monitoring and Control

The managerial function of controlling is the measurement and correction of performance in order to make sure that the enterprise objectives and the plans devised to attain them are accomplished. Planning and controlling are closely related. Without objectives and plans, control is not possible, because performance has to be compared against some established criteria. The basic control process , wherever applied and whatever is being controlled involves three steps:

Establishing Standards

Plans are yardsticks against which manager's device controls. Standards are actually the criteria for performance. They are selected points in the entire planning process. Based on these measures of performance are made so that managers can receive signals about how things are going.

Measuring Performance against the Standards

The next step in control process is the measurement of performance. If standards are appropriately drawn and if means are available to determine the progress, the appraisal of performance can be done.

Correcting Variations from Standards and Plans

If the performance is measured correctly, then it is possible to straighten the deviations.

Performance contracting is a cyclical process in which results are fed back to the government and public enterprise. This is done in order to make correction for short-term variances from contract and this process is called monitoring. This could be represented by the feed back loop of control as below :

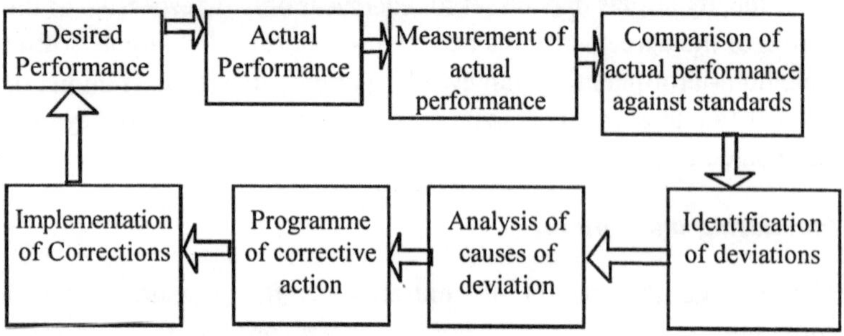

Feed Back Loop of Management Control

In the case of the Indian MoU process, the monitoring and control over the contracts is done at the Bureau of Public Enterprises. This institution is responsible for preparing the contracts, getting the contracts signed and monitoring the contracts as well. Public Enterprise Information Systems are usually organized around accounting systems. There is a need for standardization, so that data is comparable. In many countries, public enterprises are required to use the same accounting standards as applied to private businesses. The International Federation of Accountants (IFAC 1989) has recommended this, i.e. that public enterprises follow National Accounting Standards where these exist, otherwise the IFAC/IASC International Accounting Standards.

Evaluation

Evaluation is to put a value on the performance for the period. This is done by comparing actual performance with the contract goals and targets and analyzing the reasons for shortfalls and over-target achievements. Most governments see this entirely in terms of enterprise performance, not their own. In other words, performance contracts are thought of as extension of budgets. An exception is India, where a High-Power Committee, chaired by the Cabinet Secretary, examines performance of both sides impartially.

After expert analysis, there should always be a final evaluation meeting between the contracting parties to discuss performance and draw out lessons that can be applied in future periods. In the popular mind, PEs are evaluated largely on financial profitability, for want of any other clear criterion. Profit is not only a means of survival traditionally it is the way the score is kept. Even when performance contracts are set out there is a strong tendency for the public to misinterpret the resulting score as a proxy for profitability, or perhaps efficiency. In Korea, however, there appears to have been wide public acceptance of the performance indices coming out of the evaluation process, and the ranking of PEs each year.

Let us consider the example of evaluation of a PE with the following performance:

Criteria	*Unit*	*Weight*	*Score*		
			1.0	*0.8*	*0.25*
Production	Thousand (tonnes)	0.3	>>22	20	<<15
Profit	Million (currency units)	0.5	>>25	20	<<18
Project implementation	Million (currency units)	0.2	>>30	25	<<20

Source: A Handbook for Performance Contracting, UN Publication, 1995.

Production	26,000
Profit	12 million currency units
Project Implementation	26 million currency units

The scores will be calculated as,

If the actual production lies anywhere between 20,000 tonnes and 22,000 tonnes, the score will be only 0.8 (or 80 %). Only when it exceeds 22,000 tonnes will the value jump to 1.00 (or 100 %). In the above case, for production the achievement of 26,000 tonnes is above the score target for 1.0. So the score value is 1.0 × weightage = 1.0 × 0.3 = 0.3.

For profit, the score is 0.25 as the achievement is below the score target of 18 million for minimum score. The score value is 0.25 × 0.5 (weightage) = 0.125.

For project implementation the score is 0.8 as the actual is between 250 million and 300 million. The score value is 0.8 × 0.2 = 0.160.

The composite score = 0.3+0.125+0.160=0.585. In other words the entire enterprise has obtained a total of 58.5 per cent marks in overall performance.

Audit and Accountability

Audit closes the circle of public accountability. PEs are normally subject to independent and expert audit, but audit institutions typically confine the scope of their audit to the accuracy of the financial records and accounts and compliance with laws and regulations. Auditors cannot audit the efficiency or effectiveness of a PE without an operational definition of goals. Auditors welcome performance contracting, as it provides the necessary basis for performance audit of PEs.

Performance contracting raises the stakes for enterprise managers, especially where their pay depends on the final score. Internal monitoring and reporting systems is subject to increasing pressures. An effective system of internal control is the first line of defense. It is also necessary to guard against management increasing their apparent profit by changing their accounting practices; any such changes should be separately disclosed in the accounts or auditor's report.

In some countries there are parliamentary committees which review PE performance. These bodies should also welcome contracts as bases for their review. Other channels of accountability may be opened up. The success of the Korean system has been due not only to its technical features but also to the interest and support shown by the President and the Deputy Prime Minister and the media publicity attending the system. The secrecy that surrounds the performance of PEs in many countries may be dispelled through open and transparent publication of performance contracts and evaluation reports for PEs in competitive markets, confidential data may be edited out.

Rewards and Penalties

The PE managers are paid the same for poor performance as for good performance. Pay is usually based on civil service scales, which in many countries are significantly lower than those of their counterparts in the private sector. Non-pecuniary rewards do exist but are small and uncertain. PE managers are seldom removed for incompetence. Even criminal activity is seldom punished. The result is management weakness, characterized by low morale, feeling of frustration, failure to apply management skills and techniques, and dysfunctional attitudes.

Summing Up

The performance contracts contain a number of features, which encompass the various facets of PEs, like the mission, objectives, performance criteria, weightages, target values. The contracts must be made meticulously and properly evaluated if the real performance of the enterprise has to be reflected through it. During discussions with the senior officials of the enterprises dealing with the MoU it was observed that it is a highly confidential exercise. The purpose with which the system of contracts was started in India and other countries was to improve autonomy and strengthen accountability simultaneously. But the system seems to have made little impact regarding the two important issues of autonomy and accountability, which left the functionaries dissatisfied. If the system of MoU were to be implemented as per the design it would have certainly shown positive results. The problem lies at the implementation level of the system and not at its conception.

NOTES

Bureau of Public Enterprise, *Annual Survey Report,* GoI, Part 1. 1996-97 and various issues.

Estimates Committee, Second Lok Sabha, 23rd Report, p. 12.

Geeta P., Memorandum of Understanding in Central Public Enterprises: A Study of Select Public Sector Undertakings in India, Doctoral Thesis, Department of Business Management, OU, Hyderabad, October, 2000.

Gupta K.R. *Economics and Management of Public Enterprises,* Atlantic, New Delhi, 1984, p. 192.

Jones Morris, W.H, *The Government and Politics in India,* p. 195-96.

Kapur A.C, *Select Constitutions,* S. Chand & Company, New Delhi, 1983, 11th Edition, p. 250.

Narain Laxmi, *Public Enterprise Management,* S. Chand & Company, New Delhi, 1988, p. 254, p. 260 and p. 280.

Shrivastava Mohan. *Problem of Public Accountability of Public Enterprises,* Uppal, New Delhi. 1986. p. 144.

Thomas Peters and Robert Waterman: *In Search of Excellence,* New York, Harper & Row, 1982.

7

INTERNAL AUDIT AS A REFORM TECHNIQUE FOR POWER SECTOR IN INDIA

Power sector is one of the most capital intensive industry in India. Power costs are a dominant cost component of economic activities[1]. Recent statistics reveal that commercial losses of State Electricity Boards (SEBs) have exceeded Rs. 20,220 crore during 2000-01 with APSEB/APTRANSCO topping the list with estimated losses of about Rs. 3,800 crore. 19 SEBs across the country are estimated have netted Rs. 82,462 crore revenue during 2000-01 and reported transmission and distribution (T&D) losses of 23 per cent[2]. The mismatch between cost of power and tariff is cited as the main cause for such losses. The tendency towards competitive rates and the need for attaining increased productivity propelled by reforms in the Indian power sector indicate the underlying paradigm shift in sector. Reforms can be two fold: internal and external. The power sector reforms in India are based on externalities as propounded by the World Bank. The history of successful reforms shows that internal measures are first initiated prior to the application of external initiatives. There may be certain measures that could qualify as both the internal and external measures. The Optimum Performance through Internal Management Action (OPTIMA), advocates the application of internal measures as a technique to reform an enterprise. OPTIMA is an evolving approach which encompasses tools such as organisational restructuring, financial restructuring, product portfolio restructuring, labour restructuring and environmental interface restructuring. It is preferable to turnaround an enterprise through internal restructuring than taking recourse in the first instance to external restructuring. Internal restructuring is comparatively more economical, far more effective, speedier, durable and a good accomplice to external restructuring. This chapter focuses on introduction of effective internal audit in the power sector in India which is an important component of OPTIMA[3].

Backdrop

To begin with, let us examine the background of the Internal Audit (IA) function in the various power utilities. Table 7.1 presents the strength and total expenditure on IA in the different utilities.

Table 7.1 : *Strength and Total Expenditure*

Name of the Board	*IAD Strength*	*Expenditure(Rs. in Lakh)*
APSEB	66	54
ASEB	39	26
KEB	421	48
KPC	17	3
KSEB	221	NA
MSEB	103	60
NEEPC	9	5
RSEB	315	215
UPSEB	192	175

The Andhra Pradesh State Electricity Board (APSEB)/ APTRANSCO, had a gross annual expenditure of Rs. 1,600 crore per annum. Its gross annual revenue was of the same order. It employed more than 70,000 employees. Its budgeted staffing level for the Internal Audit Department (IAD) was 91. Its annual IAD staffing level during the same year was 66. Its annual expenditure on IA was of the order of Rs. 54 lakh per annum.

The Assam State Electricity Board (ASEB) incurred a gross annual expenditure of Rs. 305 crore. Its annual revenues are about Rs. 140 crore. It employed 23,000 persons. The IAD staff in the Board totals 39. The total expenditure on IAD was Rs. 26 lakh per annum.

The Karnataka Power Corporation (KPC) had 17 persons in its IAD. It was engaged only in the transmission of power. This is because in Karnataka, transmission and generation of power had been separated, and consequently two organisations were dealing with each of these functions. It had 422 employees in its IAD.

In the Maharashtra State Electricity Board (MSEB), the gross annual expenditure was about Rs. 3,000 crore. The Board received an equal amount of revenue to match its annual expenditure. It had on its rolls about 1,20,000 officers and workers. It had about 103 persons in its IAD. The total expenditure in IAD was Rs. 60 lakh per annum.

The North Eastern Electric Power Corporation (NEEPC) is a central undertaking. Its gross annual expenditure was about Rs. 35 crore and gross annual revenue was Rs. 49 crore. It had a strength of about 4000. It had only 9 persons in its IAD. The expenditure on maintenance of the IAD was about Rs. 5 lakh per annum. The Uttar Pradesh State Electricity Board (UPSEB) during the same period, incurred an annual gross expenditure of Rs. 175 lakh. It had 192 officers in its IAD.

A brief examination of the general background of IA in the SEBs point out that IAS as a function has already made its mark in these Boards. The percentage of the expenses incurred on IA, and the number of employees working in the IAD as a percentage of gross annual expenditure and total number of employees, differs from Board to Board. During the discussions with officials of some SEBs, it was indicated that in view of the increasing importance of IA in their operations, they propose to allocate higher outlays for their IADs to enable them to increase the level of staffing and provide higher sums for travel, etc.

Scope of Internal Audit Functions

The scope of IA function, although having some commonalities, differs very widely in a couple of aspects in respect of the Boards under study. In the case of the APSEB, the scope of the IAD covers aspects such as ensuring compliance with laws and regulations, administrative policies, plans and procedures, ensuring soundness and application of management controls over administration, revenues and expenditure, ascertaining efficiency in acquisition and use of resources, checking upon the effectiveness in achieving organisational objectives, and ensuring effectiveness in achieving the overall programme of the Board. IAD uses both systems and transactions based audit to accomplish these tasks. The activities open for the scrutiny of IA, include security classified information, records protected by piracy provisions, and important policy areas. About 10-15 per cent of the APSEB's activities get covered by the IA. The IAD is often involved in the preparation and review of financial statements. It also attends to activities pertaining to the control of frauds. These precisely include fraud detection and fraud investigation. The IAD is not consulted in the design and development stage of new or revised programmes and systems.

ASEB also includes in the gamut of IA, activities such as revenue audit, expenditure audit, stores audit, and special audit relating to any or all of these activities. The Board considered the expenses incurred on IA as worthwhile as it derives full value for money expended in IAD. Among the benefits accruing from IA activities to the Board, the prominent ones are savings and economies on the various heads of expenditure, improved control, and prevention of shortfalls in respect of various items of operation. The Board is not fully satisfied with the performance of IA, and the main reason for this is the inexperience of the IA staff.

KPC has the following objectives for its IAD:

1. Reviewing the soundness, adequacy and application of accounting, financial, and operational controls.
2. Examining and reporting on the extent of prescribed procedures under rules/statutory requirements in regard to financial and accounting transactions.
3. Reviewing and reporting the action taken by the departmental authorities on the points brought out in previous audit reports, both internal and external.

KSEB includes under the ambit of IA activities, revenue audit, cash audit, expenditure audit, test audit of stores and pre-audit of project-related purchases. Before undertaking IA the IAD formulates a plan of action. KSEB feels that IA provides value for money spent on its activities. The Board is also of the view that IA activities have benefited the organisation in several ways in recent years—by affecting economies, improving control, ensuring justification of additional resources required by its various departments and systems and programmes. The Board is satisfied with the standard of performance achieved by the IAD.

Under the gamut of its IA activities, MSEB includes, verification of stores, revenue and establishment expenditure. It plans IA activities on a half-yearly basis. The Board feels that the IA activities provides value for money spent.[4] It is of the view that the introduction of IAS has ensured that the different functions of the Board are discharged more efficiently. It has resulted in increased management reassurance, provided superior justification for reallocation of resources and effected savings and economies in expenditure. Though the Board is on the whole satisfied with the functioning of the IA, it is of the view that the audit personnel's lack of experience has prevented the realization of the full benefits of this function to the organization. The Board also feels that the inordinate delay in complying with IA objectives by the department does not allow it to do justice to its other activities.

In the case of the NEEPC, all the activities except the ones which require management decision, are included in the purview of IA. The corporation plans its IA activities from year to year. The corporate feels that the investment in IA has proved beneficial. Among the benefits of IA accruing to the organization, the prominent ones are: identification of significant shortfalls in compliance, efficiency and effectiveness, and improved control of procedural arrangements.

Audit Charter

The IA Charter, also known as the IA Manual, is a document specifying the role, responsibilities and authority of the IA function in an organization. All well-organized enterprises put such a charter in place before commencement, or in the process of initiating their operations. The SEBs are very vast organizations by Indian standards. Their working is complex as compared to a typical commercial organization, as they have to perform the dual act of providing a service on a commercial basis and fulfilling their social obligations. In such a situation, the presence of an IA Charter assumes greater significance. The KPC, and MSEB have prepared their own IA Manuals. The rest of the SEBs covered by our study, including APSEB, though recognising the need for a charter, have not been able to develop one. They also mentioned that they did not have any plan to prepare an IA Manual. Two of the Corporations having an IA

Charter disclosed that though there is a need to revise it within a period 1-2 years, it took them much longer where KPC revised IA Manual 3-5 years ago, KEB revised 6-10 years ago, MSEB was an exception, the IA Manual having been revised within a period of 12 months. However, the SEBs have definite views about the highest level of endorsement of the IA charter. In the case of APSEB and KEB, it was suggested that Member, Finance should endorse the IA charter. In the case of ASEB, KPC, and MSEB, the competent authority suggested for endorsement was Chairman/Chairman-cum-Managing Director. A review of the constraints imposed by the charter on the scope of IA activities on the various SEB points out that no areas were omitted from the gamut of IA.

Audit Committee

An Audit Committee normally comprises the members of senior management of an enterprise who oversee and review the operations of IA functioning. In enterprises of world fame, a special role is assigned to such companies. For instance, Unit Trust of India has such a committee, as also ACC Limited. Such committees are necessary in the case of huge enterprises in terms of operations and investment, requiring these to have an effective view of operations and to undertake an examination to ascertain the effectiveness of the control systems. These committees are normally set up by the Board and may comprise members drawn from the Accounting, Economics, and Law disciplines. The committee might also have experts with an intimate knowledge of the functioning of the industry of which the firm is a constituent. The recognition of the need to bring the IA function under the control of audit committee implies the great deal of importance that an enterprise attaches to the audit function. Our discussions with the concerned authorities in the various SEBs reveal that no Board deemed it fit to set up an audit committee to oversee the functioning of IA.

Internal Audit Plan

The presence of a strategic audit plan is a primary requirement for the success of the IA function in an organisation. Such a plan should spell out the duration, audit priorities, and the target maximum audit cycle.

In the case of the APSEB, the strategic audit plan had a target maximum audit cycle of one year. While formulating such a plan, no consideration was given to APSEB's other strategic plans. It may be noted that no audit priorities were fixed in the case of the APSEB and, therefore, no question arose concerning the importance of various factors which have to be considered for fixing such priorities. The ASEB had not given any thought to the question of formulation of such a plan. In the case of KPC, the strategic audit plan had one to two years' duration, and no reference was made to the organization's other strategic plans. While formulating the audit plan, priorities are fixed by giving maximum importance to factors such as materiality, risk, impact on other operations, public interest, recent review activity, and audit resource requirements. In the case of the KEB, the strategic audit plan had a duration of one to two years. Audit priorities were fixed giving due regard to various factors as mentioned in the case of KPC. MSEB did not have a strategic audit plan. However, it regarded materiality and public interest as very important, and impact on other operations fairly important, which were to be given due weightage in the exercise of framing any such plan. The Board suggested a target maximum cycle of two years.

NEEPC did not formulate a strategic audit plan. However, it suggested a target maximum cycle of two years and indicated a three-year maximum cycle based on its current experience.

Internal Audit Coverage

The IA coverage determines the success or failure of the IA function in any enterprise. A big gap is found between the targets and achievements in this area. The question of coverage is shrouded in mystery: "*should it be only the coverage of operations or should it also span the functioning of the various controls?*" some experts have also raised the issue of horizontal interface while talking about the coverage of IA, thereby making the suggestion that a firm's efficiency should be compared with similar firms in the same industry. Our discussions with the officials of the various SEBs pointed out to unanimity only with regard to the operational aspect of IA coverage. In the case of APSEB, the audit coverage fluctuated between 50-60 per cent of operations, as against 90-99 per cent in the case of KPC, KEB, and MSEB, 80 per cent in the case of NEEPC, and 40 per cent in the case of ASEB. The significant reasons for not completing the planned IA coverage included shortage of IA staff, staff inexperience, under-estimation of the time required to complete the planned audits, new responsibilities assigned to IA function, major administrative changes in auditable areas, IA overtaken by other reviews, etc. The strategy suggested to address the lack of coverage of auditable areas was clearing the backlog of inspections in the subsequent programmes by APSEB. In the case of KEB a Consultant was appointed to suggest ways and means to remove the backlog of IA. In NEEPC steps were taken to assess time requirements more rationally. In the case of MSEB action was taken to redress the problem by initiating training for the officers and staff. The IAD was allocated additional staff. In ASEB, though action was taken to clear the backlog, the problem was only partially solved. Some extra posts were created in IAD, selections made, and postings done. In the case of APSEB, action was being considered to increase the audit coverage, and continually audit the activities brought under such coverage. The problem of shortage of staff was temporarily handled by directing the circle superintending Engineers to draft Junior Accounts Officers for IA on a deputation basis in the absence of experienced Junior Accounts Officers at the headquarters.

Internal Audit comprises audit of operations concerning finance and accounting, administration and management, operations and services, and allied matters. In any approach to undertaking IA operations, an optimum balance should be struck with regard to the time allocated for IA of these various activities. A study of the time allocation reveals that in the absence of any sensitisation to this important aspect, APSEB, KPC, KEB, MSEB, and ASEB have not allocated any specific time. Only NEEPC indicated that 66 per cent time was allocated to IA for the financial and accounting operations, and the rest to the other operations of the organization. A stock taking of the purpose of IA was restricted to dimensions such as the integrity of information, compliance with laws and regulations, administrative policies, plans and procedures, soundness and application of management controls over assets, revenue and expenditure, economy and efficiency in acquisition and use of resources, effectiveness in achieving organizational objectives, and effectiveness in achieving programme objectives. KPC and KEB wanted to achieve all the above-mentioned purposes of IA. NEEPC had its focus on integrity of information and compliance with laws and regulations, administrative policies, plans and procedures. The other purposes of IA were considered less important. APSEB indicated that it considered soundness and application of management controls over assets, revenue and expenditure, as the driving force of the IA function.

One of the important issues in IA is how to evaluate the evaluators. When this question was posed to the various SEB's very interesting revelations were made. In the case of APSEB, the performance measures used to judge the efficiency and effectiveness of the IA function were indicated as the review of monthly returns submitted by IA units, realisation of shortages, for which replies were received from field offices. KPC, KEB, NEEPC, and ASEB realised the need for having such a performance indicator, but they were yet to develop one. In the case of MSEB the review of recovery targets and clearance of outstanding

Reporting Arrangements

The success of any IA system depends on how the arrangements for reporting the various findings are put in place. The practices in this connection reveals that in the case of APSEB, audit findings are documented and communicated to operational Management, an executive summary of an audit report is provided to the user departments; and audit recommendations are always followed up by IA. However, the Operational Management does not have to respond always to the IA findings and recommendations. The proportion of audit recommendations made in IA reports which were implemented ranged between 50-60 per cent. About 15-25 per cent of the recommendations, though accepted were not implemented. The reason for this non-implementation was the lack of resources available with APSEB. In the case of KPC, IA reports are submitted to the Chairman-cum-Managing Director as opposed to the Operational Management in the case of APSEB. The Operational Management is expected to respond to audit findings and recommendations in a timely manner, and in practice the Operational Management complies with this requirement. In the case of KEB, IA reports are submitted to the Chairman, Member, Finance, and concerned administrative officers. In the case of NEEPC, the IA reports are submitted to the Operational

Management and the external auditors. The audit findings are documented and communicated to Operational Management and followed up by IA. The Operational Management is required to respond to audit findings and recommendations in a timely manner. About 50 per cent of the recommendations made by IA were accepted. About 15-25 per cent of the recommendations, though accepted, were not implemented. A large number of recommendations were not even considered. In the case of MSEB, the IA reports are submitted to Operational Management. The audit findings are documented and communicated to Operational Management, and the audit recommendations followed up by IA. The Operational Management is required to always respond to such audit findings and recommendations. In the case of ASEB, the IA reports are issued to Member, Finance, and Operational Management. The audit findings are documented and communicated to Operational Management and such recommendations are followed up by IA. However, the Operational Management normally does not respond to the audit findings and recommendations in a timely manner.

Use of Contract Internal Auditors

When privatization of the activities of the SEBs is gaining ground in the country, it is worthwhile to consider whether the IA function could be contracted out to produce better results. All the SEBs studied by us responded in the negative when the idea of contracting out the IA function as a whole, or some of its elements, was put forward to them.

Internal Audit Unit

All the SEBs under the study had their own IA unit. APSEB had a staff of 66 persons and an expenditure of Rs. 54 lakh. It spent Rs. 45 lakh on salaries and Rs. 9 lakh on administrative and operating expenses. The IA unit of the organization had no plans to recruit and retain suitable staff. The total number of staff employed by KPC was 17, comprising 6 posted in the central office, and 11 in its various regions. The staff are interchangeable between Accounts and other departments. In the case of KEB also, the staff of IAD was interchangeable with the Accounts and other departments. The total staff of 422 persons in IAD comprised 15 posted in the central office, and 407 in the various regions. In the case of NEEPC, there were 9 officials working in IAD. The total cost of running the Department was made up of Rs. 4,08,000 as salaries and allowances, and Rs. 50,000 as administrative and operating expenses. All the 9 functionaries were posted in the central office. In the case of MSEB, the total staff of 103 persons in IAD comprised 46 working in the central office and 57 posted in the various regions of the Board. The total expenses incurred on IA were Rs. 60 lakh, made up of Rs. 49 lakh towards salaries and allowances, and Rs. 11 lakh towards administrative and operating expenses. ASEB employed 39 persons in its IAD, and all of them were based at the central office. The yearly expenses incurred was Rs. 26.40 lakh, of which Rs. 18 lakh was spent on salaries and allowances, and Rs. 8.40 lakh on administrative and operating expenses.

Qualifications and Experience of Internal Auditors

There is a trend today to staff IAD with well-qualified and experienced personnel. Most of the organizations recruit professionals and Internal Auditors and pay them very well. In the case of APSEB, most of the IAD staff have only a Bachelor's degree. In the case of KPC, excepting one executive who was holding a CA/ICWA degree, the others were graduates. In the case of NEEPC, of the nine executives employed in IAD, there were two chartered cost accountants, one ACS, one M.Com./MBA, one law graduate, and five holding a Bachelor's degree. Some professionals were of more than one professional body. In the case of MSEB, there were two chartered cost accountants, two M.Com./MBA, and one law graduate, and all the others were holding a Bachelor's degree.

Two executives were members of more than one professional body. In the case of ASEB, excepting two persons who had a Master's degree in Commerce, the others were graduates.

Training of IA Staff

The experts in IA have suggested continuous training of the IA staff. APSEB neither has any ongoing formal training for its staff nor any plan to launch such training programmes, though during the course of informal discussions the need for such training was emphasised more than once. The state of affairs in ASEB, KPC, and NEEPC was similar. KEB and MSEB had an ongoing formal training programme. An officer was assigned the task of planning and developing training programmes and organizing such programmes with the help of internal resources and external agencies. MSEB trod the same line. The IAD was fairly satisfied with the coverage of training for its staff, the training areas, the number of staff receiving training, the content of training courses, and the presentation of training courses. However, it felt that the need for training existed and it did not receive any worthwhile attention, including system-based auditing, basic performance auditing, and advanced performance auditing.

Authority of Chief Internal Auditor

A survey of the authority of the Chief Internal Auditor in the various SEBs showed that in APSEB the head of the IA function was authorised to develop audit priorities, finalise work plans and programmes, and determine boundaries and direction of audits. However, the Department did not divulge as to whether they had direct access to those who oversaw and reviewed the IA function. The chief of the IA function also controlled the region based IA units. The case of KPC was no different. In the case of NEEPC, the chief of IA had the authority to develop audit priorities, finalise work plans, and chalk out programmes, but he had no authority to determine boundaries and direction of audits. He did not have any direct access to those who oversaw and reviewed the IA function. In the case of MSEB, the chief functionary of IAD was competent to set out audit priorities, finalise work plans and programmes, and determine boundaries and direction of audits. He also had direct access to those who were appraising the performance of the IA function. He exercised control over the region-based units. The case of ASEB was similar, except for the fact that the chief of the IA function did not have access to those who oversaw are reviewed the functioning of IA.

Internal Audit Performance

Under this head, we propose to study the IA performance in the various SEBs at the Chief Executive, Head of the Department, and Operating Manager's levels.

Assam State Electricity Board (ASEB)

A full-fledged IAD began functioning in 1975. It was subsequently upgraded and is now headed by the Chief Internal Auditor, equivalent to the rank of Chief Engineer. He is assisted by the Deputy Chief Internal Auditor. The status of the Chief Internal Auditor is equal to the Head of any other Department. He reports to the chief of the Finance Department. The Department has also been strengthened and nearly six teams are simultaneously engaged in field audit. Traditional IA is conducted at least once in two years in the respective units of the organization.

Karnataka Electricity Board (KEB)

The IAD in KEB was set up in 1957. There were 221 persons on the staff of IA. It was headed by the Financial Adviser and Chief Accounts Officer, who was a BCom and FCA, and Senior Accounts Officers, who were Matriculates SSLC. They had gained two to three decades of experience in their jobs.

The chairman of the Board accepted the importance of IA as an essential instrument of financial control. He agreed that IA serves as a powerful arm to the management in appraising the activities of the organization. He favoured having the chief of IA as part of his management team, but disclosed that the IA staff was not very capable of thinking in managerial terms and did not possess the necessary technical skills. He wanted IA to be viewed as an independent appraisal activity and recommended a certain amount of independent in its functioning. He wanted highly qualified people to staff the IA function. He also wanted the IA team to be interdisciplinary, reporting only to the Managing Director. He wanted the IAD to conduct surprise checks and IA to be conducted on a continuous basis. He did not want IA to be burdened with additional responsibilities. He lamented about the fact that IA was manned by under-qualified people and about the lack of training. He was also unhappy about the practice of frequent interdepartmental transfers. The chief of the IA function complained about the lack of adequate strength in the IAD. KEB's IAD was involved in appraising its activities in terms of policies and procedures. However, it was not undertaking physical verification of assets. He admitted that the effectiveness of the team was limited to the extent of its having on the staff only Accountants. In his view, the work done by the IAD was not helpful in taking managerial decisions. He was satisfied with the work done by the IAD in connection with bringing out cases of defalcation and defraud. While he said that the employees of his Department, including himself, were happy with their status, there were only happy to some extent with job content and power to perform their work. He disclosed that the Department was going by test checking only. His audit staff while conducting the audit employed techniques such as physical examination, confirmation, searching, examination of documents, and correlation with related information. However, he accepted that his Department was not conducting systems audit and was limiting itself only to traditional audit. On being asked whether he was getting cooperation from the other Departments while conducting audit, the answer was "only to some extent" as far as Purchase, Stores, Services, Maintenance and Administration Departments were concerned. He was not getting support from Production, Personnel, and Research and Development Departments. He was also not inviting suggestions from other Operating Heads while planning IA.

The Operating Managers in KEB held that the role of IA should be that of an expert reviewer of the operations. It should suggest measures to improve the operational efficiency. They suggested an effective IA mechanism to make the organisation perform well. They recommend adequate freedom to the IAD. In their view, internal control measures are a precondition to the success of IA. IA should be given sufficient independence, but it should not be given vigilance powers. In their view, IA should be reporting to the Managing Director and staffed with technically qualified people having knowledge of operations. The audit team should have representation from each department of the organization. According to them IA is essential for an organization to evaluate the efficiency of the management system. The reports submitted by the IAD should contain the comments of the respective heads of department against the remarks made by IA. IA should be empowered to undertake operation audit. The technical competence of the IAD should be able to match this challenge. IA staff should be exposed to practical working in operations. The management hardly utilizes the IAD expertise. This may be because the persons working in the IAD are not competent, which ultimately led to IA not exercising effective control in the organization. They were skeptical about whether IA added to the effectiveness in their operations.

Maharashtra State Electricity Board (MSEB)

The chairman of the Board agreed that an effective system of IA was an important instrument of financial control. He indicated that IA served as a powerful arm to the management in appraising to associate the chief of IAD as a part of his management team. However, he suggested management training for the IA staff to enable them to come up to expectations in this regard. He expressed his unhappiness about the lack of qualified staff in the organization, and felt that this deficiency could be removed through training. In his view, the Chief of IA need not necessarily possess any professional degree, but what was more important was his attitude to the job, besides his professional background. He wanted IAD to be staffed by a multi-disciplinary team and have a reporting relationship with the Board Audit Committee. While he suggested surprise checks by the IAD, he wanted to divest it of investigations and other related activities. He wanted IA to be done on a continuing basis. He did not want IA to be given additional responsibilities, excepting for some small jobs now and then in situations of compulsion.

The IAD in MSEB had a strength of 103 persons. The expenses incurred on IAD worked out to Rs. 60 lakh. The function was headed by Director, Internal Audit, generally a retired IAS officer. He was assisted by a Chief Accounts Officer holding an M.Com. degree. One Joint Chief Accounts Officer and two Deputy Chief Accounts Officers were the other functionaries in the hierarchy. One of the Deputy Chief Accounts Officers was a Chartered Accountant. The Chief Executive agreed that an effective system of IA is an important instrument of financial control. However, due to certain limitations, it could not serve as a powerful arm to the management in appraising the activities of the organization.

Though he wanted to associate the Chief of IA as a part of his management team, he felt that the IAD staff was not creative in terms of thinking and lacked the necessary technical, communication and conceptual skills. He viewed IA as an independent appraisal activity and wanted to give the IAD a certain amount of independence. He wanted professionally qualified executives to work in the department. Preferring IA & AS officers he wanted the IAD to report to the Managing Director and did not favour surprise checks by the Department. He did not want any additional responsibilities, besides the IA tasks to be given to IAD. He was also against giving any vigilance powers to the Department.

The Director of IA revealed that no strict division was made of officers and staff employed in the IAD in terms of the functions performed by them, namely, financial audit, operational audit, systems audit, special investigations, etc. he agreed that the functions of the Department should include review of the internal controls, examining the organization's records as to the implementation of top management policies, acting as a watchdog to prevent likely frauds, planning and carrying out checking of transactions, and verification of calculations. He disclosed that all the activities were combined with the Accounts Department, and that the status of the chief of IAD was equivalent to the Head of any other Department. He had a reporting relationship with the chief of the Finance Department. He was fully satisfied with the status, job content, and the power to perform his work. He said that he was conducting audit on a continuous basis throughout the year. The IAD did not contain any technical personnel. He disclosed that his Department was conducting IA in respect of the various units once in two years, and that his Department was going by test checking. Regarding the type of techniques used by IA staff while conducting the audit, he disclosed that these included confirmation, recomputation, examination of documents, enquiry, examination of subsidiary records, and correlation with related information. He expressed his satisfaction with the cooperation he received from his counterparts in the other Departments.

There was divergence of opinion among the different Operating Managers regarding the role and importance of the IAD. However, taken as a whole, the Operating Managers did not want it to be a procedural consultant, detective agent, or an unwanted interrupter. Most of them felt that the management was under utilising the talents of the IAD. However, they suggested that IA in order to enhance its capabilities, should staff itself with technical people. They did not want any vigilance powers to be given to the IAD. The operating Managers agreed that IA reports should contain the comments of the respective Heads of Departments against the remarks made by IA before the report is submitted to the management. They wanted one representative from each Department on the IA team. Most of them felt that the management was not fully utilising the competence of the IAD. Some of them suggested that financial audit and systems audit should go together for attaining the ultimate aim. They wanted weightage to be given to practical aspects. Very importantly, unlike the other Boards, the Operating Managers suggested that purchase, transmission and distribution losses, and revenue audit in respect of their functions could be taken up.

Madhya Pradesh Electricity Board (MPEB)

MPEB considers IA an important instrument of financial control in the Board. However, they felt that it could serve as a powerful arm to the management in appraising activities of the organization only if IA is concurrent and immediate. They wanted the chief of IA to be a part of the management team, and for the IA staff to be trained in management functions and for developing technical skills. They felt that the deficiency in professional qualifications could be made up through this training. Aptitude for the job was considered very important. They wanted the chief of IA to report to the Board/Audit Committee. They felt that surprise checks should be carried out with regard to cash, verification of assets, etc.

North Eastern Electric Power Corporation (NEEPC)

The Operating Managers outlined the role of IA as that of an expert reviewer of the operations, a constructive critic, a procedural reviewer, and a procedural consultant. However, they did not approve of its role as a detective agent. Whereas they expressed their agreement of undertaking IA of Operating Departments, they wanted competent people to be on the staff of IA, having practical work experience and knowledge of enterprise operations. They wanted transparency of the IA report which, in their opinion, should contain the views of the Operating Managers against the remarks made by IA. They wanted certain vigilance powers and independence to be given to the chief of IA. They wanted technically qualified and competent people to be on the staff of the IAD, with practical work experience and sound knowledge about operations. They felt that there should be one representative from each Department of the organization on the audit team. Unlike the other SEBs, they felt that the IAD was helpful in enhancing the effectiveness of the control systems in the organization and, therefore, they welcomed the role of IA in their operations.

RSEB

The Operating Managers suggested an intensive IA. In their view, IA should be more of a technical audit dealing with release of connections, checking of connections, position of transformers, checking of consumption variation register, checking of site checking register, position of physical compliance, checking of tripping of supply with log book, checking of load shedding register, checking of connected load register, nature of application of tariff, and theft cases. The function included even the checking of stores in regard to genuineness of requirement of material and its utilization, and availability of stock. On the revenue side, they suggested paying more attention towards average charges, wrong application of tariff, wrong assessment of minimum charges, miscellaneous charges, less assessment of consumption charges, non-issue of first bill, non-compliance of meter change orders and disconnection orders.

UPSEB

UPSEB had a full-fledged IAD, which set up in 1977. The Head of the IAD was a chartered accountant and a cost accountant. He was designated as controller of audit. He was assisted by a Deputy Internal Auditor, who was also a chartered accountant, a cost accountant and an IA & AS. These two functionaries were assisted by a Chief Accounts Officer, Deputy Chief Accounts Officers (14), and Accounts Officers (16), Accountants (18), Auditors (79) and office staff (63). The chief of the IAD accepted that his Department was conducting only traditional audit and his staff had no idea of systems audit. He also accepted that his Department was not getting full-fledged support from the Purchase and Stores Departments.

In the UPSEB, the Controller of Audit was of the view that the IA was an important instrument of financial control in the organization. It served as a powerful arm to the management in appraising the activities of the organization. He pointed out that IA's mission was confined to not only review of controls. He favoured the association of the chief of the IAD as part of the management team. However, he opined that the IA staff was not fully capable of thinking in management terms as they did not have the necessary technical, conceptual and communication skills. Despite this, he considered IA as an independent appraisal activity within the enterprise for the efficient functioning of the same. He opined that the staff in the IAD should be qualified, holding professional qualifications, such as CA, ICWA, MA (Economics), MCom, Law, Engineering, etc. On being asked as to what type of qualification the Chief of IA should possess, he indicated that those qualifying in the IA & AS would be the best choice. He agreed with the view that the IAD should comprise an inter-disciplinary team. Regarding the authority to whom the Department should report, the answer was that the Board Audit Committee was the best choice, though in UPSEB this function had to report to the Director, Finance. He was for exercising surprise checks, but was critical of the permissions which had to be taken from line executives to conduct inspections of the operating units. He observed that sometimes the functions IAD could extend to investigations and Wage Board negotiations. He recommended that IA should be conducted on a continuous basis. He did not want the IAD to be burdened with any additional responsibilities arising in the shape of budget compilation and its review, liaison with statutory auditors and management, assisting with the compilation of annual accounts or helping in clearing out the backlog of accounts. He did not want any vigilance powers to be given to the IAD. The Controller of Audit revealed that the existing strength of the Department of 192 personnel was adequate.

However, he indicated that the IAD did not have qualified Internal Auditors. Regarding maintenance of rapport with other Departments, he felt that it was good only to some extent. On being asked about the functions of the IAD, he revealed that they comprised reviewing the internal control systems, verifying the financial accounts and vouchers, and physical verification of assets. Interestingly, appraisal of the activities of UPSEB in terms of policies and procedures was not considered as a function. The composition of the IAD disclosed that only accountants were there on its staff. During the discussion, it was further pointed out that IA helped in checking frauds and misappropriation and in exercising effective internal control. However, it did not help in enhancing the effectiveness of managerial decisions. The cases of defalcations and defrauds brought to the notice of management by the IAD were on the increase. In UPSEB the expenses incurred by IA were about Rs. 175 lakh per annum. The type of punishments imposed for frauds and misappropriation included stoppage of increments, stoppage of promotions, and imprisonment. The rights enjoyed by the IAD included inspection of accounts and vouchers, making surprise checks without prior permission, making a report on any individual in the case of negligence and misappropriation, and recommendation of action against such individuals.

The operating managers wanted IA to be a constructive critic and acknowledged the need for its presence. They were, however, not in favour of assigning vigilance powers to the IAD. They wanted the Department to be given adequate independence within the administrative set-up of the undertaking. The reporting relationship was to be with the Managing Director. They suggested qualified technical people on the IA team, with sound knowledge about operations, and wanted at least one representative from each Department of the organization to be in the team. They felt that the IAD was of little help in enhancing the effectiveness of the managerial capability in the organization.

Further, they hinted at the need to improve the technical competence of the IAD staff. They wanted the staff to be exposed to the practical working of operations. They felt that IA was essential for an organization to evaluate the efficiency of the system. They also wanted the comments of the respective Heads of Departments against the remarks made by IA before the report was submitted to the management. Whereas they wanted the IAD to undertake operational audit, they wanted only competent people to staff the IA function. However, as this condition could not be met, they are skeptical about the success of operational audit by IA.

Summing Up

IA is an important component of OPTIMA. This chapter shows that this function is in a very weak shape in the SEBs/unbundled power utilities. The concept of IA has not taken deeper roots. IA has not been organised suitably in terms of its location in the organisational charts and its functional relationship with other activities. IA function has been very inadequately staffed. Professionals have not found their way in IA set-up. The existing incumbents have not been exposed to any training. The budget allocations to IA as a percentage of total turnover have been very insufficient. IA charters lack clarity and IA has been equated mostly to internal checks. The concept of IA being systems audit has not found favour. Audit committees has not been set up by the power utilities and their role as a mechanism to discharge corporate governance effectively has not been much appreciated. Though the presence of a strategic audit plan is a primary requirement for the success of IA function, IA organisations have not appreciated this significance. The IA coverage has been very narrow and not exceeding 50-60 per cent of the total transactions. The reporting arrangements lack harmony and the basic purpose for which IA is conducted. IA function mostly reports to Controller of Accounts or officials attached to Director of Finance. The use of contract Internal Auditors has not made inroads. As IA is inadequately staffed the number of IA units also fall short of organisational requirements. IA staff usually does not interact with the operating staff which have a divergence of opinion about the role and importance of IA. The technical competence of IA staff is not satisfactory.

REFERENCES

1. Mishra, R.K., and Navin, B., (2001), *State Level Public Enterprises in India*, Mittal Publications, New Delhi.
2. The *New Indian Express,* Sept. 4, 2001, Hyderabad Edn., p. 11.
3. Mishra, R.K., Geeta. P. and Navin. B. (ed.) (2001), *Some Issues relating to Public Enterprises Management*, Anmol Publications, New Delhi.
4. Mishra, R.K., (1999), *Internal Audit in State Electricity Boards with Reference to Andhra Pradesh State Electricity Board,* Institute of Public Enterprise, Hyderabad.

8

ENVIRONMENTAL POLICY IN INDIA

A Critical Appraisal

India achieved its independence on August 15, 1947. During the first 50 years of its independence it set for itself the task of bringing about an economic transformation, alleviation of poverty, introduction of social justice, and integration of the country with the rest of the world. India is inhabited by about 1000 million people, and has the distinction of being the second largest country in the world, standing next only to China. The total area of the country is about 32 million sq. km. India ranks seventh in the world on this parameter. The rate of economic growth of the country was about 3.5 per cent between 1951 and 1991. However, since the introduction of the economic reforms in 1991, the rate of growth has stepped up, and currently it is hovering around 6.5 per cent per annum. The policy makers propose to push the rate of growth to 7.5 per cent during the Ninth Plan period (1997-98 to 2002-2003). The per capita income of the country is about US $ 350. The country aims to work for a strategic break through to catch up with the developed countries and achieve a stage of self-sustained growth. However, the participation of Mrs. Indira Gandhi (then Prime Minister) in the first United Nations-sponsored Conference on Human Environment held in Sweden in 1972, added a very formidable dimension to the entire agenda of economic development. The conservation and promotion of environment emerged as the single, key dominating factor in planning and implementing the economic growth policies of the country. India's commitment to the cause of conserving, promoting, and fostering the environment became much stronger by the time the Earth Summit was held in Brazil in 1992.

During the two environmental decades (1972-1992), the major issue before the country was how to strike a balance between the urgent need to secure food sufficiency, health, drinking water, and shelter, and the desire to protect the environment. The country has to provide its masses with an honourable living, on the one hand, and prevent any further degradation of its environment in the future to ensure its all-round growth, supported by adequate socio-economic and political measures, on the other.

Environmental Policy

The Environmental Policy has been an integral part of Indian society from its very inception. Barring brief periods of its invasion between 1000-1947 AD, during which time the country was ruled by the Moghuls and the British, environmental issues were never given a backseat. This trend continued even after Independence up to 1985, when a separate Ministry was created at the Centre to deal with issues related to environment.

The Environmental Policy in India can be studied under three sub-heads i.e the Environmental Policy in ancient India, the Environmental Policy in medieval India, and the Environmental Policy during the British period.

In ancient India, protection and cleaning of the environment was the essence of Vedic culture. In Hindu theology, forests, trees and wildlife protection held a place of reverence. The *Rig Veda* considers human life as a part and parcel of the environment.[1] The *Atharva Veda* considers trees as the abode of forest gods and goddessess.[2] The *Yajur Veda* concluded that the relationship with nature and animals should be not that of dominion and subjugation, but of mutual respect and kindness.[3] According to *Rig Veda,* mankind has to live in harmony with nature and they should treat it as their best friend.[4]

In *Nrisimha Puran* trees have been presented as God himself.[5] In *Geeta,* the world is described as a *peepal* tree.[6] *Vishnudhamsutra* equates planting of a tree as equal to giving birth to a child.[7] Whereas the plantation of trees was considered a sacred task in Hindu culture, cutting of trees was prohibited, and punishment was provided for such acts. *Skand Purana* contains a long list of trees cutting of which is prohibited.[8] *Yagyavalkya Smriti* treated felling of trees as a punishable offence.[9] *Ramayana* and *Mahabharata* held destruction of forests as a great sin.[10] *Charak Samhita* opined that destruction of vegetation leads to the ruin of a State.[11] *Durga Saptasati* opines that so long as the earth has mountains, forests, trees, plants, etc., human beings will continue to survive.[12] Sri Madbhagavatam says that a man could attain the state of supreme peace and God's grace only when he offers respect with exclusive devotion to seas, sky, water, earth, heavenly bodies, living beings, trees, and rivers.[13] Kautilya in *Arthasastra* has advised afforestation in non-agricultural land.[14]The Vedic culture prohibits injuring or killing of animals as they stood next to human beings in relation to mutual respect and kindness.[15] This makes it clear that protection of the environment has been an important facet of the Indian way of life.

The civilization of Mohenjodaro, Harappa, and the Dravidians which flourished in India between 2000-5000 BC, carried these traditions.[16] The Mauryan period (300 BC) was found to be the most glorious chapter from the point of view of environmental protection. The Vanyadaksha was to promote, safeguard, and conserve the forests. He classified forests set apart for the State, forests set apart of the religion, forests reserved for the supply of forest produce, forests set apart for grazing of royal livestock such as elephants, forests reserved for serving royalty, and forests open to public for bunt. Various punishments were prescribed for cutting trees, damaging forests, and for killing animals. Punishments were also provided for causing pollution and uncivic sanitation. This model of governance of the environment continued upto the Gupta era (673 BC).[17]

The Environmental Policy of ancient India stood reversed in the medieval period (1000-1600 BC). Forests were treated as no more than wooded land and properties which yielded some revenue. A few species of trees were specified as royal trees which could be cut by paying a small fee. Forests during this period shrunk steadily.[18]

The British rule over India came in 1600 AD through the East India Company and later its colonization by the British powers in the 1860s. This proved to be an era of plundering of natural resources, and at the same time turned out to be the beginning of organized forest management. Forestry, wildlife and water pollution were the chief subjects of the concentration of the British in India. The Forest Act, 1869, was the first step asserting the State monopoly over the forests, in terms of which it was empowered to acquire forests, curtailing the customary right of tribal communities to manage forests. It further expanded the power of the State by providing for a new class of forests termed as reserved forests, which were closed to the people, and empowered the forest administration to impose penalties for any transgression of the provisions of the Act.

The Forest Policy of 1894 aimed at promoting the general well-being of the people in the country, preserving the climatic and physical conditions of the country, and fulfilling the needs of the people, and accordingly classified forests as reserved forests, commercial forests, minor forests, and pastures. This policy had legitimacy of the conventional conservation practices of the local community, and it allowed uncontrolled diversion of forest lands to the Forest Act of 1927. Attempts were made during the latter half noise pollution, soil preservation, and land-use by legislating laws by the British Government, characterized by a narrow purpose and limited territorial approach. The Oriental Gas Company Act, 1857; Indian Penal Code, 1860; Indian Fisheries Act, 1897; Bengal Smoke Nuisance Act, 1905; and Bombay Smoke Nuisance Act, 1912, were cases in point. In the field of wildlife protection, the laws enacted comprised the Elephants Preservation Act, 1879, and the World Birds and Animals Protection Act, 1912. The consolidation of the Holdings Act, 1920, was enacted to have a proper consolidation of the land holdings. Thus, it is clear that the British rule aimed at appropriation and exploitation of common resources, with the primary objective of earning revenue, and did precious little to improve environmental management.

India did not have any precise environmental policy during the initial years of its Independence, but between 1947 and 1980 it initiated a series of measures to check environmental degradation. However, it was only during the Sixth Five-Year Plan (1980-85) that a full chapter was devoted in the Plan document to environment, which briefly discussed the environmental problems relating to land-use, agriculture, water, air, forestry, marine environment, minerals, renewable resources, energy, and urban and human settlements. The document also made a mention of the disappearing species and eco-system, marine eco-systems, including coastal mangroves, coral reefs, marine reserves, island eco-systems, etc. The document briefly touched upon the administrative and legislative arrangements for environmental protection. It suggested the implementation of programmes such as environmental impact assessment, environmental information system, public awareness about environmental protection, creation and management of bio-sphere reserves, and monitoring and conservation of marine ecosystems.[19] Prior to this Plan, the first-three Five-Year plans starting in 1951, 1956 and 1961 respectively, gave due priority to environment related issues such as sanitation, public health, nutrition, water supply, and housing. However environmental protection did not receive any significant attention during the Third Five-Year Plan, except for forest development and soil conservation. This policy continued in the Fourth Five-Year Plan (1969-74).[20]

The year 1972 marked a watershed in the history of environmental management in India, in which year the Conference on Human Environment was held under the aegis of the United Nations. Mrs. Indira Gandhi, the then Prime Minister of India, asserted in the Conference that poverty and need are the biggest polluters. To quote her: "The environmental problems of developing countries are not the side effects of excessive industrialization but reflect the inadequacy of development. The rich countries may look upon development as the cause of environmental destruction, but to us, it is one of the primary means of improving the environment for living or providing food, water, sanitation and shelter; of making the deserts green and the mountains habitable.[21]

Whether or not the world appreciated this point of view expressed in the Conference, India understood the implications of the global concern about the environment. The Indian Constitution was amended in 1976. Article 48A of the Indian Constitution has laid down: "The State shall endeavour to protect and improve the environment and safeguard the forests and wild life of the country.[22] A Chapter on Fundamental Duties under Article 51A(g) was added to make it mandatory on the citizens "to protect and improve the natural environment, including forests, lakes, rivers, and wildlife, and to have compassion for living creatures".[23] In 1972, a comprehensive national law, i.e. wildlife (Protection) Act, was enacted with the objective of solely protecting the wildlife. Project Tiger was launched in 1973 to ensure maintenance of the viable population of tigers in India.

For the control of water pollution, the Water (Prevention and Control of Pollution) Act, 1974 was passed. As discussed earlier, the 1980s marked a period of environmental awakening, institution-building, strengthening legal mechanisms and launching a spate of environmental programmes. The Sixth Plan (1984-85) observed: "it is imperative that we carefully husband our renewable resources of soil and water, and our plant and animal life to sustain our economic development".[24] The pendulum of forest thinking during this period swung between economic considerations and ecological perceptions. The major thrust of the plan as regards forest management and protection was on saving the natural forests from further depletion, formation of new fuel and fodder reserves to meet the growing needs of the local population, and setting up a greater number of national parks and wildlife sanctuaries. It was also proposed to link forest development with the growth of tribal economy. The Seventh Plan (1985-90) followed the approach of sustainable development in harmony with the environment. The Plan stressed the need for taking environmental considerations fully into account in the case of development programmes in all sectors. The Plan also called for involvement of the people at all levels in resource conservation and called for a greater role for the voluntary agencies/non-government organizations in the management of environmental issues. The Plan gave the highest priority to restore the forest cover to 53 per cent of the geographical area of the country from the present level of about 23 per cent. A new National Forest Policy of 1988 was formulated with the principal aim of ensuring environmental stability and maintenance of ecological balance.

In 1980 the Government of India set up a High Power Committee under the Chairmanship of the Deputy Chairman of the Planning Commission, Mr. N. D. Tiwari, to take a comprehensive view of the administrative and legislative aspects of environmental protection.[25] The committee suggested the creation of a Department of Environment at the Centre for environmental conservation and sustainable national development, creation of a Central Land Commission to conserve the national ecological base, establishing a dialogue with the public to inculcate interest in nature, inclusion of fuel and fodder supply in the Common Minimum Programme of the Central Government, and institution of a Central Authority for giving prior approval for diversion of forest land to non-forestry uses. The Government of India set up the Department of Environment on November 1, 1980. On the recommendations of the Tiwari Committee, the National Committee on Environmental Planning and Coordination was replaced by the National Committee on Environmental Planning in April 1981. The Central Pollution Control Board was set up in 1981. The National Wasteland Development Board was set up in May 1985. The National Afforestation and Ecological Development Board was set up in 1988. A Task Force was set up to elicit public support for wildlife conservation. A full-fledged Ministry of Environment and Forests was set up in 1985 to conduct Environmental Impact assessment for clearing the Plan projects. The Environmental Information System became operational through the installation of a computer terminal link with the computer system of the National Informatics Centre. Thinking was mooted to formulate comprehensive legislation on bio-sphere reserves.

Protection of grazing lands, protection of endangered species, control of toxic substances, scientific land-use, prevention of noise pollution, prevention of denudation of forests, etc. The Eighth Five-Year Plan (1992-97) identified eight major tasks to meet the challenges of environmental degradation, including protection of the natural environment, regeneration and restoration of degraded eco-systems, decentralization of control over the natural and national resources, developing and sharing a greater understanding of nature, formulation of a National Policy for Environment, and putting in place an appropriate institutional and legal framework in support of the policy, ensuring coordination and integration in governmental action aimed at conservation and sustainable use of national resources, making individuals and institutions more accountable to the people for their actions impinging on environment and eco-systems, and monitoring the state of the environment.[26] The Ministry of Environment and Forests adopted a Policy Statement for Abatement of Pollution (1992)[27] and National Conservation Strategy and Policy Statement on Environment and Development (1992).[28] The Policy Statement on Abatement of Pollution asserted the Government's commitment to abatement of pollution for preventing deterioration of the environment. The Policy Statement on Environment and Development took the responsibility for laying down the guidelines to permeate environmental considerations into the fabric of national life and the development process. In order to provide environmental reorientation policies and permeate environmental considerations into the fabric of national life and the development process. In order to provide environmental reorientation policies and practices, the Government chose the following as instruments for action:

- Environmental impact assessment of all development projects;
- Compulsory prior environment clearance of all projects above a certain size;
- Adoption of environmental compatible technologies;
- Public participation in environmental improvement programmes;
- Creation of environmental consciousness through education and mass programmes;
- Moderation of process of demand unleashed by the development process itself by taking measures to recycle waste materials and natural resources; and
- Creation of a cadre for environmental management service and effective implementation of the environmental laws.

A review of the Environmental Policy in its first leg (1947-85) points out that it relied to a great extent only on a regulatory framework. It was reactive in nature. It did not deploy economic instruments and disincentives to regulate the environment. The polluters found it economically more advantageous to pay penalties rather than comply with regulations. It failed to induce changes in production processes and thereby minimize wastage. The policy did not attempt to strike a proper balance between environmental protection and economic development. The inadequacy of the institutional framework for implementation of the laws, poor monitoring machinery, and lack of scientific and technical expertise constituted the major limitations of the policy. The new Environmental Policy contained in the Eighth Five-Year Plan, the National Forest Policy, 1988, and other basic policy documents adopted in the 1980s marked an improvement upon the earlier policies. The new Environmental Policy contains tough measures against environmental pollution, provides for an active involvement of people, makes environmental impact assessment and audit compulsory for large-sized projects, emphasizes adoption of economic instruments as a proactive strategy for the degradation of environment, and provides teeth to the institutions responsible for the management of environment.

Environmental Health

A critical assessment of the environmental health of India has been provided in terms of the parameters mentioned below:

Resource	*Status*
Land	India covers one-fortieth of global land and occupies second position in Asia after China. A major portion of this area is in humid regions (69%) of the remaining, 25% is in arid and semi-arid regions, and 6% in cold regions. Only 11% of the land is not affected by any inherent soil constraints. 34% of the land in the humid regions is affected by inherent soil constraints, followed by 80% in arid and semi-arid regions, and 86% in cold regions. So, the worst affected regions are the cold, arid and semi-arid regions. India's wasteland areas are affected seriously by salinity, alkalinity and wind; and water erosion cover an estimated 100 million hectares, of which about 42 million are still being cultivated. Four million hectares have already been swallowed up by ravines. Among Asian countries, India has the highest proportion of its irrigated land affected by salinity.
Forests	At the turn of the century, India had a forest cover of about 53% of its land area. Today, hardly 23% land is officially under the Forest Department. But only 10-12% of the area has adequate tree cover. Over one million hectares of forests are cut every year and 0.15 million hectares are lost to development projects annually. Official estimates show that forest cover has increased only by 0.7% since 1977-79, one of the lowest rates in Asia. The official estimate of annual deforestation is about 48,000 hectares (1983-87), as against the annual reforestation of 138,000 hectares. The forestry programmes of the Government are not in commensurate with the survival needs of the people dependent on forests.
Bio-diversity	India's natural bio-diversity is one of the richest in the world. This diversity is being threatened now. At mid-century, Indian farmers were cultivating 50,000 varieties of rice. By 2000 AD they will probably grow not more than 50. India has 17,270 plant species; of these 1,469 are rare and being threatened. The country has 341 known mammal species, of which 38 are being threatened; 1,178 varieties of bird species of which 72 varieties are being threatened; and 400 species of reptiles, of which 17 varieties are being threatened. There are six wet lands of international importance covering 1,93,000 hectares.
Cropped Agricultural Area	About 50% of the land area is accounted for by the cropped land, the highest proportion in Asia, excluding Bangladesh. Crop diversity is the important characteristics of Indian agriculture. The important annual crops are rice, wheat, sorghum, pulses, oil seeds, cotton, etc., and the perennial crops include tea, coffee, rubber etc. Not enough attention is paid to preserve the bio-diversity.

Resource	*Status*
Irrigation and Floods	The major sources of irrigation in India are wells, canals and tanks. About 30% of the net area is being irrigated. Of this, wells account for 49%, followed by canals (38%) and tanks (7%). The traditional source of irrigation in India, i.e., tanks has been declining in importance over the years. The increase in groundwater exploitation is growing at a faster rate when compared to canal irrigation. The Indian irrigation policy is biased toward large dams which are creating ecological problems. There are 1,357 large dams and another 160 are under construction. The ecological problems include loss of forest area, displacement of people, etc. Siltation rates of the reservoirs of major dams are three to four times higher than the projected rates. Over the period, groundwater tables are going down in most of the regions due to over-exploitation. This is leading to desertification. According to official estimates, annual average flood damage in India (1953-87) is : area affected –7.66 million hectares; population affected –31.84 million; crops affected –3.51 million hectares and Rs.367.79 crore in value terms; loss of human lives –1,439; loss of cattle –0.10 million, and total damage—Rs. 768.08 crore.
Input Use	Though India is not among the high fertiliser intensive Asian countries, intensive agricultural practices, without supplementation by organic manure, are leading to rapid depletion of soil fertility. The average annual fertiliser consumption is about 62 Kg per hectare and pesticide consumption is 0.31 Kg per hectare. Regional variations in input use intensity are very wide.
Livestock	Livestock population in India has grown at the rate of 1.16% per annum between 1951 and 1982. The consumption of livestock is fast-changing. Number of sheep and goat has grown by 31% since 1978-80, as against 6% increase in cattle and 14% increase in buffaloes and camel. This reflects the degradation of grazing lands because sheep and goat can survive better in hostile environment. As fodder becomes scarce, people and their animals turn to forests, increasing the pressure on forests.
Water	India has annual internal renewable water resources of 1,850 cubic Km. On per capita basis it is about 2,170 cubic metres which is far below the Asian average of 3,370 cubic metres. Moreover, only 18% of the renewable water is being used annually, i.e 612 cubic metres per capita. Further, India uses only one-tenth of the rainfall it receives annually. Even after 40 years from now it will be using only a quarter. 70% of all the available water in India is polluted. Increasingly, polluted rivers and lakes and large dams are seriously affecting river in fisheries, thereby affecting the livelihood of millions of people .

Resource	*Status*
Air	Though India's emissions of air pollutants on per capita basis are much lower than the Asian average, they have crossed the permitted levels in most of the cities in India. The per capita emission of carbondioxide (CO_2) is about 0.77 tonnes. CO_2 emissions from land-use change are 120 million tonnes. Methane emissions are 36 million tonnes. Levels of sulphur dioxide and particulate matter in several Indian cities already exceed permissible limits. The world's worst air pollution problem could be the wood smoke inhaled by poor Indian women while cooking, especially in rural areas. A tonne of particulate from household wood stoves may actually lead to more than 500 times the human exposure than a tonne of particulate from coal fired power station. The current car and two wheeler boom is aggravating the problem of air pollution.
Health and Sanitation	There are about 2.62 doctors per thousand population in India and about nine hospital beds per 1,000 people. The rural-urban disparities in this regard are very wide. Only 73% and 79% of the rural and urban population respectively in India have access to safe drinking water which is well below even by the Asian standards. The conditions of sanitation are still worse. Only 4% and 38% of the rural and urban population have access to sanitation facilities. 50% of the food samples are contaminated with pesticide residues, with 30% exceeding permissible limits. Thousands of workers die every year because of occupational diseases, the gravest being caused by various types of dust. One million miners suffer from silicosis. As a result, 6 out of 10 miners are physically unfit to undertake hazardous and back-breaking jobs. Mosquito-borne diseases are rapidly growing and are grossly under-reported.

Source: The State of India's Environment the First, Second and Third Citizens Reports, Centre for Science and Environment, New Delhi, 1982, 1985 and 1991; World Resources 1992-93: A Guide to the Global Environment, A Report by the World Resource Institute in collaboration with the United Nations Development Program, Oxford University Press, New York, 1992; Statistical Abstract of India, 1990, CSO Department of Statistics, Government of India, 1992).

Constitutional Provisions

India is a union of 26 States. The powers of the Central Government and the State Governments to legislate are mentioned in three separate lists. The first, or the Central List, contains the subjects on which the Union Government has exclusive powers of legislation. The second, or the State List, comprises the subjects for which the States have exclusive jurisdiction to formulate legislation. The third, or the Concurrent List, enumerates the subjects on which both the Union and the State Governments have concurrent jurisdiction. In the case of conflict between the Union and the State, the final say rests with the residuary powers vested in the Central Government. Further, the Constitution also empowers the Union Government to legislate with respect to a matter contained in the State List in national interest. Article 253 of the Indian Constitution empowers Parliament to make any law for the whole or any part of the territory for implementing any treaty, agreement or convention with any other country or countries, or any decision made at any international conference, association or other body. It is important to note that forests, protection of wildlife, animals, birds, and population control and family planning, were transferred from the State List to the Concurrent List by the 42nd Amendment to the Constitution. However, environmental subjects like agriculture, land, health and sanitation are still in the State List. One of the implications of the present constitutional provisions is that both the Centre and the State have constitutional authority to formulate and implement plans for environmental protection and development, but they have to coordinate their planning activities. The centre has to determine, in consultation with the States, the overall perspectives, objectives, and strategies for environmental planning. The detailed micro-level implementation has to be left to the States to be carried out by them, based on their perspectives of the environmental problems encountered within the broad framework decided by the Central Government. Of the three components of environment, land and water included in any list and is, therefore, with the Centre under its residuary powers.

Environment or environmental protection does not find a place in any list. It has been suggested that environmental protection should form a part of the Concurrent List. It is further felt that it is necessary to do so as India is a signatory to the Declaration of the United Nations Conference on Human Environment. The principles of the Declaration bind India to the decisions taken at the Conference that: "The natural resources of the earth, including the air, water, land, flora and fauna, and specially representative samples of the natural eco-systems must be safeguarded for the benefit of the present and future generations through careful planning and management, as appropriate.

Legal Mechanism

More than three dozen laws have been enacted to protect the environment in India. They cover all aspects of the environment, from pollution to conservation, and deforestation to nuclear waste. Some of these laws existed even before the environmental movement arrived on the scene, viz., The Forest Act, 1927; Orissa River Pollution Act, 1953; Punjab State Tube Well Act, 1954; West Bengal Control of Water Pollution Act, 1957; Jammu and Kashmir State Canal and Drainage Act, 1963; and the Maharashtra Water Pollution Prevention Act, 1969, etc. Despite these laws, by 1970 India was faced with an environmental crisis. Immediate and drastic actions were needed to cope with the magnitude of this crisis. We discuss hereunder some major Central Acts for protection of the environment, forest, wildlife, etc. These laws help us understand the evolutionary process in the development of legal mechanisms to promote and safeguard the environment.

The Wildlife (Protection) Act, 1972: This Act provides for the protection of wild animals and birds and matters connected therewith or ancillary thereto. It provides for notification of sanctuaries, national parks, and common reserves and areas by the State Government.

The Water (Prevention and Control of Pollution) Act, 1974: The purpose of this Act is to ensure prevention and control of water pollution and maintenance or restoration of wholesomeness of water by preventing discharge of domestic and industrial effluents in rivers, streams and other sources of drinking water, and water for support of fish life, for housing and irrigation. It provides for deterrent penalties for contravention of the provisions of the Act. The Act also provides for setting up of Central and State Water Testing Laboratories to enable the Pollution Control Boards to assess the extent of pollution.

The Indian Forest Act, 1927: This Act was enacted to preserve and safeguard the forests. It deals with reserved forests, village forests, protected forests, and forests of private owners. Several amendments have been incorporated to bring it in line with the Forest Policy of the Government.

The Forest (Conservation) Act, 1980 : This Act was adopted to check indiscriminate dereservation and diversion of forest land for non-forest purposes. The State Governments are required to submit formal proposals for declaration of reserved forests and diversion of forest land for non-forest purposes to the Ministry of Environment and Forests for approval. The Act was amended in 1988 to incorporate strict penal provisions against violation.

The Air (Prevention and Control of Pollution) Act, 1981: This law was enacted to deal with preservation of the quality of air and the control of air pollution. The presence in the air, beyond certain limits, of various pollutants discharged through industrial emission and certain human activities connected with traffic, heating, use of domestic fuel, and refuse have an adverse effect on the health of the people, vegetation, and also animal life.

The Environment (Protection) Act, 1986: This is a general legislation on environmental protection which, among others, provides for coordination of activities of the forest, regulatory agencies, creation of an authority or authorities with adequate powers for environmental protection, regulation and discharge of environmental pollutants and handling of hazardous substances, speeding up the response in the event of accidents threatening environment, and deterrent punishments to those who endanger human environment, safety and health. The Act empowers the Central Government to take all such measures as it deems fit for the purpose of protecting and improving the quality of the environment and preventing and controlling environmental pollution.

The Water (Prevention and Control of Pollution) Cess Act, 1977: This law was enacted to provide for levy and collection of a cess on water consumed by persons for carrying on industries and by local authorities, with a view to augmenting the resources of the Central Pollution Control Board and the State Pollution Control Boards for the prevention and control of water pollution. The funds raised through cess are allocated to the Central and State Pollution Control Boards.

The Public Liability Insurance Act, 1991: This Act was enacted to provide for public liability insurance for the purpose of providing immediate relief to persons affected by accidents occurring while handling any hazardous substance, and matters connected therewith or incidental thereto. Annexure 8.1 provides the gist of important legislation related to environment in India.

Institutional Framework

It has taken more than two and a half decades for the country to develop a modicum of institutional framework for the management of environment in India. The institutional framework for the management of environment in India is composed of a four-tier structure. First, there are the apex institutions set up by the Government of India. At the second level are the institutions established by the various State Governments. The autonomous institutions set up under the aegis of the Central/State Governments are operating at the third level. Finally, the voluntary agencies/non-governmental organizations are involved, dealing with a wide range of environmental management issues. The Central Government's Ministry of Environment and Forests deals with the formulation and implementation of policy on environment from time to time. It was set up in January 1985. It consists of two Departments, viz., the Department of Environment and the Department of Forests and Wildlife. Its main activities comprise conservation and survey of flora and fauna, forests, wildlife, prevention and control of pollution, afforestation, and regeneration of degraded areas, protection of the environment and research related to these topics. The Ministry has set up the Ganges Board for the cleaning of the river Ganga. It has set up regional offices in the five major zones of the country, located at Bangalore, Bhopal, Bhubaneshwar, Lucknow, and Shillong. The Headquarters is located at New Delhi. The regional offices take care not only of forestry concerns but also environmental management and pollution control functions. As a part of the environmental management and pollution control functions, the Ministry monitors and regulates on-going forestry development projects and schemes with a specific emphasis on conservation of forests. It assists the States and the Union Territories in the preparation of proposals involving diversion of forest lands for non-forestry uses. It also assists the States and the Union Territories in the preparation of a management plan for monitoring forests. They are controlled within the framework of guidelines issued by the Central Government from time to time and provide support to the States and Union Territories in the matter of strategy and retrieval of data covering forestry. The Ministry coordinates its working with the Department of Science and Technology, Ministry of Agriculture and Department, Ministry of Space, Ministry of Energy and Power, and the Planning Commission.

Annexure 8.2 details the role, organization and main activities of the Ministry of Environment and Forests of the Government of India.

Most of the State Governments have Departments/Ministries of Ecology, Environment and Energy. Such Department/Ministry formulates the policy for the management of environment and forests at the State-level and is also endowed with the responsibility of its implementation. Such Departments/Ministries are also burdened with the responsibility of inculcating awareness about the importance of environment among the public, conducting training programmes on environment, environmental appraisal of development projects, and pollution monitoring and control.

The autonomous institutions in the country include the Forest Survey of India. Botanical Survey of India, Geological Survey of India, Environment Training and Protection Research Institute, National Environmental Engineering Research Institute, and a host of other institutions. The Botanical Survey makes an assessment of the botanical resources of the country. The Geological Survey of India carries out investigations in various fields, with special reference to agriculture and forests. It is also engaged in exploring the land resources of the country. The Forestry Survey of India undertakes country-wide comprehensive Forest Resources Survey at regular intervals for proper planning and policy formulation. It prepares a comprehensive State of the Forest Report, including National Vegetation Map, once in every two years. It undertakes work in regard to the preparation of forestry inventory of the various States. The Forest Development Corporations in the various States are engaged in scientific management of forest resources on commercial lines. They deal with the trading of timber and other forest produce and are engaged in raising forest plantations. In what follows we present a brief description of the apex institutions endowed with the task of conservation and promotion of the environment in India.

The Indian Council of Forestry Research and Education provides proper impetus and thrust to research activities and education and functions as an apex body to guide research activities. It has six institutes, Dehradun, Institute of Wood Science and Technology; Bangalore, Institute of Forest Genetics and Tree Breeding; Coimbatore, Institute of Deciduous Forests, Jabalpur; Institute of Arid Zone Forestry Research, Jodhpur; and Institute of Rain and Moist Deciduous

Forest Research, Jorhat. The council also oversees forestry education in the country which has been taken up by 20 State Agricultural Universities.

The National Land-Use and Wastelands Development Council works through the National Land-Use and Conservation Board and the National Wastelands Development Board. They deal with issues concerning the health and scientific management of the country's land resources. The State Land-Use Boards have been established to build up and strengthen their capability to promote and implement land-use policy and related programmes, and coordinate and review such programmes at the State-level.

The Indian Board for Wildlife advises the Central and State Governments on ways and means of promoting conservation and effectively controlling poaching of wildlife through coordinated legislation and administrative measures. It also advises on the setting up of national parks, sanctuaries and zoological gardens.

It provides inputs to the Government on policy regarding export or living animals, trophies, skins, furs and other products of wildlife. It reviews from time to time the progress in the field of wildlife conservation in the country and suggests such measures for improvement as are considered necessary. The State Boards for Wildlife have been set up in almost all the States with similar functions. They are also responsible for enforcing laws against poaching and killing of animals and birds in protected areas.

Thc Wildlife Institute of India was set up at Dehradun by the Government of India to boost the training and research efforts in wildlife conservation and management.

The Animal Welfare Board of India is responsible for the implementation of the Prevention of Cruelty to Animals Act, 1960. It also imparts training in various aspects of animal welfare. The State-level Animal Welfare Boards have been set up to strengthen the working of the Animal Welfare Board of India.

The Central Zoo Authority monitors the management of zoos in the country and also to enforce certain minimum standards of upkeep. It derecognises zoos which fail to improve by enforcing the relevant provisions of the Wildlife (Protection) Act.

The National Eco-Development Board ensures that economic development takes place in harmony with ecological plans. The

Board is also required to bring about optimal utilization and management of primary natural resources like land, water and forests, leading to sustained growth rather than mere short-term gains.

The Central Pollution Control Board and the State Pollution Control Boards have been set up under the Water (Prevention and Control of Pollution) Act, 1974. The Central Pollution Control Board is empowered to enter any place and inspect any equipment, industrial plant, record, register, document or any other material object and to take samples of air, water, soil or any other substance for the purpose of analysis, from any factory premises or places. It provides technical assistance to the State Pollution Control Boards, organises training programmes, mass awareness programmes, and dissemination of information in respect of matters relating to water and air pollution. The State Pollution Control Boards operate at the State-level. They lay down standards for treatment of sewage and trade effluents and emissions from automobiles, industrial plants or any other polluting source. They evolve efficient methods of disposal of sewage and trade effluent on lands, and develop reliable and economically viable methods of treatment of sewage, trade effluent, and air pollution control equipment.

The Environmental Training and Protection Research Institute Hyderabad, was set up in 1985 with the objective of designing and conducting training programmes concerning the various components of environment, with special emphasis on mounting programmes on environmental impact assessment, environmental audit and environmental education. The institute takes up studies on environmental protection. It draws participants from the Departments overseeing environmental protection and training belonging to the Central Government and the various State Governments. It has developed linkages with the various Institutes in India.

The National Environmental Engineering Research Institute (NEERI), Nagpur, was set up under the aegis of the Government of India with the responsibility of conducting a training programme on Environmental Impact Assessment for Industrial Projects. It advises the Central Government and the State Governments about the suitability of the various industrial and irrigation projects from the point of view of environmental promotion and protection. The Supreme Court of India and the various High Courts have sought advice from the institute on various public interest litigation and legal disputes relating to a number of projects.

Componential Status

Environment constitutes the external force influencing man's existence and sustenance. The discussion on componential status provides a critical assessment of the state of management of water, air and forest resources, land-use and the position with regard to pollution.

In India, water is a basic input for life. Water is the most scarce resource in India. The groundwater resources have been over-used. Whereas urban India faces severe shortage of water, rural India does not have the requisite access to it. The four metros of the country, viz., Delhi, Mumbai, Calcutta and Chennai, supply water to their inhabitants for a couple of hours every day. In recent years they have been supplying water once in two/three days for a few hours. The inhabitants in some areas of Rajasthan have to walk a couple of kilometres to fetch a pitcher of water. Only 8 per cent of the rain water is used for irrigation and drinking water purposes. Mega schemes like Ganga-Kaveri link have the potential of solving the water problem but have not been implemented. The cooperation from Indian citizens has not been sought in managing the available water. Much of the water available for drinking and irrigation is polluted. Even the Ganges water has not been spared from contamination. The Water (Prevention and Control of Pollution) Act, 1974, is the first attempt to comprehensively deal with water management in India. The policy recognises the source of origin of the basin as the basic function unit of planning for water resources development and calls for proper measures to optimize utilization of these resources not only for the benefit of people living in the basin but also transfer of surplus water to meet the requirements of the water-deficit areas. The policy deals with the problems of water logging and soil salinity leading to the degradation of agricultural land, planning and implementation of new irrigation or multi-purpose projects, development and exploitation of groundwater resources and quality of water.

Air is the life blood of human beings. Air quality in the urban areas of India is deteriorating on an alarming scale, India adds every year four million of sulphur dioxide, seven million particulates, one million tonnes of carbon monoxide, 0.5 million tonnes of nitrogen oxide and 2.2 million tonnes of hydrocarbon into the air from domestic, industrial, and transportation sources. Calcutta, Mumbai, Pune, Coimbatore, Madurai, Delhi, Ludhiana, Punjab, Yamuna Nagar, Faridabad, and Hyderabad account for nearly 85 per cent of air polluting industries. Industries account for nearly 45 per cent of the total air pollution load. These include petrochemical complexes, fertilizer plants, textile mills, leather units, thermal power plants, and mining and chemical industries. In Calcutta 1000 tonnes of pollutants are discharged every day. The pollution levels are higher than that of New York or London. Delhi has earned the distinction of being the fourth most polluted city in the world. The Government has not brought out a separate policy statement on management of air resources. The Air (Prevention and Control of Pollution) Act, 1981 has given a new impetus to deal with the management of air resources under which the Central and State Pollution Control Boards administer a system of monitoring activities and enforcing through fines and criminal prosecutions the prevention of air pollution. Air quality data have been analysed and interpreted to assess the distribution and concentration of pollution levels in the major cities of India.

The Forest Policy of 1998 aims at increasing the forest cover. When India won its Independence the forest cover was 33 per cent. Annexure 8.3 shows that the reserved forest area has come down to 19.5 per cent. Annexure 8.4 points out that the per capita forest area in hectares is 0.09. Arunachal Pradesh, Assam, Goa, Himachal Pradesh, Kerala, Madhya Pradesh, Manipur, Meghalaya, Mizoram, Nagaland, Orissa, Sikkim, Tripura, Andaman and Nicobar, and Dadra and Nagar Haveli have forest cover higher than the national average. However, some major States such as Andhra Pradesh, Bihar, Rajasthan, Uttar Pradesh, West Bengal and the Union Territory of Delhi have forest cover far below the national average. Out of 413 districts, as many as 30 districts exist without forest cover. Most of these pertain to Bihar, Haryana, Madhya Pradesh, Karnataka and Uttar Pradesh.

Managing environmental pollution has become a difficult problem to cope with. Though noise pollution standards have been laid down under the Air (Prevention and Control of Pollution) Act, 1981, the industrial and non-industrial sources of noise are numerous and adequate enough to disturb the day-to-day life of the living beings in the country. Loudspeakers are extensively used for political meetings, marriages, religious functions, music programmes and advertising. Trucks, buses, heavy vehicles and passenger cars, produce undesirable noise to the annoyance of the people. Aircraft noise is a disturbance to the people living around airports in the country. The noise pollution in the country has resulted into a noise hazard, leading to permanent hearing loss and nuisance affecting efficiency, comfort and enjoyment. 50 per cent of the students in noise-polluted areas fail to concentrate on their studies. In Mumbai, 36 per cent of the population in the city constantly encounter noise pollution. Of these, 75 per cent felt lack of concentration, 69 per cent complete disturbance of sleep and 65 per cent restlessness. The high intensity of noise pollution has affected the Khajuraho temple in Madhya Pradesh which is reported to have developed cracks due to sonic booms. The metropolitan cities of Mumbai, Calcutta and Chennai are amongst the most noisy cities in the world. It is estimated that in Mumbai, with more than six lakh vehicles and a large number of trains plying every day, the noise level ranges from 57 to 91 dB. The noise level in Chennai varies from 52.7 dB to 190.4 dB. In Delhi it ranges between 50 and 120 dB. Calcutta has an average noise level of 87 dB.

Industrial pollution has reached dangerous proportions. The Central Pollution Control Board has identified more than 10,000 industries causing pollution. A large number of industries discharge the sewerage into the rivers. Whenever officials from the Boards visit the industries to inspect and collect samples of treated and untreated effluents, they are quite often made to wait at the gate of the industry till the industry makes arrangements either to close the process causing pollution or commission the treatment plant. The industry's attitude is one of great callousness. Even the multinationals in the country have acted indifferently in this regard. The Bhopal gas tragedy of 1984 shook not only India but also the entire world. Thousands of people died due to leakage of MIC gas from the gas tanks of the Union Carbide plant at Bhopal. The impact of the leakage was such that a large part of the Bhopal population, numbering two hundred thousand people, developed serious problems affecting their eyes, and various limbs. Of the people affected, 3,000 were pregnant women. The children born of some of these women had various deformities. Many of the victims of the Bhopal gas tragedy have yet to get compensation. In September 1997, the Visakhapatnam Refinery of Hindustan Petroleum Corporation Limited was found responsible for the death of 16 workmen in its oil storage tanker. Due to lack of proper maintenance, the plant continued to remain in operation resulting into these deaths.

One of the major environmental problems in India has been inappropriate use of its land resources. Annexure 8.5 shows that of the 329 million hectares of land is environmentally degraded. It is estimated that by the year 2000 the per capita total availability of land would decline to 0.33 hectare and cultivable land to 0.15 hectare. Andhra Pradesh, Madhya Pradesh, Maharashtra, Rajasthan, Tamil Nadu and Uttar Pradesh have wastelands higher than the rest of the States. Though the National Wastelands Development Board was set up in 1985 to deal with the problem, and the State Land-Use Boards have been set up in almost all the States and the Union Territories, the country has yet to make significant progress in employing its wastelands for productive purposes. One of the aspects of the land utilization is land pollution. It has been revealed that India loses annually about 50 million tonnes of foodgrain on account of loss of top soil. It is estimated that salinity afflicts 18 million hectares of land in command areas existing in Gujarat, Madhya Pradesh, Meghalaya, Punjab, Haryana, and Andhra Pradesh. Irresponsible mining activities have rendered thousands of acres of land unusable. Land pollution is a national phenomena in India. Thermal plants have created the problem of fly-ash, rendering thousands of acres of land inarable. The cement plants in the country have created health hazards for their workers.

Population has been an important dimension of India's environmental problem. The population explosion is chiefly responsible for poverty, illiteracy, and lack of educational facilities. Even a modest fulfilment of the basic needs of the masses has resulted in over-exploitation of its natural resources. The introduction of the New Economic Policy, 1991 and India's signing the GATT later, have opened up the floodgates of further exploitation of India's natural resources. It is expected that industries causing pollution in the developed countries will get shifted to India and huge foreign investments would come in sectors which are resource-based. Man himself is responsible for environmental degradation by exploiting all the natural resources and discharging the waste products into the environment beyond its assimilative capacity. In order to keep up the quality of environment Government have introduced different legislation and regulations to safeguard the environment. Other techniques introduced by the Government for pollution control include subsidies to the polluters by the way of straight grants or tax incentives.

Apart from that polluters should take action voluntarily to protect the environment i.e., willingness to comply with the environmental standards, and appropriate technological support . The following instruments of action, now required to be popularized for the accomplishment of the converted goal of sustainable development.

The Environmental Impact Assessment (EIA) is one of the most valuable, and interdisciplinary decision-making tools. It can be applied at the project level for the selection of project site, consider the alternate process technologies and alternate options for the target development. EIA can also be used to ensure regional planning for sustainable development in the context of ecosystem carrying capacity.

The Environmental Audit mechanism which ensures post-project environmental quality monitoring and may be considered as a feedback to the EIA, done during the planning stage. Environmental audit might also be considered as a management tool. Again waste minimization audit could be the first step for successfully accomplishing the goal of waste minimization.

The simplest waste minimization efforts include good house keeping, segregation of waste streams, training of the sensitive employees etc. only after these relatively inexpensive measures are taken, the changes in production methods etc. might be contemplated.

Environmental Impact Assessment

Environmental Assessment is a systematic, reproducible and interdisciplinary process of evaluation of potential impacts of proposed action, and its practical region.

Key Steps in Environmental Assessment Process

The first step is to identify the real problem through meetings involving proponent, public, and responsible government agencies. Purpose, Need and Justification of the action will be established in this step.

A detailed idea about the area where environmental action has to be undertaken should be framed which provides the baseline for the impact analysis

The Environmental impact should be clearly analysed and compared with the alternatives. These impacts could be either "Primary" or "Secondary". Primary impacts are usually associated with constructions, Operations etc., quantifiable, direct and occur at the same time and place of action. On the other hand, "secondary impacts" are indirect or induced changes in the environment, population, economic growth, land-use etc. Impacts can be again short-term or long-term, depending upon the persistence or duration of the impacts.

A balanced decision covering all aspects of policies, goals, and needs over the long terms based on evaluation of all available alternatives should be taken. The entire process of environmental assessment should be thoroughly documented, and that would start with the preparation of draft on EIA and also include review of the "Draft" by all concerned personnel, departments etc., and monitor the follow-up action.

Methods for Forecasting and Assessing Environmental Impact

The process of environmental impact assessment involves the following four distinct elements:

- Identification of impacts
- Measurement of impacts
- Interpretation of impacts
- Communication of assessed impacts

Environmental Audit

The term "environmental audit" derived its name from "financial audit", and bears some similarity with the latter. An "environmental audit" is an independent, systematic method of verifying that, environmental regulations, internal policies and good operating practices are being followed.

The concept of an environmental audit had its beginning in late 1970s in USA, when the consequences of mismanaging environmental responsibilities have prompted several companies to develop audit programmes of their own, as a preventive tool. Since then the interest in environmental audit has increased tremendously in all developed countries and such auditing has now become a specialized field.

In India, a notification under the Environmental (Protection) Rules, 1986, has been issued in 1992, requiring industries to submit annual report of environmental auditing of their activities/operations, each year, beginning with 1992-93. The term audit report has been changed to "statement' in a subsequent amendment in the year 1993. The industries are now supposed to submit their "environmental statement" for a financial year ending on 31st March, to the concerned State Pollution Control Board, on or before 30th September every year. As per the provision of the rule, practically none of the industries are exempted from submitting the above "environmental statement".

Environmental auditing not only safeguards the environment, and substantiate the compliance with the regulations but it also determines the status of performance of the process system, as well as that of the pollution control system. It identifies potential cost savings by the way of waste minimization or reuse/recovery/recycle of the wastes. It also provides the technical data base for use in plant modification, emergencies etc. Environmental auditing thus has got far reaching benefits to the industry—to the society—and to the nation at large. Auditing with a greater detail, which goes much beyond mere identification of regulatory violations may be termed as "management audit".

An audit is different from "assessment". The latter implies an overview with direct checking while former implies statistical verification and direct checking with greater details. An effective audit must collect its own sample and verify the existing sampling data.

Environmental auditing thus may be viewed as a "management tool" internally, and "liaison" externally with the public and the regulatory bodies. It helps in pollution control, improve production, safety and health and conservation of natural resources by the way of:

- Ensuring waste prevention and reduction.
- Assessing compliance with regulatory requirements.

- Facilitating control of environmental practices by the company's management, and Planning environmental information to the public.

General Approach to Environmental Auditing

Environmental auditing essentially consists of three main phases:

(i) Programme planning, or pre-audit preparations,
(ii) On-site activities, or site visit, normally involving interviews with personnel inspection of facilities, data sampling, etc., and
(iii) Post-visit activities, involving evaluation of audit data and reporting of findings.

Statutory Environmental Statement

Under the provision of the Environment (Protection) Amendment Rules, 1993, the mandatory environmental statement (i.e., audit report) are to be submitted in a specified format, and consists of the following nine parts:

(i) Part A, in which the particulars about the industry, in respect of ownership, industry category, production capacity etc., are required to be furnished.
(ii) Part B, in which information about water and raw material consumption is to be furnished. The water budgeting and product-wise or unit-wise material balance is not essential for filling in entries in this part but would help while filling other parts. The water budgeting is however difficult but not impossible to work out. Quite often actual measurements at site become necessary for this purpose.
(iii) Part C, in which information in regard to pollution discharged to environment from each unit is to be furnished. Both quantity and concentration of air and water quality parameters are to be included. The discrepancies, if any, should be highlighted and the reasons explained.
(iv) Part D demands information about hazardous waste generation, if any, both from the process and the pollution control facilities.
(v) Part E, deals with Solid Wastes from processes and pollution

control facilities: information about quantities recycled or reused or solid have to be furnished.

(vi) Part F once again deals with hazardous as well as solid wastes, and seek information about disposal practice adopted for both the above categories of wastes.

(vii) Part G partially attempts to get information about the cost of pollution control and its effect on the cost of production.

(viii) Part H invites proposal for additional measures or investments for environmental protection and pollution control.

(ix) Part I is intended to include any other information not included in any other parts, which might improve the quality of the environment.

New Framework

The twenty-first century and the next millennium await an environmental-friendly India. This requires a paradigm shift in India's environmental thinking, policy-making, its implementation and the level of general awareness of India's people about environmental problems. A new environmental framework will have to be evolved to attain these goals.

Involving People

The present initiatives on environment suffer from a lack of involvement of people.[29] Unless such initiatives ensure the active involvement of people, it is difficult to achieve the desired results. The users of water could better ensure the enforcement of the Water (Prevention and Control of Pollution) Act. Air pollution could be substantially brought down if the owners of vehicles are held responsible for keeping the levels of emission within the limits. The responsibility for keeping noise pollution within limits needs to be imposed on the village Panchayats, tribal leaders, municipalities and municipal corporations. The "family" should be considered as the basic unit for evolving and implementing population planning and control measures. The management of forest resources should be left to the people within the forest area and their neighbourhood. This will ensure the protection of forests and also bring down substantially the costs of surveillance.[30] The money saved could be used for regeneration of forests and promoting flora and fauna and bio-diversity. During the last ten years, some Indian States such as West Bengal, Andhra Pradesh, Uttar Pradesh, Tamil Nadu, Madhya Pradesh and Karnataka, have experimented with joint forest management, under which some forests have been handed over to the people living in and around the forest areas. This has significantly brought down the expenses incurred by Government on the protection of forests, and reduced the incidence of felling of trees and poaching of wild animals. In Karnataka, the joint forest management technique works through the institution of Village Forest Committees. Every Village Forest Committee grows 50,000 teak saplings and 5,000 hybrid cashew saplings every year. The Village Forest Committees restrict the entry of outsiders inside their village boundaries. For collecting various minor forest produce where such entries are inevitable, they fix a time schedule and also certain fees which the outsiders have to pay. The joint forest management has resulted in regeneration of forests because of the complete protection provided by the people.

Appraisal and Implementation of Projects

Most of the projects in the country are set up with the help of financial institutions. The Industrial Development Bank of India, Industrial Finance Corporation of India, Industrial Credit and Investment Corporation of India, State Level Development Banks, viz., State Financial Corporations, State Industrial and Infrastructure Corporations, and Commercial Banks. The mega projects receive funding from even the international financial institutions, such as the World Bank, International Finance Corporation, Asian Development Bank, etc. These financial institutions often fund environmentally unsound projects. They do not ensure that the project outlay incorporates sums set apart for the disposal of industrial wastes ad effluents. In the case of environmental disasters caused by such projects, the responsibility should be owned by such funding institutions.

The construction of large and medium irrigation projects have displaced innumerable persons. Similarly, setting up of sanctuaries and game parks, and other development projects, have added fuel to the fire. According to one estimate, the development displaced persons of projects since 1952 has numbered 15.5 million. Of this, less than half a million people have been rehabilitated so far. The backlog of people to be rehabilitated is more than ten million. Such a displacement has resulted in landlessness, joblessness, homelessness, marginalization, and social risk articulation.[31] Baba Amte and Medha Patkar have been waging a relentless battle to impress upon the Government to review their development policies and plans resulting in such displacements.[32]

Strengthening Institutional and Legal Mechanisms

There is a need to strengthen the apex mechanisms both at the Central and the State levels. The Ministry of Environment and Forests should be manned by professionals and not by Government officers of the Indian Administrative Service (IAS), as is being done now.

The long-term difficulty in this scientific department appears to be members of the IAS for whom the Ministry of Environment and Forests is just another stepping stone closer to the powerful Ministry of Finance. To discourage questioning scientists, the Ministry has posted willing non-expert scientists in the key divisions, especially those that involve ample international negotiations and foreign travel. The day is not far off when the Environment Minister will need to have an impact assessment done for the Ministry's work-force. Some of the square pegs in the round holes in the Ministry could be seen from the fact that a Plant Chemist heads Education; an Environmental Health and Hazardous Wastes expert looks into Medicinal plants, a botanist heads Waste Minimization and Pollution Control, an Aquatic Zoologist evolves vehicular pollution norms, a Toxicologist and Agricultural Scientist heads R&D, a Documentation Expert in Toxicology heads Hazardous Waste, and a Bio-diversity Expert looks after Monitoring. The Secretary, Additional Secretary and Joint Secretary of the Department are all drawn from the IAS, having had no significant background of the requisite knowledge and experience. The Ministry should be reorganized to effectively tackle the problems concerning the management of water, air, and forest resources.

Coordination and Capacity Building

The apex organizations at the level of the Central Government dealing with the management of environment have to interact with a multitude of Ministries and Organizations. For instance, the Ministry of Environment and Forests at the Centre, has to interact, in order to achieve its objectives of preserving and fostering environmental forces, with the Ministry of Family Planning and Health, Ministry of Finance, Ministry of Industry, Ministry of Law and Justice, Ministry of Surface Transport, Ministry of Railways, Ministry of Civil Aviation, Ministry of Agriculture and Development, etc. It should have the capability to impress upon its sister Ministries the importance that an effective management of environment could play in achieving the overall national goals of growth and development. It should also develop the capability to understand the different aspects of management of pollution, water, air, forests. It should liaise effectively with the autonomous institutions. These suggestions should be replicated by the apex organizational at the State-level. The State Governments for the purpose of inducing elements of harmony and integration in the environmental policies should work hand in hand with the Central Governments should not shirk from implementing the measures suggested by the Central Government in this regard.

A number of non-governmental organizations have come up in the 1990s to actively engage themselves with the implementation of various institutional protection and development programmes, expressing environmental concern and conducting environmental research, education and training. Their number exceeds a mark of 5000. They mainly undertake activities relating to conservation and promotion of forests. Most of them are very small in size. Financially they depend upon small grants extended by the Central/State Governments. They suffer from a dearth of professional as well as administrative staff.

Installing Comprehensive Management Information System

Environment covers in its gamut wide-ranging subjects starting from water to bio-diversity. The management of environment in such case requires comprehensive information. There is a need to assess the need for this variegated information, and the hardware and software needed to be put in place for the collection and dissemination of such information. In India though an adequate institutional base has been created to tackle the environmental problems, no mind has been given to collect the requisite on a continuing basis for using them as an input for decision-making for superior environmental management. The lack of coordination among the forest institutions is the key reason for such happening. For instance, the National Remote Sensing Agency (NRSA) has a Forest Division having vast data on the forest cover in the country. The Division has not disseminated even an iota of information under its possession. It has also not liaised with the Forest Department of the various States and the Ministry of Environment and Forests, Government of India. NRSA is an autonomous society working under the aegis of the Department of Space of the Government of India.

Strengthening of Environmental Management in Enterprises

Environmental Management is a useful technology through which the management can meet the current and future challenges. For strengthening organization's operations and to achieve environmental targets, a quality management system is required. There are three standard drafts for EMS. The first internationally recognized environmental standards is BS 7750, specifications for Environmental Management systems. This was issued by the British Standards Institute in 1992. In the middle of 1993 the International Organization for Standardization (ISO) established a technical committee (ISO/TC/207) to develop EM standards. In 1994, six sub-committees of ISO/TC/207 issued two draft standards, namely;

ISO 14000: Environmental Management Systems General Guidelines on Principles, Systems and Supporting Techniques.

ISO 14001: Environmental Management Systems Specifications with Guidance for Use.

A March towards Environmentalism

As developing countries struggle to built up development paths that provide both prosperity for their citizens and good environmental background, they are not willing to accept the existing methods towards environmentally friendly development. So they want a new approach towards economic development and environmental protection. Taking this aspect into consideration some of the methods that can be adopted are:

People Participation

Success or failure of any action depends more on the commitment of the concerned authority, including local communities, than that of the Central/State Governments. Protecting natural habitats, forests and even river basins requires genuine community involvement in planning and implementation.

Incorporating Environmental Concerns

Before framing economic policies, tax policies, regulatory policies, national accounting, environmental aspect should also be given top priority so that whatever techniques that will come into action during enforcement of a particular project/production process will have best results.

Education and Training

The environmental programmes are based on top-down to bottom approach, which suffers from a lack of dialogue between the functionaries at the top and the functionaries at the bottom. These programmes are seldom revised on the basis of the feedback received from the people on the ground. This phenomenon has acted as a great constraint to environmental progress. There is a need to promote environmental education right from the school to the university-level. The Government Departments, autonomous institutions, and public and private enterprises, also need to educate their employees about the importance of the environment. The research institutions in the country engaged in environmental studies, work in isolation and have failed to see the broad picture. Their researches have not transformed the environmental scenario fundamentally. The research personnel do not interact with the environmentalists and the grassroot people. They do not take sufficient caution in putting their knowledge into practice with little or modest costs. In recent times the Government of India has set up the Indian Institute of Forest Management at Bhopal to prepare environmental managers to deal with environment. This institute also conducts post-graduate training programmes leading to an award of the Post-Graduate Diploma in Forest Management. This makes the beginning to supply professionally trained people. India needs to replicate the US approach of initiating mass education in environment at the post-graduate level. There is a move to introduce environmental education at the primary school level in India, which in our view is a very appropriate step to nurture the right ethos about environment from the very beginning or citizenhood.

Economic and Social Incentives

The environment is an anchor for the growth and development of the country, whereas people in the different walks of life have been recognized for their contribution to the society, the environmentalists have drawn a complete blank at the hands of the Central Government, the various State Governments and Socio-economic and political fora. The Ministry of Environment and Forests has a record of consistently giving up under the pressure from economic ministries and other economic organizations such as the Confederation of Indian Industry and the Federation of Indian Chambers of Commerce and Industry. Now no environment clearance is required for projects having an investment outlay upto Rs. 200 crore. Annexure 8.6 shows that the environmental impact assessment exercise is tardy and too cumbersome.

The public budgets have not provided a foolproof system of economic incentives and disincentives to promoters and the polluters of the environment respectively. The Bhopal gas tragedy of December 1984, killing more than 5,000 inhabitants, and permanently damaging one or more organs of the bodies of about 50,000 citizens, is a case in point. The contribution of Indian environmentalists has been acknowledged by the organisations the world over. Magasasay awardees, S.L. Bahuguna and Medha Patkar, who have dedicated their lives to the cause of conservation and promotion of the environment have had to face great inequities at the hands of the Central and the State Governments. Even the industry and business has turned a deaf ear. The outlays set apart for the promotion and conservation of environment have been trivial. The manifestos issued by the various political parties bidding for the parliamentary elections of February/March 1998 revealed that none of them want to make any commitment to promote and conserve the environment, reduce the population, and increase the outlay on this head. The continuation of administered prices has led to abuse of environmental resources. Inequitable distribution of income has given entitlement to the rich segment of Indian society to use environmental resources far in excess of their needs. The economic organizations such as the Bureau of Industrial Costs and Prices and Tariff Commissions do not give any cognisance to environmental cost. The Indian corporates do not add the environmental cost to their cost of production. There is a need for these enterprises to implement ISO-14000.

Conclusion

To conclude, India has to go a long way to make its environmental policy work effectively to provide the desired results. This requires a paradigm shift in the recent thinking about environment. Reforms in the legal and constitutional provisions governing the environment, strengthening of the existing environmental framework relating to it, and a more effective approach concerning management of the different constituents of environment needs to be introduced on a war footing having to change the state of the environment. The legal mechanisms, ineffective and outdated, are marked with a plethora of counter-productive laws. The institutional mechanisms lack coordination, focus, capacity-building and relevance. They have not been able to create a mass awareness among the Indian people to treat environment as an integral part of their lives. The state of componential management of environment is shocking. The air, water and noise pollution are far above the permissible limits. The forest cover is both inadequate and decreasing. The rate of growth of population is alarming. The wastelands constitute a significant part of the total land. A poor country like India cannot afford to waste $10 billion every year caused by damage to its environment (see Annexure 8.7). All efforts are required to be made to stop any further environmental degradation. The twenty-first century and the next millennium await an environment-friendly India, requiring a paradigm shift in the environmental thinking, policy-making, its implementation and the level of general awareness of India's people about environmental problems.

REFERENCES

1. Tiwari, B.N. "Hindu Culture and Ecology" in Sharma, Gautam (Ed.), Environment, Man and Nature, Reliance, New Delhi, 1989. pp. 23-27.
2. *Ibid.*
3. *Ibid.*
4. *Ibid.*
5. *Ibid.*
6. Geeta Press, *Geeta,* Chapter XI, Gorakhpur, 1998.
7. Tiwari, B.N., *op cit,* Citing *Vishnudhamsutra,* 19.4, p. 26.
8. *Ibid.*, referring to *Skandpurana,* Chapter XIV, XV and XVII, p. 26.
9. *Ibid.*, citing *Yagyavalkya Smriti* V:227, p. 26.
10. Geeta Press, *Tulsikrit Ramayana* (1998) and *Mahabharata* (1990), Gorakhpur *Ibid,* citing *Charak Samhita, Vimanstnam,* chapter 33, Verse 11, pp. 26-27.
11. *Ibid.*, citing *Manusmriti,* Chapter 2, Verse 56, and Chapter 4, Verses 56 and 31.
12. *Ibid.*, citing Sri *Madbhagavatam,* Verse 41-43, p. 27.
13. *Ibid.*, citing *Kautilya's Arthasastra,* Adhyaksha Prachar, Chapter 2, Para 20, p. 31.
14. *Ibid.*, citing *Yjurveda,* Chapter 13, Verse 47 , p. 27.
15. Thakur, Kailash, *Environmental Protection Law and Policy in India,* Deep and Deep, New Delhi, 1997, p. 104.
16. Gupta, V.K., *Kautilyan Jurisprudence,* Delhi, 1987, pp. 155-156, as cited by Thankur, Kailash, *op cit.*, p. 174.
17. Lal, J.B., *India's Forests: Myth and Reality,* Natraj, Dehradun, 1989, pp.15-27.
18. Planning Commission (Government of India, New Delhi), *Sixth Five Year Plan* (1980-85), p. 34.
19. Planning Commission (Government of India, New Delhi), *Fourth Five Year Plan* (1969-74), p. 29.
20. Rosencraz, *et al.*, (Ed.), *Environment Law and Policy in India,* Tripathi, Bombay, 1991, p. 39.
21. Ministry of Law and Justice (Government of India, New Delhi), *The Constitution of India,* 1989, pp. 14-15.
22. *Ibid.*, p. 152.
23. Planning Commission (Government of India, New Delhi), *Sixth Five Year Plan, op. cit.*, pp. 34-35.
24. Department of Science and Technology (Government of India, New Delhi), *Report of the Committee for Recommending Legislative and Administrative Machinery for Ensuring Environment Protection,* 1980, p. 108.
25. Planning Commission (Government of India, New Delhi), *Eighth Five Year Plan,* p. 95.
26. Ministry of Environment and Forests (Government of India, New Delhi), *Policy Statement for Abatement of Pollution,* 1992.

27. Ministry of Environment and Forests (Government of India, New Delhi), *The National Conservation Strategy and Policy Statement on Environment and Development,* 1992.
28. Dwivedi, O.P., and Khator, Renu, India's Environmental Policy, Programs and Politics, in Dwivedi, O.P, and Vajpeyi, D.K., (Ed.), *Environmental Policies in the Third World,* 1995, Westport (USA), p. 66.
29. Mukherjee, S.D., Strategy for Joint Forest Management, in Kurup, V.S.P., (Ed.), *New Voices in Indian Forestry, Society for Promotion of Wastelands Development,* New Delhi, 1996, p. 78.
30. Shiva, Vandana, Conserving India's Environment, *The Indian Journal of Public Administration,* July-September 1989 (Special Number on Environment and Administration), New Delhi, p. 383.
31. Saksena, K.D., *Environmental Planning, Policies and Programmes in India,* Shipra Publications, Delhi, 1993, pp. 160-210.
32. Shrivastava, Paul, Industrial and Environmental Crises, Rethinking Corporate Social Responsibility in Fischer, Frank and Black, Michael (Ed.), *Greening Environmental Policy—The Politics of a Sustainable Future,* London, 1995, pp. 193-196.

ANNEXURE 8.1

Important Legislations (Acts) related to Environment

Legislation (Act)	*Gist of the Act*
Forest Act (1927)	This Act stipulates that no forest land or any portion thereof may be used for non-forest purposes. It provides for the constitution of any advisory committee to advise the Government on cutting the trees.
Forest (Conservation) Act (1980)	This Act has been passed to control deforestation which causes ecological imbalance and results in environmental degradation. It has provisions to put restrictions on the use of forest land for non-forest purpose.
Wild Life Protection Act (1972)	Provides for the constitution of a Wildlife Advisory Board, regulation of hunting of wild animals and birds, laying down procedures for declaring the areas as sanctuaries and national parks, and regulation of trade in wild animals.
Water (Prevention and Control of Pollution) Act (1974)	Provides for the establishment of Central and State Pollution Control Boards for the Prevention and control of water pollution. The Act seeks to control pollution primarily through standards to be laid down by the Boards and the consent orders issued by them. Stiff penalties are imposed for violation. The Boards are given ample powers for investigation and inspection and to take samples and to establish laboratories for analyzing the samples.
Air (Prevention and Control of Pollution) Act (1981)	Air pollution is to be controlled primarily through standards laid down by the Boards and for violating the provision relating to the consent by the Boards, stiff penalties have been provided.
Environment (Protection) Act (1986)	Provides for (a) covering some of the major areas of environmental hazards not covered by the existing laws; (b) linkages in handling matters of industrial and environmental safety and control mechanisms to guard against slow, insidious build up of hazardous substances, especially of new chemicals in the environment; and (c) an authority not only to coordinate the activities of the various regulatory agencies but to assume the lead role for studying, planning, and implementing long-term requirements of environmental safety and to give directions to and to coordinate a system of speedy and adequate response to emergency situations threatening the environment.

Source: Economic and Political Weekly, Mumbai, January 10, 1998.

ANNEXURE 8.2

Role, Organization and Activities of the Ministry of Environment and Forests, Government of India

The Ministry of Environment and Forests is the nodal agency in the administrative structure of the Central Government, for the planning, promotion and coordination of environmental and forestry programmes.

The main activities of the Ministry are: Conservation and survey of flora, fauna, forests and wildlife, prevention and control of pollution; and Afforestation and regeneration of degraded areas and protection of environment.

These tasks are being fulfilled through: Environmental impact assessment, eco-regeneration, assistance to organisations implementing environmental and forestry programmes; Promotion of environmental and forestry programmes; and Promotion of environmental and forestry research, extension, education and training to augment the requisite manpower, dissemination of environmental information, international cooperation and creation of environmental awareness among all sectors of the country's population.

An overview of the activities of the Ministry and its associated offices/organisations points out that the Ministry performs the following tasks: Survey of natural resources (flora and fauna and forests); Conservation of natural resources including forestry and wildlife (bio-sphere reserves, wetlands, mangroves and coral reefs, bio-diversity conservation, combating desertification, forest conservation, wildlife conservation, animal welfare); Environmental impact assessment; Prevention and control of pollution (supervision of the Central Pollution Control Board), Hazardous substances management; Regeneration and development (National River Conservation Directorate; National Afforestation and Eco-Development Board); Environmental research (National River Conservation Plan, forestry research, wildlife research, National Natural Resources Management System); Education, training and information (forestry education, training and extension, wildlife, education and training, non-formal environmental education and awareness); Environmental information; Legislation and institutional support; International cooperation; Advisory inputs; and Civil construction.

ANNEXURE 8.3

Distribution of Geographical Area and Actual Forest Cover

State/UT	*Geographical area (sq km)*	*Actual forest cover (sq. km)*			*Actual forest cover as % of geographical area*
		1993	*1995*	*1997*	
Andhra Pradesh	275068	47256	47112	43290	17.2
Arunachal Pradesh	83743	68661	68621	68602	82.0
Assam	78438	24508	24061	23924	31.2
Bihar	173877	26587	26561	26524	15.3
Goa, Daman and Diu	3814	1250	1250	1255	32.6
Gujarat	196024	12044	12320	12578	6.1
Haryana	44212	513	603	604	1.2
Himachal Pradesh	55673	12502	12501	12521	23.7
Jammu and Kashmir	222235	20443	20433	20440	9.2
Karnataka	191791	32343	32382	32403	16.9
Kerala	38863	10336	10336	10334	26.8
Madhya Pradesh	443446	135396	135164	131195	30.5
Maharashtra	307690	43859	46843	46143	14.3
Manipur	22327	17621	17558	17418	78.9
Meghalaya	22429	15769	15714	15657	70.3
Mizoram	21081	18697	18576	18775	88.7
Nagaland	16579	14348	14291	14221	86.5
Orissa	155707	47145	47107	46941	30.3
Punjab	50362	1343	1342	1387	2.7
Rajasthan	342239	13099	13280	13353	3.8
Sikkim	7096	3119	3127	3129	44.0
Tamil Nadu	130058	17726	17045	17064	13.6
Tripura	10486	5538	5538	5546	52.8
Uttar Pradesh	294411	33961	33986	33994	11.5
West Bengal	88752	8186	8276	8349	9.2
Andaman and Nicobar Islands	8249	7624	7615	7613	92.4
Chandigarh	114	5	7	5	4.4
Dadra and Nagar Haveli	491	206	204	204	42.4
Delhi	1483	22	26	26	1.5
Lakshadweep	32	NA	NA	NA	—
Pondicherry	493	NA	NA	NA	—
All India	3287263	640107	638879	633397	19.5

Source: Forest Survey of India, 1993.

ANNEXURE 8.4

Recorded Forest Area

State/UT	*Geographical area (sq km)*	*Recorded Forest Area (sq km)*	*% of forest area to geographical area*	*Population*	*Per capita Forest area (ha)*
Andhra Pradesh	275068	63726	23.2	66304664	0.10
Arunachal Pradesh	83743	51540	61.5	858392	6.00
Assam	78438	30708	39.1	22294562	0.14
Bihar	173877	29226	16.3	86338853	0.03
Chandigarh	144	31	27.2	640725	.005
Dadra and Nagar Haveli	491	207	42.2	138542	0.15
Delhi	1493	42	2.8	9370475	—
Goa, Daman & Diu	3814	1256	32.9	1270061	0.10
Gujarat	196024	19388	9.9	41174060	0.05
Haryana	44212	1687	3.9	16317715	0.51
Himachal Pradesh	55673	37591	67.7	511079	0.74
Jammu and Kashmir	222235	20174	9.1	7718700	0.26
Karnataka	191791	38646	20.2	44817396	0.09
Kerala	38863	11222	28.9	29011237	0.04
Lakshadweep	32	—	—	51681	—
Madhya Pradesh	443446	155414	35.0	66135862	0.23
Maharashtra	307690	63861	20.3	78706719	0.08
Manipur	22327	155414	67.9	1826714	0.03
Meghalaya	22429	9496	42.3	1760626	0.54
Mizoram	21081	15935	75.6	686217	2.32
Nagaland	16579	8625	52.0	1215573	0.71
Orissa	155707	59555	38.2	31512070	0.19
Punjab	58362	2842	2.5	20190795	0.01
Pondicherry	493	—	—	789416	—
Rajasthan	342231	31539	9.2	43980640	0.07
Sikkim	7096	2650	37.3	403612	0.66
Tamil Nadu	130058	22599	17.5	55638318	0.04
Tripura	10486	6292	60.0	2744827	0.23
Uttar Pradesh	294411	51502	17.5	138760417	0.04
West Bengal	88752	11379	13.4	67982732	0.02
Andaman and Nicobar	8249	7171	86.9	277989	2.58
Total	3287263	770078	23.4	843930861	0.09

Source: Forest Survey of India, 1993.

ANNEXURE 8.5

Estimates of Wastelands in India

(*Hectares*)

State/UT	*Non-forest Degraded area*	*Forest degraded Area*	*Total*
Andhra Pradesh	76.82	37.34	114.16
Assam	9.35	7.95	17.30
Bihar	38.96	15.62	59.58
Gujarat	71.53	6.83	78.36
Haryana	24.04	0.74	24.78
Himachal Pradesh	14.24	5.34	19.58
Jammu and Kashmir	5.31	10.34	15.65
Karnataka	71.22	20.43	91.65
Kerala	10.53	2.26	12.79
Madhya Pradesh	129.47	71.95	201.42
Maharashtra	115.60	28.41	144.01
Manipur	0.14	14.24	14.38
Meghalaya	8.15	11.03	19.18
Nagaland	5.08	8.78	13.86
Orissa	31.57	32.27	63.84
Punjab	11.51	0.79	12.30
Rajasthan	180.01	19.33	199.34
Sikkim	1.31	1.50	2.81
Tamil Nadu	33.92	10.09	44.01
Tripura	1.08	8.65	9.73
Uttar Pradesh	66.35	14.26	80.61
West Bengal	21.77	3.59	25.36
UTs	8.89	27.15	36.04
Total	936.91	358.89	1295.80

Source: Society for Promotion of Wasteland Development, New Delhi, 1984.

ANNEXURE 8.6

Major Environmental Costs in India

Problem	*Impact on health and/or production*	*Lowest (US$ mn)*	*Highest (US$ mn)*
Urban air pollution	Urban health impacts	517	2,102
Water Pollution (health impacts)	Urban and rural health impacts, especially diarrhoeal diseases	517	2,102
Soil degradation	Loss of agricultural output	1,516	2,362
Rangeland degradation	Loss of livestock carrying capacity	238	417
Deforestation	Loss of sustainable timber supply	183	244
Tourism	Decline in tourism revenues	142	283
Total costs of environmental degradation		5,872	13,758
Total cost (% of GDP)		2.64%	6.41%
Average cost (% of GDP)		9,716	(4.53%)

Source: Rao, P.S., "Take A Long, Deep Breath", *The Economic Times,* Hyderabad, June 12, 1998, p. 7.

9

CHANGING PUBLIC ENTERPRISE POLICY IN INDIA IN THE 1990s

Some Reflections

The 1990s has been a decade of tumultuous change. The entire economic paradigm has undergone a basic shift from Command Economy to Market Economy. The Government's role is also in a state of transition from that of a 'producer state' to a 'facilitator state'. Eventually, the Indian 'state' is likely to become a 'regulatory state'. This paradigm shift has influenced even the public enterprise policy. The 1990s have brought in their wake a sea change in the public enterprise policy.[1] Between 1947 and 1991, public enterprises proliferated in the various areas of economic activity and occupied all possible vacant spaces. Not only did they grew phenomenally in terms of numbers, but investments in these enterprises also increased substantially. About 50 per cent of the capital formation took place in public enterprises. The rate of growth of employment was about 5 per cent in these enterprises as against the national average of 1 per cent for the Indian economy. The magnitude of investments in these enterprises assumed a compound rate of growth of 15 per cent per annum. However, these enterprises turned out to be net non-savers as their financial profitability was negative. The chronic-loss making compelled the Government to change its outlook towards these enterprises. As a part of the new economic policy announced during 1991-1992 and subsequent to its continuation, the Government announced a series of measures to restructure public enterprises. This chapter proposes to first take stock of these measures and then attempt a critical analysis on their effectiveness.

Reform Measures and Public Enterprises

We present below a summary of reform measures[2] initiated to restructure and transform public enterprises during the period 1990- 2000.

Policy Measures in 1990s

Between 1990 and 1999 there have been frequent changes in the Government, barring July 1991 to June 1996 during which period a minority Government was at the helm of affairs. The year 1990 saw two governments, both of which were the by-products of coalition. During the year, the thought of employee stock ownership in public enterprises gained momentum and worker's participation in management assumed ascendancy. The concept of regulated growth in investment in public enterprise marked its emergence.

Between 1991 – 1996 the fiscal crisis reached its peak in 1991 and the Government had to approach global financial institutions for stabilisation and structural adjustment. As a part of the conditionalities imposed, the Government had to announce some important measures to restructure public enterprises.

Portfolio

It was decided to review the portfolio of public sector investments with a view to focus on strategic, hi-tech and essential infrastructure. Consequently, enterprises which were operating in competitive sectors of the economy where the private sector had registered its emphatic presence were decided to be hived off. This policy pronouncement provided a forceful hint to public enterprises to review their spectrum of activities with the objective of unloading non-core and peripheral functions. It was expected that the follow up of this measure would result in making public enterprises lean and mean. The Government felt that a selective public enterprise portfolio would bring down the transactions cost, improve the quality of control and add to the efficiency of the public enterprise system. Reference to the Board for Industrial and Financial Reconstruction (BIFR). At the beginning of the 1990s itself, a large number of public enterprises had fallen sick. They constituted about 25 per cent of the then operating public enterprises. The trends in the financial results of the remaining public enterprises revealed the likelihood of more public enterprises falling sick. The Government did not have an exit policy for public enterprises and it refrained from following the path adopted by the private sector. It, therefore, decided to use the BIFR route, which provided a fair opportunity to public enterprises to evolve suitable revival packages and implement them or else wind up with a social safety net. Unlike the private sector which throws away the baby with the bathwater, the Government suggested public enterprises to have a human face. Each enterprise was directed to formulate its own social safety net comprising voluntary retirement, and retaining and redeployment schemes for workers. The fiscal deficits did not leave much scope for public enterprise to depend on the Government for funding. The Government permitted public enterprises to access international capital markets and make forays into the Indian capital market. The partial disinvestment in public enterprises was introduced as a double-edged sword aimed to reduce, on the one hand, the fiscal deficits of the Government, and enhance the degree of 'publicness' in public enterprises, on the other, through wider participation in their shareholdings by general investing public, banks, mutual funds, workers and financial institutions.

Upgradation of Technology

For the introduction of the state-of-the-art technology, it was decided that public enterprises would be given a free hand and the funds for such upgradation would come from the disinvestment proceeds or restructuring packages approved by the global financial institutions.

Governing Boards

It was realised that strengthening the institution of the Governing Boards was necessary in order to professionalise public enterprises and make them effective business entities. A number of steps were suggested for revamp. It was decided that the number of Government nominees was not to exceed two. Further, part-time directors were expected to bring in a breath of fresh air to the public enterprises and were to have a greater say. More room was made for the representation of professionals, who were expected to provide sound business advice. The representation of different interest groups also received attention and the workers' representation on the Boards was accepted in principle.

Accountability and Autonomy

To solve this tangle, the Government emphasised the need for widening and deepening the concept of Memorandum of Understanding (MoU). It wanted the contracts to be negotiated well in advance and subsequent delegation and decentralisation of powers within the enterprise. It advocated sincere involvement of public enterprises in the formulation and implementation of MoU to thwart unnecessary public criticism on the count of public accountability, conferment of greater autonomy to these enterprises gradually over a period of time with regard to matters concerning capital expenditure, mobilisation of funds, formulation of incentive schemes, joint ventures, etc, 1997. The Janata Dal Government, during this period, initiated some important measures and made public its unambiguous stand of speeding up the disinvestment process through majority stake in shareholdings.

Disinvestment Commission

The Government set up through an executive order, the Disinvestment Commission which was responsible for reporting its scheme on the disinvestment of select public enterprises. It was also empowered, among other things, to suggest to the government the appointment of global advisors.

Navratnas and Miniratnas

In order to prepare giant public enterprises for global competition and enable them to assume the role of Indian multinationals, the Government identified 9 enterprises (namely, Bharat Heavy Electricals Limited, Steel Authority of India Limited, Mahanagar Telephone Nigam Limited, Videsh Sanchar Nigam Limited, National Thermal Power Corporation, Bharat Petroleum Corporation Ltd., Hindustan Petroleum Corporation Ltd., Indian Oil Corporation Ltd, Indian Petrochemicals Corporation Ltd., Oil and Natural Gas Corporation) as navaratnas and 97 enterprises as miniratnas, based on their record with regard to constant profitability and size of capital. Later, the list of navaratnas was extended from 9 to 11 to accommodate MTNL and VSNL. Subsequently, the number of miniratnas was scaled down from 97 to 45. The rationale behind identification of these enterprises as navaratnas and miniratnas was to increase their economic and operational autonomy in proportion to their financial and commercial success, as also to provide them special leverage to face competition in Indian and global markets by freeing them from bureaucratic and procedural hurdles.

Guidelines

The Government appointed the Vittal Committee to examine the guidelines issued to public enterprises from time to time. The Vittal Committee suggested that 762 guidelines out of the 892 issued to public enterprises be slashed. However, the Government abolished 696 guidelines.

Distribution of Dividends

The profit-making public enterprises had to declare 30 per cent of the net profits as dividends as opposed to the earlier practice of capitalising profits.

1998

The coalition Government during this year had to do a lot of tight rope walking with the left front and therefore had to adopt a mild posture with regard to off-loading public enterprises from its portfolio.

Rehabilitation Package

The Government decided to prepare rehabilitation packages for sick public enterprises to give them a chance for revival instead of going for their quiet closure/privatisation.

Redefining the Scope of the Disinvestment Commission

The Government wanted the Commission to make suggestions regarding disinvestments of only those enterprises which it referred to the Commission. The Commission was divested of its powers to recommend the names of global advisors.

1999

The rightist Government of the day is in all preparedness to accelerate the tempo of the disinvestment programme and reduce the scope of public enterprise activities in the Indian economy.

Privatisation

For the first time, during the 1990s, the Government in its budget presented to the parliament used the word 'privatisation'. The Government went all out to show its commitment to privatise public enterprises and restore the powers of the Disinvestment Commission.

Competition

The Government initiated the process of evolving a competition policy. It exhorted public enterprises to be competitive.

Salaries and Wages

While accepting the Mohan Committee report on wage revision in public enterprises, the Government left it to each and every public enterprise to examine its paying capacity to meet the burden arising out of its implementation. The Government categorised public enterprise into 3 divisions: public enterprises earning profits continuously for three years; public enterprises recording mixed performance; and public enterprises suffering from sickness. Those enterprises which were consistently earning profits could implement the revision, the mixed performance enterprises were required to take the approval of the respective ministries and the sick enterprises had to get the burden of implementation incorporated in the rehabilitation packages.

We propose below to critically evaluate the success in the implementation of these measures and assess their overall impact on the functioning of public enterprises.

2000

The Government decided to discontinue the National Renewal Fund (NRF) in its present form and place the funds required for retraining/

rehabilitation of employees who had availed VRS under the Department of Public Enterprises (DPE). The DPE would involve itself in this work from 2001-2002 with a plan fund of Rs.11.50 crore. It would be concerned with the employees of the Central Public Enterprises (CPEs). The Ministry of Labour and the Ministry of Small Scale Industries would concern themselves with the employees of State Level Public Enterprises (SLPEs).

The Committee of Secretaries decided to declare a deadline for the closure of sick non-revivable PEs and provide a window for VRS/ voluntary separation scheme (VSS), which if non-availed by a worker would entitle him to the normal retrenchment compensation.

In the budget presented to the Parliament for the fiscal year 2000-2001, the Government decided to bring down its equity in all non-strategic PEs to 26 per cent or lower, if necessary. The Government further announced that the entire receipts from disinvestment and privatisation will be used for meeting expenditure in social sectors, restructuring of PEs and retiring public debt.

Reform Measures—Impact on P.E. Performance

Critics say that economic reforms have eluded public enterprise. They assert that the sequencing of economic reforms was not in order. Quoting the experience of reform exercises carried out in other countries, they opine that economic reforms in India should have begun with the restructuring of public enterprises. They suggest that having public enterprises in the first phase of economic reforms, we should not commit the lapse of not including it in the second wave of economic reforms, which is likely to be initiated during 1999 - 2000. Giving due regard to this valid criticism, we now present an assessment of the success of the various measures initiated as a part of public enterprise policy during 1990-1999 and assess their impact on public enterprises.

Portfolio

The public enterprise portfolio has not suffered any setback as the various governments in power from time to time have lacked willingness to divest themselves of certain public enterprises. It must be stated that coalition politics has been a major limiting factor.

Though certain enterprises have been identified for closure, the Government's inaction has resulted in their perpetuation. This callousness has affected the morale of the workers and the managerial force might result in the realisation of non-optimal revenues from the sale for the State. However, public enterprises have indirectly benefited from this policy measure. A large number of public enterprises have been practicing cold privatisation. They are divesting themselves of unimportant activities such as maintenance of a fleet of vehicles, contracting out canteens, etc.

Reference to BIFR

As on 31.03.1998, 62 industrial public enterprises, whose net worth had become negative, were registered with the BIFR. Of these, 32 were the sick, taken-over units, accounting for 50 per cent of the total registered cases with the BIFR. The BIFR approved the revival package in respect of 21 public enterprises, of which two enterprises, namely Bicco Lawrie Limited and Mica Trading Corporation Limited, have turned around, and one enterprise, namely Damodar Cements and Slags, has been divested. In the case of the remaining 18 enterprises, the revival schemes approved by the BIFR, are at different stages of implementation. The BIFR recommended winding up in respect of 9 public enterprises, of which in the case of the Ujjain Pipe and Foundry Company Limited of the Indian Iron and Steel Company, the High Court of Kolkata has passed the order for winding up and an official liquidator has taken possession of the assets and records of the company. The other cases are before various authorities such as the concerned High Courts and the appellate authorities. The BIFR has also issued winding up notice in respect of 4 subsidiaries of the National Textiles Corporation. In two cases, where revival packages were already sanctioned, the BIFR reopened as their implementation could not be proceeded with. These were the Industrial Drugs and Pharmaceuticals Limited and the Orissa Drugs and Pharmaceuticals Limited. In the case of the Nagaland Pulp and Paper Company Limited and the Bharath Immunologicals Limited, applications for registration were dismissed by the BIFR as they were found to be non-maintainable. The BIFR has not been able to take quick action with regard to the formulation of the rehabilitation packages and maintainability of cases due to several handicaps. It is advisable to set up a separate authority to deal with the cases of sickness in public enterprises. This authority could probably be named the 'Public Enterprise Turn Around Board'.

Mobilisation of Funds, Disinvestments and Public Participation

Under the new economic dispensation, public enterprises are reducing their dependence on Government funding. Instead of assistance and budgetary support they are now approaching national and international capital markets. The infusion of Government equity and debt add up to 4 per cent of the total investments in public enterprises as opposed to about 15 per cent earlier. The internal resources and the extra budgetary sources now fund about 70 per cent of the annual incremental funding needs. For working capital support, public enterprises are reducing their dependence on the medium-term loans from the Government and approaching commercial banks and the all-India development banks. The floatation of commercial paper is catching up with public enterprises. Some public enterprises have conducted road shows for mobilising funds abroad through their eligibility under the external commercial borrowings provisions approved by the Government from time to time. More and more public enterprises are getting listed on stock exchanges. Between 1991-92 and 1999-2000, disinvestments yielded Rs. 20,698 crore against the target of Rs. 48,320 crore. In 2000-2001, the Government has so far (up to February 28, 2001) realised around Rs. 677.50 crore by selling out its stake in Modern Foods to Hindustan Lever Limited and Bharat Aluminium Company Ltd. to Sterlite Industries Ltd. The target for 2000-2001 is Rs. 10,000 crore. The Government's new strategy of disinvestment centres around identifying strategic buyers who could eventually take over the ownership and control of PEs. The Government employed some new interesting concepts such as special purpose vehicles, and cross holdings. These, in effect, meant realisation of funds from public enterprises through book adjustments and paper entries, giving no heed to the suggestion that mobilisation of funds through disinvestment should be coming from the market place. As a result, one of the objectives of disinvestment that of widening the share ownership and strengthening the capital market could not be achieved. The Disinvestment Commission's performance presents a discouraging picture. None of its several reports has drawn the attention of the Government. Its recommendations concerning professionalisation of the Boards, provision for elected directors, selection of top managerial personnel, autonomy in price fixation, accountability, setting up of a pre-investigation board, strengthening the investor interface have been put in the cold storage.

Upgradation of Technology

To become global giants, it is necessary that public enterprises acquire new technologies and brands. Unfortunately, there is hardly any enterprise which can boast of uniqueness of its brand, the development of which requires a long time and huge investments. The R&D expenditure in public enterprises has not improved in terms of the ratio of R&D expenses to the total revenues earned. Further, the studies on total factor productivity show that the contribution of technology in the growth of productivity has remained marginal. One of the ways to keep up-to-date with technology is to promote tie-ups and joint ventures with the technology leaders. BHEL has been trying to have such an agreement with leading technology firms concerning its various products.

Governing Boards

Despite the Government's announcement of its best intention of according the rightful place to the governing boards, little has been done on that front. Several enterprises have remained 'topless'. The several positions of the functional directors have not been filled up, and the tenures of the directors have remained awfully short. Further, the appointments on the Board have not been expertise based. The Boards were not empowered to fill up the vacant positions and appoint various top functionaries. The positions of non-official directors continue to remain unfilled in respect of atleast 22 miniratnas. The Search Committee has selected non-official directors in 15 miniratnas, but the final list is still being processed in the concerned ministries/ departments. Their powers continue to be regulated by the Articles of Association and the Memorandum of Association. The boards in public enterprises have yet to provide any evidence that they realise the importance of corporate governance. No public enterprise board has presented so far an evaluation of its functioning by a third agency.

Accountability and Autonomy

The MoU was introduced to iron out the conflict between accountability and autonomy. However, the expected results have not fructified. On the part of the Government, its lack of will to provide due support to public enterprises in order to enable them achieve the various targets set for the financial year has come in the way of the success of the MoU system. On the part of the public enterprises, their lack of sincerity reflected by their lack of will to share the relevant information, has failed this new instrument. Though, a large number of public enterprises have been awarded an 'A' grade subsequent to the fulfilment of targets set out in MoUs, the total factor productivity has not registered any noticeable change. The initiation of measures such as navratnas and miniratnas have also fallen short of expectations, as the good intentions of the DPE have been countered more than once by the concerned administrative ministries. To add to the woes, even the navaratna package does not provide any evidence of the Government's intention of loosening its control. The newly constituted governing boards of navaratna enterprises have retired civil servants as part-time directors. Some officials have found a place on the governing boards of more than one navaratna. Surprisingly, the Government, even after the announcement of this autonomy measure in 1996, has not been able to complete the process of formation of the miniratna boards by filling up all positions.

Privatisation

The Government announced its intention of wholesale privatisation in its budget presented to the Parliament in February 1999. While doing this it did not provide a timeframe and its scheme of prioritisation. Thoughtless privatisation is likely to create severe repercussions for the Indian economy. It is necessary that the French model of privatisation is studied in detail and some salient characteristics of the model, such as establishment of a Statutory Privatisation Commission and formulating a calendar for privatisation, is adopted. The Government has displayed its ill intentions of not legitimising the process of disinvestment through an enactment. The half-hearted implementation of the Mohan Committee Report is yet another indication as to how the Government has mishandled reforms in public enterprises. Its lip-sympathy to the cause of introduction of a safety net for workers bidding adieu to public enterprises is another example of its casual approach to public enterprise reforms.

The lack of consistency of the various governments as depicted in the Chart 9.1 entitled "The Effects of Coalition Politics on Public Enterprise Activity" provides strong evidence that public enterprise reforms have yet to take off in the country.

Chart 9.1 : The Effects of Coalition Politics on Public Enterprise Activity

S. No.	*Name of the Govt. Policy Initiative*	*Congress (I) (1991-96)*	*United Front(D) (1996-97)*	*United Front (G) (1997-98_*	*Bharatiya Janata Party {1998-to-date)*
1.	**Public Enterprise(PE) Portfolio**	Select divestment	Reduction of portfolio to a bare minimum	Select divestment	Complete divestment
2.	**Boards of Directors**	Professionalisation of Boards	Induction of industrialists/ general interests	Continuation of domination of bureaucrats	Bigger role to Public Enterprise Sèlection Board and pruning the role of vigilance agencies in the appointment of directors.
3.	**Chief Executive Officer**	Appointment for 5 years	Toplessness in PEs	Long tenures for CEO	Mixed Policy of uncertain and long tenures
4.	**Memorandum of Understanding (MoU)**	Introduction of MoU as performance monitoring mechanism	Continuation of Congress(I) policy without rewards and punishment	UF(D) policy continued	UF(D) policy continued
5.	**Disinvestment**	Partial disinvestment and announcement of a full-fledged statutory commission on Disinvestment reduced the role of Government functionaries and bureaucrats.	Majority-stake disinvestment; appointment of Disinvestment Commission with executive powers only	UF(D) policy continued	Majority-stake disinvestment with Special Purpose Vehicle/Trusts and preference to internal investors. The Government established Department of Disinvestment to speed up the process of disinvestment.

Chart 9.1 (*contd.*)

S. No.	*Name of the Govt. Policy Initiative*	*Congress (I) (1991-96)*	*United Front(D) (1996-97)*	*United Front (G) (1997-98)*	*Bharatiya Janata Party (1998-to-date)*
6.	**Closure of Sick Units**	Closure of continuous cash-loss making PEs	Closure of units approved by the Board for Industrial and Financial Reconstruction (BIFR)	Uncertain about its stand on closure of sick PEs	Hastening the pace of closure of sick units
7.	**Navaratnas and Mini-ratnas**	No identification of enterprises to be treated on different footing	Identification of Navaratnas (11 PEs) and Miniratnas (97 PEs) subsequently reduced to 45 PEs	Continuation of UF(D) policy without the initiation of relevant measures	Restructuring of Navaratna/ Miniratna PE Boards.
8.	**Government intervention through guidelines**	Continue such intervention	Deletion of irrelevant guidelines	892 guidelines reduced to about 130.	UF(G) policy continued
9.	**Reduction of Budgetary Support**	General policy of reduction of budgetary support	Introduction of element of selectivity in the general reduction of budgetary support	UF(D) policy continued	UF (D) policy continued while Government expenditure being stepped up to overcome recession
10.	**De-monopoli-sation**	Continuation of monopoli-sation of PEs in certain sectors	Selective de-monopolisa-tion in sectors such as power, telecommuni-cation banking and finance, transport, etc.	UF(D) policy continued	Massive demonopolisation of PEs
11.	**Globalisation**	Economic liberalisation in PEs	Did not take relevant measures for globalisation such as changing of Articles of Association of PEs,	Policy of UF(D) continued	Policy of UF(G) continued

Chart 9.1 (*contd.*)

S. No.	*Name of the Govt. Policy Initiative*	*Congress (I) (1991-96)*	*United Front(D) (1996-97)*	*United Front (G) (1997-98)*	*Bharatiya Janata Party (1998-to-date)*
			amendment of Article 12 of the Indian Constitution, reduction of multiple audits, etc.		
12.	**Internal Restructuring**	Commercialisation of PEs and programme to corporatise and privatise PEs were announced but no freedom to purchase goods, hire and fire employees, etc., was extended	Heavy subsidies to consumers of PE goods continued although public enterprise policy was framed in favour of commercialisation and corporatisation	Onslaughts on PEs of UF(D)	Onslaughts on PEs of UF(G) continued

To conclude, the changing policy with regard to public enterprises has not had the desired success as it has lacked continuity and involvement of both the Government and the Public Enterprise system and as a consequence it has provided sub-optimal results.

NOTES

1. Department of Public Enterprises (Ministry of Heavy Industries and Public Enterprises, Government of India), Working Group Meeting for Tenth Five Year Plan on Public Sector Reforms and Privatisation, January 2001, New Delhi, pp. 5-16.
2. *Public Enterprise Survey,* Volume 1, Department of Public Enterprises (Ministry of Heavy Industries and Public Enterprises, Government of India), 1998-99, New Delhi, pp. 2-3.

10

SECURITISATION

A New Instrument for Financial Sector Reforms

Concept of Securitisation

Securitisation is the buzzword in today's World of Finance. Though, it is not a new financial development in the developed economies, it is certainly a new concept for the emerging markets such as India. The technique of securitisation holds a great promise for a developing country like India. Securitisation is "Structured Project Finance". This financial instrument is structured or tailored to the risk-return and maturity needs of the investors. The popular use of the term Structured Finance in today's financial world is to refer to such financing instruments where the financer does not look at the entity as a risk, but tries to align the financing to specific cash accruals of the borrower. The present-day meaning of securitisation is a blend of two forces: Structured Project Finance and Capital Markets. The process of securitisation creates the strata of risk-return and different maturity securities that is marketable into the capital markets as per the needs of the investors.

History of Securitisation

The history of securitisation depends upon what is the meaning of securitisation adopted. However, in the sense in which it is understood presently i.e. structured finance, the securitization developed in the United States (US) real estate financing market and from there it spread not only all over the world but to diverse applications also. However, in Europe, a form of Mortgage funding has existed for a long number of years which has remarkable similarities to the present form of securitization though the two are not the same. The instrument has existed in Denmark for more than 200 years. Likewise, the instrument has a long history in Germany.

The US is the biggest market of Securitisation in terms of volume, application and participation. A financial instrument was developed with an urge to create a secondary market in mortgage financing. The catalysts in the process formed Government agencies for buying and selling federally insured mortgages. The history of the US Government efforts to introduce a secondary market in mortgages goes to 1934 when the National Housing Act created the Federal Housing Administration (FHA). The FHA insured housing loans made by private lenders and thus absorbed the inherent risks in housing finance. In 1938, the Federal National Mortgage Association was created to buy and sell federally insured mortgages. In 1968, the erstwhile Federal National Mortgage Association (FNMA) was split into two separate bodies—a new FNMA and the Government National Mortgage Association (GNMA).

In 1970, GNMA did its first securitization transaction on a "Pass Through" structure. GNMA pass through were securities backed by Mortgage insured by FHA. These pass through had the full credit and the backing of the US Government, since GNMA had guarantee both the repayment of principal and timely payment of interest. The 1970 programme (GNMA-I) is still in operation. In 1983, GNMA launched another pass through programme called GNMA-II. These programme are further classified based on the type of mortgages pooled therein, such as single family loans, mobile home loans, project loans, etc.

Though the FNMA was the oldest of all the US Government agencies, it was the last to enter the securitisation market. In 1968, the original FNMA was split into a new FNMA and GNMA. FNMA is privately owned with its stock quoted on the New York Stock Exchange. However, due to an implicit support from the US Government and historical affiliations with the Government, the credit standing of FNMA is seen to be better than private corporations, however, slightly inferior to that of the Government agencies like GNMA. The first FNMA mortgage backed securities (MBS) was issued in 1981. The agency played a crucial role in promoting securitization of adjustable rate mortgages and variable rate mortgages.

Need for Securitisation

The market size per investor comes down as the number of investor goes on increasing. The small investor is not a professional investor. His basic requirement is to invest in an instrument, which is easy to understand, and is easily liquidatable. This need of the investor, innovated into a new financial instrument is known as "Securitisation". Securitised Instruments are preferred for a number of reasons as explained below.

Borrowers require high amount of capital: This is clearly outside the range of the small investors. This difficulty was sorted out by the financial intermediation of the Bank/Financial Institutions (FIs) where the bank would pool the resources of the investors savings and in turn they lead the capital pooled to the borrowers.

Small investor is not a professional investor: The small investor understands homogeneous, liquid, easy to understand and market tradable instrument. The importance of liquidity is high for the small investor. FIs cannot liquidate the investment directly to the investor in a small run as this would definitely lead to asset-liability mismatch. Thus, an easy to understand homogeneous financial instrument with easy liquidity features holds a great promise in the world of finance. Moreover a credit rating label on such a Financial Instrument increases the investors' confidence in such an investment.

The Instrument possess a greater economic significance: Securitisation tends to eliminate fund-based intermediation. The intermediary in the process turns down to a specialized service oriented firm and thus charges some reasonable fees, which is lower than the fund based intermediation costs as detailed below:

- Securitisation encourages savings the investors gets best benefits by investing in securitised paper.
- Securitisation changes the roles of the financial intermediary from a fund-based activity to a service based activity. A service-oriented market is more efficient than a fund based market.
- Securitisation diversifies risk by creating different tranches in the transaction.
- Securitisation focuses on the use of the resources and not their ownership. The investors does not look at the originator, but his interest lies in the performance of the asset.

Features of Securitisation

As a new financial instrument, securitization is characterized by a myriad special features:

1. *Homogeneous Products:* The securitised instrument is designed in a homogeneous quantity and market acceptable lot.
2. *Marketability and Merchantable Quality:* The Instrument is homogeneous market acceptable lot and as it generally consists of the rating label, it is merchantable quality also. For Merchantable Quality the instrument should also possess the feature of the wide distribution also.
3. *Special Purpose Vehicle (SPV):* The instrument is issued by a SPV, the structure of the SPV is designed in such a manner that the SPV remains "Bankruptcy Remote" from the Originator. Thus the Investors Beneficial Interest is protected in this manner.
4. *Recourse:* Securitisation is an asset based structured financing concept. The investors holds the beneficial interest in the assets so it should be a non-resource featured. Limited Recourse is done by the Originator to enhance the credit rating of the transaction.
5. *Issue Features:* The following types of firms could resort to securitization:

   (i) Real Estate Finance Companies,
   (ii) Auto Finance Companies,
   (iii) Credit Card Companies,
   (iv) Hoteliers,
   (v) Power Generating and Telecom Companies,
   (vi) Banks, and
   (vii) Infrastructure Project Companies like Toll Road Companies.

6. *Investors:* Most of the Investors in the securitised instruments are professionalised Investors which include FIs, Mutual Funds, High Net Worth Investors, etc.

Forms and Process of Securitisation

There are two Forms of Securitization: (i) Pass Through Structure and (ii) Pay Through Structure.

The Pass Through Structure has to follow the following implementational path:

- Investors get a proportional interest in pool of receivables,
- Monthly Collections are divided proportionally among the Investors,
- All the investors receive proportional payments—no slower or faster payments,
- Refinement can be done in the form of 'Senior' or 'Junior' investors to enhance the credit rating of the transaction,
- Pre-payments are passed on to the Investors, and
- No reinvestment of cash collected.

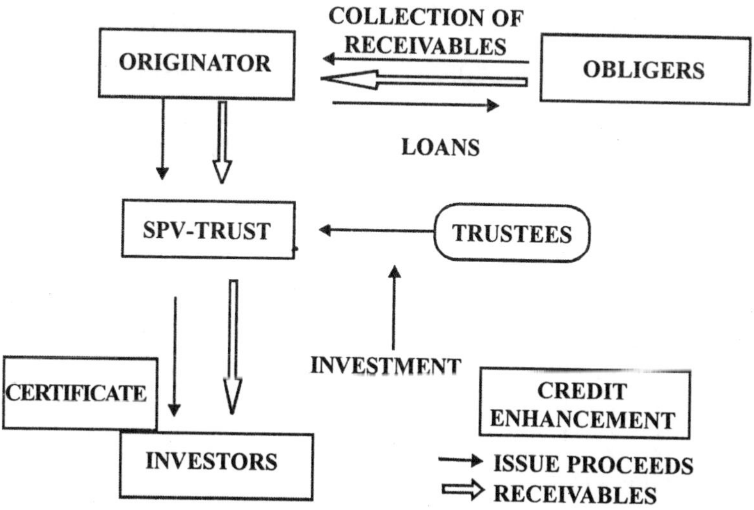

Diagram 10.1 : Implementation Path for Pass Through Structure

Pay Through Structure

The Pay Through Structure follows the below-mentioned implementational path:

- Investors get a proportional interest in pool of receivables,
- SPV reinvests the amount collected generally in a AAA rated paper (Guaranteed Investment),

- Investors are serviced on the dates of the schedule payment, the payment for this is released from the Receiving and the Paying Bank Account,
- Pre-payments are reinvested in the Guaranteed Investment Paper, and
- SPV is an active conduit.

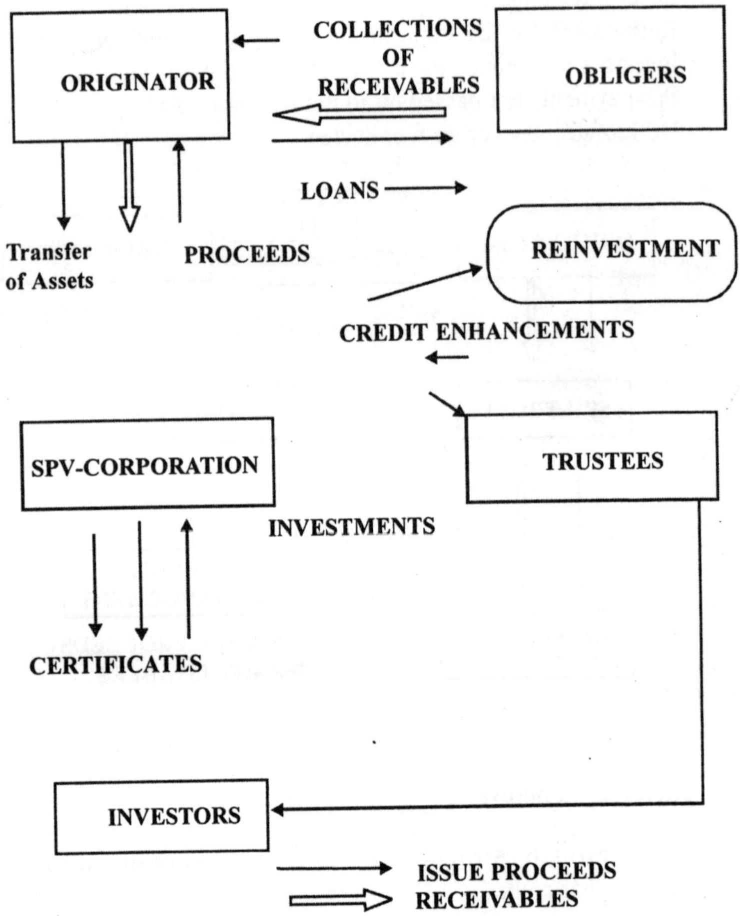

Diagram 10.2 : Implementation Path for Pay Through Structure

The process of securitisation is operationally very easy. Assets are originated by company, and funded on that company's balance sheet. This company is normally referred to as the "Originator". Once a suitably large portfolio of assets has been originated, the assets are analysed as a portfolio, and then sold or assigned to a third party which is normally a special purpose vehicle company (an "SPV") formed for the specific purpose of funding the assets. The SPV is sometimes owned by a trust, or even, on occasions, by the Originator. Administration of the assets is then sub-contracted back to the Originator by the SPV.

The SPV issues tradable "securities" to fund the purchase of the assets. The performance of these securities is directly linked to the performance of the assets and there is no recourse (other than in the vent of breach of contract) back to the Originator.

Investors purchase the securities, because they are satisfied (normally by relying upon a rating) that the securities will be paid in full and on time from the cash flows available in the asset pool. A considerable amount of time is spent considering the different likely performances of the asset pool, and the implications of defaults by borrowers on the corresponding performance of the securities. The proceeds upon the sale of the securities are used to pay the Originator.

The SPV agrees to pay any surpluses which arise during its funding of the assets back to the Originator, which means that the Originator, for all practical purposes, retains its existing relationships with the borrowers and all of the economies of funding the assets (i.e. the Originator continues to administer the portfolio, and continues to receive the economic benefits (profits) of owning the assets). As cash flows arise on the assets, these are used by the SPV to repay funds to the investors in the securities.

The process in general can be described to consist of the following stages:

— The process begins when the lender (or originator) segregates loans/lease/receivables into pools which are relatively homogeneous in regard to types of credit, maturity and interest rate risk.
— The pools of assets are then transferred to a Special Purpose Vehicle (SPV) usually constituted as a trust. The originator may

float the SPV as a subsidiary in the form of a limited company. Another option could be for the SPV to be floated jointly by the originator/individuals/banks/institutions who are interested in the securitisation deal.

— Based on these, the SPV issues asset backed securities in the form of debt, certificates of beneficial ownership and other instruments. The securities issued may be with or without recourse.
— Interest and principal payments on the loans, leases and receivables in the underlying pool of assets are collected by the servicer (who could also be the originator) and transmitted to the investors.
— Credit enhancement can add features to boost investor confidence. This could be in the form of a provision of recourse, a guarantee requiring the originator to cover losses, a letter of credit from a bank, or over collateralisation.

There could be three basic methods of transfer of assets:

— Novation,
— Assignment, and
— Sub-participation.

Novation is the clearest way of selling a loan and effectively transferring both the rights and obligations. In novation, the existing loan between originator and borrower is cancelled and a new agreement between the investor and borrower is substituted. The buyer steps into the shoes of the original lender or seller who ceases to have any obligations to the borrower. The loan is, therefore, excluded from the balance sheet of the seller.

An assignment transfers from the seller to buyer, all rights to principal and interest. Assignments for the purpose of disposing of assets may fall into two basic legal categories. The first is statutory assignment, transferring both legal and beneficial title. A statutory assignment will pass and transfer from the seller to the buyer all the legal rights to principal and interest. In most cases, it will also pass on all the legal remedies available against the borrower to ensure discharge of debt. In other words, the buyer acquires the full legal and beneficial interest in the loan. The second is equitable assignment, transferring only beneficial title. It does not transfer legal rights. Thus, a buyer may not be able to proceed directly against a borrower. The seller must be joined in action. However, the seller is not liable for debt.

Sub-participation does not transfer any of the seller's rights, remedies or obligations against the borrower to the buyer. But, it is an entirely separate, back-to-back, non-recourse funding arrangement, under which the buyer places funds with the seller. In return, the seller passes on to the buyer, payments under the underlying loan, which the borrower makes to him. But, the loan itself is not transferred.

Securitisation in India

Available data indicates that ICICI had securitised assets to the tune of Rs. 2,750 crore in its books as at the end of March 1999. Assets to the tune of Rs. 1,200 crore was in the process of being bought over up to end of FY-1998-99. CRISIL is reported to have rated about 1,200 crore of securitised transactions up to 1998. In addition, there have been several unrated transactions.

The first widely reported securitisation deal in India dates back to 1990 when Citibank securitised auto loans and placed a paper with GIV mutual fund. Since then, a variety of deals have been undertaken. Asset classes chosen have concentrated mostly on auto and hire purchase receivables of NBFCs. According to some estimates, 35 per cent of all securitisation deals between 1992 and 1998 related to hire purchase receivables of trucks and the rest towards other auto/ transport segment receivables.

Apart from these, some innovative deals have been struck. Earlier, in 1994-95, SBI Cap structured an innovative deal where a pool of future cash flows of high value customers of Rajasthan State Industrial and Development Corporation was securitised. An oil monetisation deal has been structured where the future flows of oil receivables accruing to a company was securitised. Real estate developers have securitised receivables arising out of instalment sales. The recent securitisation deal of Larsen & Tubro has opened a new vista for financing power projects. The deal was a securitisation of lease receivables even before the plant was completed. Thus, this securitisation deal financed even the asset creation.

National Housing Bank (NHB) has made efforts to structure the pilot issue of mortgage backed securities (MBS) within the existing legal, fiscal and regulatory framework. Under the proposed transaction, mortgage debt shall be transferred/assigned/sold to NHB by Housing Finance Companies (HFC) (originator) pursuant to an agreement/ contract in the 'debt simplicitor form'. NHB will act as an issuer of pass through certificates (PTCs) and as a trustee on behalf of the investors. There is a view that there will be a conflict of interest if NHB, a regulator also acts as a trustee. However, as stated in the RBI discussion paper on universal banking, the ownership, regulatory and supervisory framework of the development financial institutions are under review.

On the basis of the Indian experience, the following features of securitisation appear noteworthy.

1. Most deals have involved the transfer of beneficial interest on the asset and not the legal title.
2. Most transactions have followed the pass-through mechanism.
3. In fact, many transactions have followed the escrow mechanism where receivables are transferred to an escrow account for payment to the buyer.
4. According to Duff & Phelps India, a rating agency, past deals have mostly been direct purchases of receivables by institutions and bigger NBFCs.
5. Routing the transaction through a Special Purpose Vehicle is yet to gain popularity.
6. There appears to be no secondary market for securitized debt.
7. The market is unregulated and lacks transparency in terms of volume, price, parties to the transaction, etc.
8. The settlement procedures are not clear.
9. There are no standard accounting and valuation norms.

Future Prospects of Securitisation in India

Since late eighties, when securitization made its beginning in India, the number as well as the size of transactions has grown over the years. This trend is likely to continue and the market would witness considerable growth in the coming years. Currently the annual disbursement of truck loans is estimated to be around Rs. 21,000 crore and the same for the car loans has been estimated to be around Rs. 23,000 crore. The outstanding housing loans to individuals as of now are estimated to be around Rs. 20,000 crore. These figures are indicative of the volume of securitization that is possible. It would help in the development of the ABS (Asset Based Securities) market particularly the mortgage backed securities (MBS) market, if some incentives are given to these instruments in the form of fiscal incentives like tax concessions. For example, MBS could be declared as eligible investments by provident funds and pension funds and could be declared as Infrastructure Bonds. The question of stamp duty continues to perplex the minds of the financial sector managers and the policy makers.

So far, companies have securitized assets to raise funds without adding to borrowings. This helped companies which had high debt equity ratio. The motivating factor in some securitization transaction in the past was the ability to book profits upfront. While these could continue to be demanded drivers for securitization. Securitization is likely to be increasingly used for better asset liability management. As securitization replaces long to medium term assets by cash, the weighted average maturity of assets of the company comes down. This is a big comfort, as typically, Non-Banking Finance Companies (NBFCs) were funding three-year assets with one year fixed deposits. Further, the NBFCs which are required to bring down the excess deposit level could use the proceeds of securitization to retire the fixed deposits.

Traditionally in the fund business segment of the financial services sector in India a single entity was engaged in the entire gamut of activities viz., raising funds, locating borrowers, credit appraisal of the borrowers, servicing of the loans and recovery. Owing to the rapidly changing environment, some kind of realignment is likely to happen in this sector. One could see some specializations emerging in the market. In developed economies, particularly in the mortgage market, there is a lot of specialization. Typically in these markets a single entity could not perform more than one or two of the activities mentioned earlier. This is also in line with the increasing emphasis on "core competence". Instead of an entity engaging in all the activities, it makes sense to focus on a few areas where it has competitive advantage.

The trend is already visible in the auto loan sector. Owing to many regulatory changes, many NBFCs are finding it difficult to raise funds at competitive rates. These NBFCs, however, have a relatively low cost distribution network in place to originate and service loans. On the other hand, large companies and Foreign Banks find that it is not economical to create a large distribution network in terms of extensive branch network across the country due to their high cost structure. However, these companies, given their size, parent support, managerial talent and a high credit rating have a much stronger funding capability.

Securitization could be effectively used to combine these two complementary pool of resources. NBFCs could originate loans and securities them and sell to large companies. And they could use the proceeds of the sale to originate more loans and the process could go on. The small NBFCs could continue to service the loans which would ensure a steady flow of fee income.

While many transactions are under way in the auto loan sector, this trend has also extended to housing sector also. In housing finance the funding required is of a much longer tenure and thus far more difficult to raise.

Benefits From and Limitations Of Securitisation

Securitisation is designed to offer the following advantages to the seller, investor and debt markets.

(i) For seller or originator, securitisation mainly results in receivables being replaced by cash thereby improving the liquidity position. It removes the assets from the balance sheet of the originator, thus liberating capital for other uses, and enabling restructuring of the balance sheet by reducing large exposures or sectoral concentration. It facilitates better asset liability management by reducing market risks resulting from interest rate mismatches. The process also enables the issuer to recycle assets more frequently and thereby improve earning. Finally, transparency may be improved since securitisation results in identifiable assets in the balance sheet.

(ii) For investor, securitisation essentially provides an avenue for relatively risk-free investment. The credit enhancement provides an opportunity to investors to acquire good quality assets and to diversify their portfolios.

(iii) It also provides opportunity for matching cash flows and managing ALM since a securitised instrument carries regular monthly cash flows and has varying maturities. The prevalence of secondary markets would offer liquidity.

(iv) From the point of view of the financial system as a whole, securitisation increases the number of debt instruments in the market, and provides additional liquidity in the market. It also facilitates unbundling, better allocation and management of project risks. It could widen the market by attracting new players on account of superior quality assets being available.

Conclusion

Securitisation could go a long way in transforming financial sector in India by enhancing liquidity and profitability of the institutions in this stage of liberalisation, on the one hand, and reducing the cost of capital for the Indian corporate and individual borrowers, on the other. It would also help solve the problem of Mini-Performing Assets of the Indian banks which are almost Rs. 80,000 crore. The Government should take appropriate steps to remove legal hurdles and also the stamp duty and the firms resorting to the securitisation should ensure that the securitised assets have necessary characteristics for the purpose.

BIBLIOGRAPHY

Agrawal, R.C., *State Enterprises in India,* Book, Allahabad, Chaitanya Publishing House, 1961.

Appa Rao B., *Small Enterprise Promotion in Andhra Pradesh—Role of Andhra Pradesh State Financial Corporation.*

Adiseshiah, Malcolm S., *Privatisation and State Enterprises,* Calcutta, IIM, 1989.

Andhra Pradesh. Bureau of Economics and Statistics, *Book Report on the Performance of State Public Sector Non-Departmental Undertakings for the Years 1982-83 to 1985-86 in Andhra Pradesh,* Hyderabad, 1989.

Andhra Pradesh. Bureau of Economics and Statistics, *Brochure on Public Sector Undertakings Andhra Pradesh*: Owned, Managed and with Shares by the Government of Andhra Pradesh 1969-71 and 1970-71, Hyderabad, 1973.

Andhra Pradesh. Bureau of Economics and Statistics, *Public Sector Undertakings in Andhra Pradesh*: Owned, Managed and with Shares by Government of Andhra Pradesh 1967-68 and 1968-69, Hyderabad, 1973.

Andhra Pradesh. Department of Public Enterprises, *Andhra Pradesh State Public Enterprises: Performance 1988-89,* Hyderabad, Department of Public Enterprises, 1989.

Andhra Pradesh. Department of Public Enterprises, *Andhra Pradesh State Public Enterprises: Performance 1991-92,* Hyderabad, Department of Public Enterprises, 1992.

Andhra Pradesh. Department of Public Enterprises, *Andhra Pradesh Public Enterprises: Performance 1992-93,* Hyderabad, Department of Public Enterprises, n.d.

Andhra Pradesh. Department of Public Enterprises, *Andhra Pradesh State Public Enterprises Performance 1990-91,* Hyderabad, Department of Public Enterprises, n.d., Gratis.

Andhra Pradesh. Department of Public Enterprise, *Andhra Pradesh State Public Enterprises : Performance 1989- 90,* Hyderabad, n.p.

Assam. Department of Public Enterprises, *Annual Report of State Public Enterprises in Assam 1980-81 to 1986-87,* Guwahati, Assam Government Press, 1990.

Andhra Pradesh. Department of Public Enterprises, *Background Papers for Draft White Paper on Public Enterprises,* Hyderabad, DPE, 1989.

Andhra Pradesh. Department of Public Enterprises, *Andhra Pradesh State Public Enterprises Performance 1987-88,* Hyderabad, Government Central Press, 1989.

Andhra Pradesh. Department of Public Enterprises. Andhra Pradesh State Public Enterprises: Performance 1988-89, Hyderabad, Department of Public Enterprises, 1989.

Andhra Pradesh. Department of Public Enterprises. Andhra Pradesh State Public Enterprises: Performance 1991-92, Hyderabad, Department of Public Enterprises, 1992.

Andhra Pradesh Industrial Development Corporation Limited: Projects under implementation.

Andhra Pradesh. Public Enterprise Management Board, Andhra Pradesh State Public Enterprises, Performance during 1985-86, Hyderabad, PENB, 1986.

Andhra Pradesh Public Enterprises, *Andhra Pradesh Public Enterprises Report on Performance* 1997-98, Govt. Public Enterprise, 1998.

Andhra Pradesh Public Enterprises, *Andhra Pradesh Public Enterprises Report on Performance* 1998-99, Hyderabad, PEMB AP, 1999.

Andhra Pradesh. Public Enterprises Management Board. *Andhra Pradesh State Public Enterprises: Performance during 1985-86,* Hyderabad, Secretariat Press, n.d.

Andhra Pradesh. Public Enterprises Management Board. *Performance of A.P. State Public Enterprises During 1985-86.* Hyderabad, n.d.

Andhra Pradesh Public Enterprises Management Board, *Andhra Pradesh State Public Enterprises: Performance during 1986-87,* Hyderabad, n.d.

Andhra Pradesh. Public Enterprise Management Board, *Andhra Pradesh State Public Enterprises:Performance During 1986-87,* Hyderabad, n.d.

Andhra Pradesh Public Enterprise Management Board, *Andhra Pradesh State Public Enterprises:Performance During 1984-85,* Hyderabad, n.d.

Andhra Pradesh Public Enterprise Management Board, *Andhra Pradesh State Public Enterprises: Performance during 1985-86,* Hyderabad, PENB, 1986.

Andhra Pradesh, *State Level Conference of Public Enterprises* 11th April 1988, Technical Session-1: Background Papers.

Babu Dev_N.D.R.A.M., State level public sector reforms status and case studies, *IPE Journal,* Vol. 23 No. 1&2, April-June; 2000.

Basu S.K. and Sarkar A. and Sinha H.N., *Report on the Monetary and Non-Monetary Work Incentives in Public Enterprises of West Bengal,* Calcutta, Book Exchange, 1971.

Batra, Satish K. (Ed.) and Jain, Tej K. (Ed.)., *State Enterprises—The Emerging Scenario,* Jaipur, Printwell Publishers, 1988.

Bhanu Prasad Committee, *Management of State Level Public Enterprises, Report.*

Barua, R.K., Development and performance of SLPES in Eastern western in India, *IPE Journal,* Vol. 11 No 2, April-June; 1988.

Bhambhri, C.P., *Parliamentary Control over State Enterprise in India,* Delhi, Metropolitan Book Co., 1960.

Bhandari, K.C., *Nationalisation of Industries in India,* Calcutta, Academic Press, 1962.

Bhat, K.S. and and Satyanarana, P.V., Janatha Scooters Limited, *IPE Journal,* Vol. 1 No. 4, April-Dec.; 1978.

Bhat, K.S. and Nandagopal, R., *Role of Chairman and Managing Directors in State Level Public Enterprises: A Discussion,* Hyderabad, IPE, 1991.

Bhatra, G.S., *Leading Issues in Public Enterprises: Control and Accountability,* Book, New Delhi, Anmol, 1993.

Capoor, H.K.L. (Chairman), India. Ministry of Home Affairs. Department of Personnel and Administrative Reforms, *Report of the Standing Group on Management of Public Enterprises in the States,* New Delhi, Govt. of India Press, 1979.

Chauhan, *Organisation and Working of Public Enterprises in Gujarat,* Book, Vallabh Vidyanagar, Sardar Patel University, 1978.

Chinta Rao, N., *Working Capital Management: (A Study of Selected State Enterprises of Karnataka),* Book, Nagarjuna Nagar, Nagarjuna University, 1988.

Damodar Dass, C., Study of Performance Improvement in APSRTC through Computerised Maintenance Management, Hyderabad, IPE, 1993.

Devendra Babu, State level public sector reforms-status and case studies, *Journal of IPE,* Vol. 23 No. 1&2, Jan-June; 2000.

Diwakar Rao, P.L., (Ed.), *Public Sector in Andhra Pradesh: A Handbook and Directory,* Secunderabad, 1988.

Diwakar Rao, P.L. (Ed.), *Public Sector in Andhra Pradesh:A Handbook and Directory* (With Special Supplement on Central Sector).

Diwakar Rao, P.L. (Ed.), *Public Sector in Andhra Pradesh,* Book, Secunderabad, Utility Publications, 1988.

Diwakar Rao, P.L. (Ed.), *Public Sector in Andhra Pradesh : A Handbook & Directory,* Sec'bad, M/s.Utility Publications Ltd, 1988.

Dutt, R.C., *State Enterprises in a Developing Country:The Indian Experience 1950-90,* Book, New Delhi, Abhinav Publications, 1990.

Dutta, Abhijit, *Privatisation of Public Enterprises: An Empirical Study relating to Some Selected Privatised SLPEs in Orissa,* Bhubaneswar, Utkal University, 1995.

El-Namaki, M.S.S., Restructuring of State-owned Enterprises: Cross Country Analysis and Conceptual Frame, *Journal of IPE,* Vol. 22 No. 3&4, July-Sept; Oct.-Dec; 1999.

Entreprisation of the State Electricity Boards, *Journal of IPE,* Vol. 25 No. 1&2, Jan-June; 2002.

Gangadhar, V. and Yadagiri, M., Disinvestment in Andhra Pradesh State Level Public enterprises, *IPE Journal,* Vol. 25 Nol 1&2, Jan-March; April-June; 2002.

Gavini, Augustine L., *Ancillaries of Public Enterprises in Andhra Pradesh—A Study in Structure, Growth and Performance,* Hyderabad, O.U., 1990.

Gujarat State Road Transport Corporation, *Statistics of GSRT Corporation,* Ahmedabad, n.d.

Gujarat. Bureau of Public Enterprises, *Public Sector Enterprises Fourth Annual Report 1980-81,* Gandhinagar, Government Central Press, n.d.

Gujarat. Bureau of Public Enterprises, *Public Enterprises Sixth Annual Report 1982-83,* Gandhinagar, 1984.

Gujarat. Bureau of Public Enterprises, *Public Enterprises Fifth Annual Report 1981-82,* Gandhinagar, Government Central Press, 1983.

Gujarat. Bureau of Public Enterprises, *Public Enterprises Eighth Annual Report 1984-85,* Gandhinagar, 1987.

Gujarat. Bureau of Public Enterprises, *Public Sector Enterprises Fourth Annual Report* 1980-81, Book, Gandhinagar, Government Central Press, n.d.

Gupta, Nirmal K. and Ahmad Abad, *Management Research: Contemporary Issues,* Book, Delhi, South Asia Publications, 1994.

Gupta, Sheh, Financial Working of Public Utilities, Book, Jaipur, Printwell, 1992.

Guptha, G.C., *Role of Andhra Pradesh Enterprises Management Board—A Critical Appraisal,* Hyderabad, IPE, 1986.

Gorwala, A.D., India. Planning Commission, *Report on the Efficient Conduct of State Enterprises,* New Delhi, 1951.

Gowri Sankara Rao P., *State Level Public Enterprises of Kerala:* (A Study on the Problems of Financial Management), Nagarjuna Nagar, Nagarjuna University, 1989.

Hassan Shabir, *Public Enterprises in Economic Development,* Book, Delhi, Anmol Publications, 1987.

Hemlata Rao, *Financial Performance of Public Enterprises,* Jaipur, Printwell Publishers, 1987

India. Comptroller and Auditor General, *Digest of important observations by the Comptroller and Auditor General of India on the performance of the State Electricity Boards 1980-85,* New Delhi, Indian Audit and Accounts Department, 1987.

India. Comptroller and Auditor General, State Government Public Enterprises—Concepts, Performance and Accountability, New Delhi, Indian Audit and Accounts Department, 1989.

India. Comptroller and Auditor General, *Report of the Comptroller and Auditor General of India for the Year Ended 31 March 1989, No.4 (Commercial) of Government of Andhra Pradesh:* Andhra Pradesh State Civil Supplies Corporation Limited and Andhra Pradesh State Essential Commodities Corporation Limited, Hyderabad, Government Central Press, 1991.

India. Comptroller and Auditor General, *Report of the Comptroller and Auditor General of India,* (Commercial) Government of

Punjab, Chandigarh, Controller of Printing & Stationery, 1974-75, 1977-78, 1980-81, 1981-82, 1983-84, 1984-85, 1990-91, 1991-92, 1995 (No. 2).

India. Comptroller and Auditor General, *Report of the Comptroller and Auditor General of India of Union Government No. 6 (Commercial) of 1990:* Delhi Transport Corporation, Delhi, Controller of Publications, 1991.

India. Government of Kerala, *Review of Public Enterprises in Kerala* 2001-2002, Thiruvanthapuram, 2003.

India. Kerala, *A Review of Public Enterprises in Kerala.* Thiruvanthapuram, Govt. Press, 1998.

India. Kerala, A Review of Public Enterprises in Kerala, Thiruvanthapuram, Govt. Press, 1998.

India. Maharashtra, *Performance of State Public Enterprises* 1994-95, Mumbai, Government Press, 1996.

India. Maharashtra, Performance of State Public Enterprises—1994-95, Mumbai, Government Press, 1996.

Institute of Public Enterprise, *Colloquium on State Level Public Enterprises:* June 25-26, 1982, Hyderabad, IPE, 1982.

Institute of Public Enterprise, *Course on Project Appraisal for State Level Public Enterprises in Karnataka,* Hyderabad, IPE, 1984.

Institute of Public Enterprise, *Programme on Budget and Budgetary Control for Executives of AP SLPEs: 25-27 April, 1985,* Hyderabad, IPE, 1985.

Institute of Public Enterprise, *Management Development Programme for Young Executives from AP SLPEs - Phase-I (APPEMB): 27-10-92 to 31-10-92,* Hyderabad, IPE, 1992.

Institute of Public Enterprise, Programme on Management of SLPEs, Programme Material, March 6-11, 1989, Hyderabad, IPE, 1989.

Institute of Public Enterprise, one Week Course on SLPE Management, Programme Material, 4-9 January 1988.

Institute of Public Enterprise, Programme Material, Programme on SLPE Management for IAS Officers: October 12-17, 1987.

Institute of Public Enterprise, Top Management Programme for SLPE's in North Eastern Region, Programme Material, February 20-24, 1989.

Institute of Public Enterprise, Workshop on SLPEs, Programme Material, October 7, 1988, Hyderabad, IPE, 1988.

Institute of Public Enterprise, One-Week Programme on SLPEs, Programme Material, 24-29 October, 1988.

Institute of Public Enterprise, One Week Course on SLPE Management, Programme Material, 4-6 February, 1988.

Institute of Public Enterprise, Programme on Management of SLPEs, Programme Material, 19-24 June, 1989, Hyderabad, IPE, 1989.

Institute of Public Enterprise, Programme on Management of SLPEs, Programme Material, 10-15 July, 1989, Hyderabad, IPE, 1989.

Institute of Public Enterprise, Programme on Problem Solving Based Training for SLPE Managers, Programme Material, 23-27 October, 1989 Hyderabad, IPE, 1989.

Institute of Public Enterprise, Programme on Corporate Planning in SLPEs: Sponsored by Department of Public Enterprises and Government of Andhra Pradesh.

Institute of Public Enterprise, Workshop on Project Appraisal for SLPEs, August 22-26, 1983.

Institute of Public Enterprise, Programme on Budget and Budgetary Control for Executives of AP SLPEs, Programme Material, 25-27 April, 1985, Hyderabad, IPE, 1985.

Institute of Public Enterprise, Financial contribution requirement of SLPEs in India 1993, Report, Hyderabad, IPE, 1993.

Institute of Public Enterprise, *Programme on Management of SLPEs:* March 6-11, 1989, Hyderabad, IPE, 1989.

Institute of Public Enterprise, *Andhra Pradesh Public Enterprise Yearbook* 1984, Hyderabad, 1984.

Institute of Public Enterprise, *One Week Course on State Level Public Enterprises Management for IAS Officers:* June 13-18, 1988, Hyderabad, IPE, 1988.

Institute of Public Enterprise, *One Week Course on SLPE Management: 4-9 January 1988,* Hyderabad, IPE, 1988.

Institute of Public Enterprise, *Programme on SLPE Management for IAS Officers: October 12-17, 1987,* Hyderabad, IPE, 1987.

Institute of Public Enterprise, *Top Management Programme for SLPE's in North Eastern Region: February 20-24, 1989,* Hyderabad, IPE, 1989.

Institute of Public Enterprise, *Workshop on SLPEs: October 7, 1988,* Hyderabad, IPE, 1988.

Institute of Public Enterprise, *One-Week Programme on SLPEs: 24-29 October, 1988,* Hyderabad, IPE, 1988.

Institute of Public Enterprise, *Programme on Management of State Level Public Enterprises: 22-28 August, 1988,* Hyderabad, IPE, 1988.

Institute of Public Enterprise, *One Week Course on SLPE Management: 1-6 February, 1988,* Hyderabad, IPE, 1988.

Institute of Public Enterprise, *Programme on Management of SLPEs: 19-24 June, 1989,* Hyderabad, IPE, 1989.

Institute of Public Enterprise, *Programme on Management of SLPEs: 10-15 July, 1989,* Hyderabad, IPE, 1989.

Institute of Public Enterprise, *Programme on Management of State Level Public Enterprises Level II: 7-12 August, 1989,* Hyderabad, IPE, 1989.

Institute of Public Enterprise, *Programme on Management of State Level Public Enterprises Level II: 21-26 August, 1989,* Hyderabad, IPE, 1989.

Institute of Public Enterprise, *Programme on Problem Solving Based Training for SLPE Managers: 23-27 October, 1989,* Hyderabad, IPE, 1989.

Institute of Public Enterprise, *Programme on Working Capital Management for Executives of State Level Public Enterprises of North Eastern Region: 18-23 January, 1990, Hyderabad,* IPE, 1990.

Institute of Public Enterprise, *Programme on Corporate Planning in SLPEs: Sponsored by Department of Public Enterprises and Government of Andhra Pradesh,* Hyderabad, IPE, 1991.

Institute of Public Enterprise, *Course Material on Finance and Accounting,* Hyderabad, IPE, 1991.

Institute of Public Enterprise, *Report on Financial Performance of State Level Public Enterprises in India (1980-81 to 1985-86):* Statistical Statement, Hyderabad, IPE, 1991.

Institute of Public Enterprise, *Privatisation: Reorientation of State Level Public Enterprises: August 24-28, 1992,* Hyderabad, IPE, 1992.

Institute of Public Enterprise, *National Seminar on PE Reform and Privatisation in State Level Public Enterprises: Strategies and Techniques,* Hyderabad, IPE, 1992.

Investment Pattern of Public Undertakings in India: A Study of Orissa Enterprises, Delhi, Mittal Publications, 1987.

Jain, Ravi K., *Working Capital Management of State Enterprises in India,* Jaipur, National Publishing House, 1988.

Jessica Mary V., Performance of State Financial Corporations: A Study of APSFC and KSFC, Hyderabad, O.U., 1992.

Karnataka Electricity Board, *Pocket-Book of Electricity Statistics 1979,* Bangalore, 1979.

Karnataka State Bureau of Public Enterprises, *Public Sector Enterprises First Annual Report Bangalore,* n.d.

Karnataka State Bureau of Public Enterprises, Public Sector Enterprises Second Annual Report 1981-82, Bangalore, n.d.

Karnataka. Bureau of Public Enterprises, *Public Enterprises Survey 1998-99 Annual Survey on the Working of the State Public Sector Enterprises,* Bangalore, BPE, 2000.

Kerala. Bureau of Public Enterprises and Centre for Management Development, *Review of Public Enterprises in Kerala,* Trivandrum, 1980-81, 1981-82, 1982-83, 1983-84, 1984-85, 1985-86, 1986-87, 1987-88, 1988-89, 989-90, 1991-92, 1995-96.

Kiran Kumar, K., Cash Management in Selected State Level Manufacturing Public, Enterprises in Andhra Pradesh:Thesis Submitted to the Osmania University for the Award of Doctor of Philosophy in Commerce, Hyderabad, Osmania University, 1990.

Kumara Swamy V., *Study of Rajahansa Services in Hyderabad City Transport,* Hyderabad, IPE, 1993.

Maharashtra. State Bureau of Public Enterprises, *Performance of State Public Enterprises (1989-90),* Bombay, Government, Central Press, 1991.

Maharashtra, *Performance of State Public Enterprises* 1995-96, Mumbai, Govt. Press, 1998.

Maharashtra, *Performance of State Public Enterprises* 1996-97, Mumbai, Govt. Press, 1998.

Maharashtra. State Road Transport Corporation, *Twentytive Years of State Transport,* Book, Maharashtra Bombay, 1974.

Maharashtra. State Bureau of Public Enterprises, *Performance of State Public Enterprises (1989-90),* Bombay, Government Central Press, 1991.

Maharashtra. State Bureau of Public Sector Enterprises, *Performance of State Public Sector Enterprises (1986-87),* Bombay, Government Central Press, 1988.

Maharashtra. State Bureau of Public Enterprises, *Performance of State Public Sector Enterprises (1987-88),* Bombay, Central Government Press, 1989.

Maharashtra. State Bureau of Public Enterprises, Performance of State Public Enterprises 1992-93, Government of Maharashtra, Bombay, Government Central Press, 1994.

Maharashtra. State Bureau of Public Enterprises, Performance of State Public Enterprises 1991-92, Government of Maharashtra, Bombay, Government Central Press, 1992.

Maharashtra, Performance of State Public Enterprises 1996-97, Mumbai, Govt. Press, 1998.

Maruthi Ram, P., *Financing of Public Enterprises—a Study of the Impact on Cost of Funds in Select Central and Andhra Pradesh Government Enterprises,* Hyderabad, Osmania University, 1987.

Mathur, B.L. (Ed.), *Organisation and Management of Public Enterprises. Vol. III - Performance Evaluation of Public Enterprises,* Jaipur, Arihant. 1996.

Mathur, D.C., *Wages in the Public Sector (A Study of Rajasthan State Enterprises,* New Delhi, Mittal Publications, 1990.

Memorandum of understanding for central and state Level public enterprises, August 24 - 25, 2000.

Memorandum of Understanding for Central and SLPEs. Hyderabad, IPE, 2003.

Minhas, Anil and Singh, Amrik and Chumber, Gurbax Ram and Chanana, Sanjeev, *Financial Committees at State Level,* Book New Delhi, Deep & Deep Publications, 1990.

Mishra, R.K. and Navin, B., *Restructuring State Level Public Enterprises,* New Delhi, Anmol, 2002.

Mishra, R.K. and Pakki Reddy, G., *Technical Note on the State Level Public Enterprises in Andhra Pradesh,* Book, Hyderabad, IPE, 1988.

Mishra, R.K. and Pakki Reddy, G., Role of Public Enterprises in the Financing of the Seventh Plan : a case of the State Level Public Mishra, R.K., and Ravishankar, S., Institute of Public Enterprise, Capacity Utilisation in State Level Public Enterprises in Andhra Pradesh, Hyderabad, 1987.

Mishra, R.K. and Nandagopal R., *State Level Public Enterprises in Bihar,* Hyderabad, IPE, 1990.

Mishra, R.K. and Nandagopal R., (Study Team), Institute of Public Enterprise, *Financial Performance of State Level Public Enterprises in India,* Hyderabad, IPE, 1990.

Mishra, R.K. and Nandagopal R., (Study Team), Institute of Public Enterprise, *Budgeting in State Level Public Enterprises in Andhra Pradesh and Tamilnadu, Hyderabad,* IPE, 1991.

Mishra, R.K. and Nandagopal, R. and Suri, Babu P. (Study Team) Institute of Public Enterprise, *Study Report on Financial Contribution and Requirements of State Level Public Enterprises in India.* 2 Vols., Hyderabad, IPE, 1993.

Mishra, R.K., Financial restructuring of State Level Public Enterprises, *IPE Journal,* Vol. 17 No. 3&4, July-Sept; Oct-Dec;1994.

Mishra, R.K., and Ravishankar, S. and Nandagopal, R. (Eds.), *Management of State Level Public Enterprises in India,* Book New Delhi, National Publishing House, 1989.

Mohammed, Latif Syed A., *Performance of Joint Sector Enterprises promoted by selected SIDCs: (A study of objectives, management and financial performance),* Hyderabad, Osmania University, 1992.

Murthy, K.S.N., *Industrial Relations in Andhra Pradesh State Electricity Board,* Hyderabad, IPE, 1985.

Murthy, S.S., Cash Generation in APSRTC, *IPE Journal,* Vol. 8 No. 3, July-Sept; 1985.

Nandagopal, R., Special problems in Coordination among PEs, *IPE Journal,* Vol. 9 No. 4, Oct-Dec;1986.

Nandagopal, R. and Vudali, Mohan V.K., Institute of Public Enterprise, Programme Material, Internal Audit in SLPES of Andhra Pradesh, Hyderabad, 1991.

Narayana Murty, A.S.Y., *Project Report on Industrial Sickness—Causes and Cures* (a study in APSFC's experience), Hyderabad, IPE, 1984.

Omprakash, *Theory and Working of State Corporations: With Special Reference to India,* London, George Allen and Unwin Ltd., 1962.

Orissa. Planning and Coordination Department. *Public Enterprises Profile 1985-86 compiled up to 31-3-1986,* Cuttack, Government Press, 1987.

Orissa. Planning and Coordination Department. *Public Enterprises Profile 1986-87 compiled up to 31-3-1987,* Cuttack, Government Press, 1988.

Orissa. Planning and Co-ordination Department, *Public Enterprises Profile 1987-88 (Compiled upto 31-3-1988),* Cuttack, Government Press, 1989.

Orissa. Planning and Coordination Department, *Compilation of Circulars Relating to the State Public Sector Undertakings* (Compiled upto the 30th April,1980).

Orissa. Department of Public Enterprises, Public Enterprises Profile 1989-90, Government of Orissa, Cuttack, Government Press, 1990.

Parthasarathy, R., (Consultant), Institute of Public Enterprise, *Study of Wages of and other Monetary and Non-Monetary Benefits and Concession given to the Employees of Andhra Pradesh State, Tamilnadu, Karnataka, Madhya Pradesh and Maharashtra State Electricity Boards,* Hyderabad, IPE .

Prasada Rao, P., *Management Audit for State Level Public Enterprises: A Case Study of Leather Industry Development Corporation,* Hyderabad, IPE, 1991.

Programme on Strategic Planning for GMs and MDs of Kerala SLPEs Part I and II, February 12-17, 2001, Programme on management control : one week Executive Development programme for manager cadre for SLPEs of Kerala, February 19-24, 2001.

Programme Material, Institute of Public Enterprise, *Workshop on Project Appraisal for SLPEs:* August 22-26, 1983, Hyderabad, IPE, 1983.

Punjab. Bureau of Public Enterprises, *Second Report on the Working of State Public Sector Undertakings 1980-81.* Chandigarh, Government Press, 1981.

Punjab. Bureau of Public Enterprises, *Sixth Report on the Working of State Public Sector Undertakings 1986-87,* Chandigarh, 1989.

Rajanath, K., Changing Role of Marketing in Public Enterprises in a phase of economic liberalization, *IPE Journal,* Vol. 13 No. 2, June;1990.

Rajasthan Agro Industries Corporation A Performance Appraisal, *IPE Journal,* Vol. No. 2&3, Oct-Dec;1977; Jan-March;1978.

Rajasthan. Bureau of Public Enterprises, *Public Sector Undertakings at a Glance 1982,* Jaipur, 1982.

Rajasthan. Bureau of Public Enterprises, *Public Enterprises Profile 1986-87,* Jaipur, Government Central Press, 1988.

Rajasthan. Bureau of Public Enterprises, *Public Enterprises Profile 1984-85,* Jaipur, Government Central Press, 1986.

Rajasthan. Bureau of Public Enterprises, *Public Enterprises Profile, Jaipur,* Government Central Press, 1985.

Rajasthan. Bureau of Public Enterprises, *Public Enterprises Profile 1983-84* Jaipur, Government Central Press, 1985.

Rajasthan. Bureau of Public Enterprises, *Public Enterprises Profile 1986-87,* Jaipur, Govt.Central Press, 1988.

Rajasthan. Bureau of Public Enterprises, *Public Enterprises Profile* 1988-89, Jaipur, 1990.

Rajasthan, Bureau of Public Enterprises, *Public Enterprises Profile 1997-98* State Enterprises Department, Jaipur, BPE, 1999.

Rajasthan, Bureau of Public Enterprises, Public Enterprises Profile 1997-98, State enterprises department, Jaipur, BPE, 1999.

Ramamurti, Ravi (Ed.) and Vernon, Raymond (Ed.), *Privatization and Control of State-Owned Enterprises,* Book, Washington, 1991.

Ramana Rao, T.V., Industrial Relations in Andhra Pradesh State Electricity Board.

Ramamohana, Rao U. and Viswanadham, V., Responsiveness of inventory management: A case study of Hyderabad Allwyn, *IPE Journal,* Vol. 15 No. 2, June; 1992.

Restructuring of State Level Public Enterprises, Seminar held on June 30 - July 1, 1995, Hyderabad, IPE, 1995.

Roy, R.C., *State Public Enterprise in India,* Book, New Delhi, Uppal Publishing House, 1985.

Sahoo, K.M., Grievance Handling—A case study of Rourkela steel Plant, *IPE Journal,* Vol. 7 No. 3, July-Sept; 1984.

Sai, S.S.T., Note on the performance of PE in AP during 1977-78 to 1979-80, *IPE Journal,* Vol. 5 No. 1, Jan-March;1982.

Sai, Baba P., *Cost Control and Cost Reduction in a State Transport Undertaking: A Case Study of APSRTC,* Hyderabad, IPE, 1988.

Sankar, T.L. and Nandagopal, R. and Mishra, R.K., *Management of state level public enterprises in India,* Jaipur, Printwell, 1992.

Sankar, T.L. and Nandagopal, R. and Mishra, R K., *Performance and Development of State Level Public Enterprises in India,* Hyderabad, IPE, 1989.

Sankar, T.L. and Nandagopal R. and Mishra R.K., *Performance and Development of State Level Public Enterprises in India,* Hyderabad, IPE, 1989.

Sankar, T.L. and Nandagopal, R. and Mishra, R.K., Institute of Enterprise, *State Level Public Enterprises in India: An Overview,* Hyderabad, 1989.

Sankar, T.L. and Mishra R.K., and Nanda Gopal R., *Working of State-Level Manufacturing Public Enterprises : Promise and Performance,* Hyderabad, IPE, 1991.

Sankar, T.L., and Nanda Gopal R. and Mishra R., *State Level Public Enterprises in India: An Overview,* Bombay, 1990.

Sankar, T.L., and Mishra R.K. and Nandagopal R., *Working of State-Level Manufacturing Public Enterprise: Promise and Performance,* Book, Hyderabad, IPE, 1991.

Sankar, T.L. and Mishra R.K. and Nandagopal R., *Can State Level Public Enterprises in India Earn a Rate of Return,* Hyderabad, IPE, 1990.

Sankar, T.L., and Santana Babu, G. and Trivikram, K. (Study Team), INSTUTE OF PUBLIC ENTERPRISE, *Andhra Pradesh State Textile Development Corporation: A Study,* Hyderabad, IPE, 1982.

Sankar, T.L. and Parthasarathy R. (Study Team), Institute of Public Enterprise, *Study of Wages and Other Monetary and Non-monetary Benefits and Concessions given to the Employees of Andhra Pradesh State, Tamil Nadu, Karnataka, Madhya Pradesh and Maharashtra state Electricity Boards.* 2 Vols., Hyderabad, IPE, 1990.

Sankar, T.L. and Mishra, R.K. and Nandagopal, R., *Role and Relevance of State Level Public Enterprises in the 1990.*

Sankar, T.L. and Mishra R.K. and Nanda Gopal R., *Can State Level Public Enterprises in India Earn a Rate of Return,* Bombay, 1990.

Sankar, T.L., Institute of Public Enterprise, *Management of State Level Public Enterprises and its Privatisation,* Hyderabad, IPE, 1993.

Sankar, T.L. and Mishra, R.K. and Nandagopal, R., Modalities of PE reforms and privatisation of SLPEs, *IPE Journal,* Vol. 15 No. 4, Dec;1992.

Sankar, T.L. and Nandagopal, R. and Mishra, R.K., *Management of State Level Public Enterprises in India,* Book, Jaipur, Printwell, 1992.

Saraswathy Rao, Y., *Public Enterprises: A State Level Perspective,* Delhi, B.R. Publishing Company, 1986.

Sarma, S.D., *Study of Project Appraisal Systems in Financial Institutions with special reference to APSFC,* Hyderabad, IPE, 1985.

Satish Chander, T., Performance of Andhra Pradesh Committee on Public Undertakings—Qualitative and Quantitative Dimensions, *IPE Journal,* Vol. 14 No. 3, Sept; 1991.

Satish Chander, T., Legislative Control Over Corporate Sector, Jaipur, RBSA, 1994.

Satyanarayana, J., *Working of the Andhra Pradesh State Road Transport Corporation,* New Delhi, Concept Publishing Co., 1985.

Selvarani, S., *Employees Welfare Measures in Select Public Enterprises in Andhra Pradesh,* Hyderabad, O.U., 1993.

Sharma, G.D., *Working of State Enterprises in Rajasthan,* Book, New Delhi, Sterling Publishers Pvt. Ltd., 1975.

Shirley, Mary M., World Bank Managing State-owned Enterprises, Washington, 1983.

Shirley Mary, M., *Managing State-Owned Enterprises,* Washington, World Bank, 1983,

Shiva Ramu, S., *State Enterprises in Karnataka: An Introduction to State Intervention,* Bangalore, IIM, 1983.

Shiva Ramu, S., *State Enterprises in Karnataka:An Introduction to State Intervention,* Bangalore, IIM-B, 1983.

Shiva Ramu, S., Management of State Level Public Enterprises in Karnataka, *IPE Journal,* Vol. 7 No. 2, April-June;1984.

Simha, S.L.N., *Development Banking in India with Special Reference to a State Level Institution*—Karnataka, Madras, Institute for Financial Management and Research, 1976.

Singh, Mohinder, *Some Aspects of Public Enterprises in India: A Plea to Reforms,* Book, New Delhi, Uppal, 1993.

Singh, Nagendra P., Financial Management in State Enterprises, *A Case Study of Bihar State Road Transport Corporation,* Delhi, Capital Publishing House, 1989.

State Level Conference of Chairman and Chief Executives Enterprises, (11-4-1988), State Level Conference of Chairman and Chief Executives Enterprises (11-4-1988).

Sujatha Rao, T., *Annotated Bibliography on Public Enterprise in India,* Hyderabad, IPE, 1994.

Surendranath, S., Financial Management of P.E. in Bihar, *IPE Journal,* Vol. 6 No. 1, Jan-March;1983.

Surinder Kumar, Financial performance and pricing policy Haryana and Punjab Electricity undertakings, *IPE Journal,* Vol. 8 No. 3, July-Sept; 1985.

Surya Kumar, K., Labour relations in Select AP State Enterprises, *IPE Journal,* Vol. 5 No. 2, April-June; 1982.

Suryanarayana, M., *Monograph on Andhra Pradesh State Financial Corporation A Catalyst of Industrial Development in Andhra Pradesh,* Hyderabad, IPE, 1986.

Swamy, K., *Financial Performance of Manufacturing State Level Public Enterprises in Andhra Pradesh,* Hyderabad, JNTU, 1992.

Swamy, K., *Financial Performance of Manufacturing State Level Public Enterprises,* Book, Delhi, Delta Publishing House, 1994.

Tamil Nadu. Finance Department, *Review of Public Sector Enterprises in Tamil Nadu 1976-77,* Madras, 1978.

Tamil Nadu. Bureau of Public Enterprises, *Review of Public Sector Enterprises in Tamil Nadu 1979-80,* Madras, Tamil Arasu Press, n.d.

Tamil Nadu. State Bureau of Public Enterprises, *Handbook of Instruction for State Public Sector Undertakings and Statutory Boards,* Madras, n.d.

Tamil Nadu. Bureau of Public Enterprises, *Review of State Public Sector Enterprises in Tamil Nadu 1986-87,* Madras, Government Central Press, n.d.

Tandon, B.C., *Public Enterprises in India,* Allahabad, Chaitanya Publishing House, 1987.

Tarun M.S. Gorg P.K. & Bodia B.S., Measuring changes in Financial Health, *IPE Journal,* Vol. 13 No. 4, Dec;1990.

Tze Ker Sin., *Public Enterprises in Asia, An introductory Survey,* Singapore, Institute of Southeast Asian Studies, 1978.

Vanamala, M. and Pakki Reddy, G. and Uma Shankari, P. and Rasool Saheb, T.S. (Study Team), Institute of Public Enterprise, *Contributions of Public Enterprises to Economic Development of Andhra Pradesh* (Sponsored by Department of Finance, Government of Andhra Pradesh) 2 Vols., Hyderabad, IPE, 1984.

Vanamala, M., *Public Sector Enterprises: An Enquiry into the Corporations for Weaker Sections in Andhra Pradesh,* Anantapur, Sri Krishna Devaraya University, 1989.

Venkateshwarlu, M., Valuation of state level public enterprises: A case study of Hyderabad Allwyn, *IPE Journal,* Vol. 15 No. 2, June;1992.

Vasanth Kumar, R., Study of the Over-run in Projects Promoted by APSFC, Hyderabad, IPE, 1993.

Venkatswamy G., *Management of State Government Enterprises.* New Delhi, Archives Publishers, 1987.

Venkatratnam, C.S. and Appa Rao B., Twenty five years of APSFC: An evaluation, *IPE Journal,* Vol. 5 No. 3, July-Sept; 1982.

Venkatswamy, G., *Management of State Government Enterprises in Andhra Pradesh.* Performance of A.P. State Public Enterprises during 1985-86.

Vuylsteke, Charles and Nankani, Helen, World Bank, *Techniques of Privatization of State-owned Enterprises.* 3 vols. Vol.I - Report on techniques of privatization and related issues. Vol.II - Country and case studies. Vol.III Bibliography and other reference material, Washington, 1988.

Umesh, D., *Identification of Market Segment for APTEX Shirts,* Hyderabad, IPE, 1993.

Uttar Pradesh. Bureau of State Enterprises, *Annual Report on the Working of UP State Enterprises 1978-79,* Allahabad, Superintendent of Printing and Stationery, 1981.

Wettendhall, Roger, On the centrality of state level enterprises in the Australian public enterprise experience, *IPE Journal,* Vol. 23 No. 1&2, April-June;2000.

What is the future of public utilities in Western Europe, *Journal of IPE,* Vol. 23 No. 3&4, July-Sept; Oct-Dec; 2000.

INDEX